Families, education and social differences

The other published volumes in this series are:

Contemporary issues in teaching and learning
Edited by Peter Woods

Diversity and change: education, policy and selection
Edited by John Ahier, Ben Cosin and Margaret Hales

This reader is one of three, and has been prepared as part of the Open University course *Exploring Educational Issues*, a broadly based multi-disciplinary course which can be studied as part of BA or BSc degrees.

It is part of an integrated teaching system; the selection is therefore related to other material available to students. Opinions expressed are not necessarily those of the course team or of the Open University.

If you would like to study this course or find out more about The Open University, please write to Course Reservations and Sales Centre, PO Box 724, Open University, Walton Hall, Milton Keynes, MK7 6ZS, or telephone 01908 653231. A copy of *Studying with the Open University* is available from the same address.

Families, education and social differences

Edited by Ben Cosin and Margaret Hales
at The Open University

London and New York
in association with
The Open University

First published 1997
by Routledge
11 New Fetter Lane, London EC4P 4EE

Simultaneously published in the USA and Canada
by Routledge
29 West 35th Street, New York, NY 10001

© 1997 Selection and editorial matter, The Open University;
individual chapters, their contributors

Typeset in Garamond by
Ponting–Green Publishing Services, Chesham,
Buckinghamshire
Printed and bound in Great Britain by
Clays Ltd, St Ives PLC

British Library Cataloguing in Publication Data
A catalogue record for this book is available from the
British Library

Library of Congress Cataloging in Publication Data
Families, education, and social differences/edited by
    Ben Cosin and Margaret Hales.
        p.   cm. – (Exploring educational issues)
    Includes bibliographical references and index.
    1. Early childhood education–Parent participation.
    2. Early chilhood education–Parent participation–Great
Britain.   3. Early childhood education–Social aspects.   4.
Early childhood education–Social aspects–Great Britain.
I. Cosin, Ben.   II. Hales, Margaret.   III. Open University
IV. Series.
LB1139.35.P37F35   1997
372.21–dc20   96–33064   CIP

ISBN   0–415–15540–1

Contents

List of illustrations   vii
Acknowledgements   viii
Introduction   1

1 Socialization and the family: change and diversity   4
   D. H. J. Morgan

2 Nursery school education in Nigeria: impact on families and
   society   30
   S. K. Akinsanya

3 Why nursery education?   37
   C. James

4 Training to work in the early years   49
   A. Curtis and D. Hevey

5 Parents and professionals   64
   A. Edwards and P. Knight

6 Learning begins at home: implications for a learning society   77
   T. Alexander

7 Special needs: personal trouble or public issue?   89
   L. Barton and M. Oliver

8 Educational inequality as a social problem: the case of England   102
   M. Hammersley

9 Is Britain a meritocracy?   116
   P. Saunders

10 Educational reform, gender equality and school cultures   132
   M. Arnot, M. David and G. Weiner

11 Feminist theories   149
   L. Measor and P. J. Sikes

12 Boys will be boys? Racism, sexuality and the construction of masculine identities among infant boys   164
   P. Connolly

13 Swimming against the tide: liberal parents and cultural plurality   190
   J. Grimes

14 Educational experiences of ethnic minority students in Oxford
   D. McIntyre, G. Bhatti and M. Fuller   197

15 Family matters
   H. S. Mirza   221

   Index   244

Illustrations

FIGURES

3.1 A child's drawing 43
3.2 Aims of nursery education 46
5.1 Types of parental involvement 71
6.1 Policy focus network 87
14.1 Relationships of A Level to GCSE results 201

TABLES

1.1 Households by type 8
1.2 Patterns of remarriage, 1961–84 10
9.1 Intergenerational social mobility rates based on father's class 118
9.2 Social mobility disparity ratios 119
9.3 Mean ability scores by class of origin and class of destination 119
9.4 Social mobility disparity ratios above and below threshold ability score for class I/II entry 121
9.5 A logistic regression model predicting class IV/V children entering class I/II 123
9.6 A logistic regression model predicting class I/II children entering class I/II 125
9.7 A multiple regression model with Hope–Goldthorpe rank scores as dependent variable 127
9.8 A multiple model including qualifications and status of first job 128
10.1 Perceptions on the part of LEAs of the impact of educational and related social reforms 136
10.2 The perceived impact of curricular and educational reforms in primary schools 137
10.3 The perceived impact of curricular and educational reforms in secondary schools 137
14.1 Numbers in each ethnic group of students 198
14.2 GCSE results for different ethnic categories 199
14.3 Ethnic categories, gender and GCSE results 199

Acknowledgements

While the publishers have made every effort to contact copyright holders of material used in this volume, they would be grateful to hear from any they were unable to contact.

Chapter 1 Morgan, D. H. (1988) 'Socialization and the family: change and diversity', in M. Woodhead and A. McGrath (eds) *Family, School and Society*, London: Hodder & Stoughton.

Chapter 2 Akinsanya, S. K. (1980) 'Nursery school education in Nigeria: impact on families and society', Paper presented at the Annual Meeting of the National Association for the Education of Young Children, San Francisco.

Chapter 3 James, C. (1984) 'Why nursery education?' *Inspection and Advice* 20 (1).

Chapter 4 Curtis, A. and Hevey, D. (1992) 'Training to work in the early years', in G. Pugh (ed.) *Contemporary Issues in the Early Years: Working Collaboratively for Children*, London: Paul Chapman.

Chapter 5 Edwards, A. and Knight, P. (1994) 'Parents and professionals', in *Effective Early Years Education*, Buckingham: Open University Press.

Chapter 6 Alexander, T. (1996) 'Learning begins at home: implications for a learning society', in J. Bastiani (ed.) *Home–School Work in Britain: Review, Reflection and Development*, London: David Fulton.

Chapter 7 Barton, L. and Oliver, M. (1989) 'Special needs: personal trouble or public issue?' in *Voicing Concerns: Sociological Perspectives on Contemporary Education Reforms*, Wallingford, Oxon: Triangle.

Chapter 8 Hammersley, M. (1996) adapted by the author from Chapter 1 of P. Foster, R. Gomm and M. Hammersley (1996) *Constructing Inequality: An Assessment of Research on School Processes*, London: Falmer.

Chapter 9 Saunders, P. (1996) 'Is Britain a meritocracy?' in *Unequal but Fair? A Study of Class Barriers*, London: Institute of Economic Affairs.

Chapter 10 Arnot, M., David, M. and Weiner, G. (1996) drawn by the authors from their report, *Educational Reform and Gender Equality in Schools*, Manchester: Equal Opportunities Commission.

Chapter 11 Measor, L. and Sikes, P. J. (1992) 'Feminist theories', in *Gender and Schools*, London: Cassell.

Chapter 12 Connolly, P. (1997) 'Boys will be boys? Racism, sexuality and the construction of masculine identities among infant boys', in J. Holland and M. Blair (eds) *Debates and Issues in Feminist Research and Pedagogy*, Clevedon: Multilingual Matters in association with the Open University.

Chapter 13 Grimes, J. (1995) 'Swimming against the tide: liberal parents and cultural plurality', specially commissioned article for this volume.

Chapter 14 McIntyre, D., Bhatti, G. and Fuller M. (1993) drawn by the authors from *Cultural Capital, Ethnicity and Early Education: Educational Experiences of Ethnic Minority Students in the City of Oxford*, Oxford University Department of Educational Studies: Oxford Paper in Education. We should like to acknowledge the University of Oxford, Oxfordshire LEA, Oxford CCR and the Paul Hamlyn Trust for financial support; Oxford Upper Schools, Oxfordshire LEA and especially the young people interviewed for their practical help; Diane Schuster for sharing the work with us; Steering Group – Mr Alan Kaye, Mr Tariq Modood, Ms Sanchia Pearse, Mr Alan Lane and Professor Richard Pring – for wise guidance.

Chapter 15 Mirza, H. S. (1992) 'Family matters', in *Young, Female and Black*, London: Routledge.

Introduction

When children enter formal education they leave the safety of their family and begin to travel the long road of adjusting and acclimatizing to the world of others: other people, other ideas, other standards, other cultures. It almost seems that this process is a longer and more difficult one today. This reader develops that relationship between families and educational provision – in the widest sense – as well as the relationship of education to inequalities and differences. These two major themes have been the concern of sociologists of education since the beginning of that discipline but any bibliography will show that those themes are regularly reinterpreted. We do not pretend to cover the whole range of those revisitations but merely to give instances of common concern which demonstrate those relationships.

The chapters in this book are concerned with contemporary issues. Together with the companion volumes on teaching and learning (Woods 1996) and on policy structure and control (Ahier, Cosin and Hales 1996) this book gathers together articles selected with a view to being accessible to a wide audience. The book will be of interest to teachers, student teachers, students of education at both undergraduate and postgraduate levels and all those with a general interest in education, such as parents and governors.

The selection and organization of the chapters are related to our concern to explore educational issues; the most general point is the variety of social backgrounds and assumptions brought to educational activity and interaction by parents, pupils, teachers, and other school staff. Such a variety leads almost automatically to the emergence of issues, including issues of controversy and even conflict. So we have adopted the following themes: the family as educator; before school; family–school links; education and inequality; education and social class; the gender agenda and education and 'race'.

A general view of the variety of family situations found in societies is often assumed to be uniform. In fact families and households vary a good deal according to views recently expressed by scholars. Morgan (Chapter 1) gives us such a general view. However, against such a social background, we may note the concern expressed in the chapters by Edwards and Knight (Chapter 5) and by Alexander (Chapter 6) to advocate and in part to analyse the reduction in the barriers between homes and schools. We also note that it is customary in educational discourses for the practical and the policy oriented to envelop analysis and description. Edwards and Knight draw our attention to ways in which the apparently uncontentious policy of associating parents more closely with the schooling of their children may discriminate unfairly between groups of parents. It may even deprive parents of a position of vantage as uninvolved consumers where they have the greater freedom of action and choice that such an apparently marginal position may offer.

Similarly it might be argued that teachers have become used to the relaxed styles both of teaching and of parenting that have developed at least since the 1960s in England. They find difficulty in discerning the often very effective parental support for pupil learning that lies behind the apparent distance that more reserved parents, such as many Indian parents, maintain.

As a result of her studies in Nigeria, Akinsanya (Chapter 2) argues that the 'traditionalist' orientation found among the nursery teachers in Lagos arises broadly from the concerns of Lagos parents (the schools operate within a market system). By contrast James (Chapter 3) looks at the more 'progressive' practices and assumptions, in a system largely, though by no means wholly, oriented towards state provision. Readers may want to consider how general is the connection between traditionalism and private schooling on the one hand, and progressivism and public provision on the other, or whether this contrast is specific to a particular couple of decades.

In the light of critiques of and complaints about liberal and permissive education that have emerged in the English education system, it would be shallow to assume that it is only Indian parents who have something to learn regarding styles of learning and styles of interaction between parents and teachers. Curtis and Hevey (Chapter 4) cite the historical decline of and confusion in training for the care of young children; they argue that the nature of the work itself makes it difficult to apply standards of the NVQ type to assess workers in this area.

In the area of education and inequalities Barton and Oliver (Chapter 7) remind us of the discussion where the socially imposed character of aspects of people's situations are often regarded as purely physical and organic.

Hammersley (Chapter 8) charts the emergence of educational inequality as a social problem, reflecting both cultural standards and social/occupational requirements. He notes the expansion of factors held to cause, indeed to be culpable for, the different average fortunes of children from different social classes; this process is repeated for other social differences such as gender and ethnicity.

Saunders (Chapter 9), though dealing with different aspects of the topic of class background and educational achievement, emphasizes 'family disposition' as distinct from 'family composition' or 'family position' within the class structure.

Connolly (Chapter 12) stresses the activity of his 'Bad Boys' in playing up to stereotypes of black aggressiveness and sexuality; for Connolly it is they, more than their detractors, who construct these identities.

The version of the research paper by Arnot, David and Weiner (Chapter 10) illustrates the impact of educational changes, notably the Educational Reform Act 1988, on gender differences in education. Again the emphasis is on the differential social implications of measure regarded by some, notably their advocates, as purely technical and neutral in their social impact. Measor and Sikes (Chapter 11) summarize a sample of feminist perspectives designed to analyse these gender differences. To broaden the discussion, McIntyre, Bhatti and Fuller (Chapter 14) give us a more detailed and in-depth study of the specific experiences of South Asian pupils in an English city. But in the chapter by Grimes (Chapter 13) we observe a cultural difference noted between English and Asian parents in this regard; English parents seem much more prepared to transcend these barriers than Asian parents, for whom the traditional division of labour between parents and teachers as professionals remained, it would seem, a valid and valued demarcation. Again, the difference of cultural understandings suggests that to ask 'Which is right? Which is wrong?' is to make understanding difficult. The social, cultural and educational background seems to be an essential part of the meaning of choices and customs.

Mirza (Chapter 15) proposes the most extreme form of the dominance of social–cultural background (the unreliability of reports, perhaps especially of ideologically engaged and of action-research-derived reports) over the apparent referent or object designated. She argues that where females are the head of the household, social class of the family, notably the children, must be interpreted in relation to them, not in relation to a male whose commitment to breadwinning may be less than that of the females. She points out that the relation of households to class position is mediated through cultural factors, paying particular attention to the cultural aspects of the life of Afro-Caribbean people in Britain.

Difference, inequality, family life and organization: the ever-changing relations between these aspects of social and educational life continue to affect teaching and learning and those concerned with them. We trust that you will find these revisitations worthwhile.

Chapter 1

Socialization and the family

Change and diversity

D. H. J. Morgan

INTRODUCTION

There are few matters of public concern or debate where the family does not
enter. The Chancellor of the Exchequer's annual Budget is always assessed in
terms of its impact on 'the average family'. Lack of discipline in schools or
hooliganism in the streets is often blamed upon some failing 'in the family'.
Concerns about child abuse raise questions about the rights of parents as
against the rights of children and the roles of professionals in relation to both
parents and children. There are continuing concerns about the care of the
elderly and the disabled and the responsibilities of family members in these
matters. The 'family', of course, is also a matter of private interest and
concern, an abiding and ever-renewed topic of conversation.

The aim of this article is to explore some of the different ways in which
people in contemporary society, largely contemporary British society, understand the word 'family' and to look at some of the broader social and historical
currents that lie behind these ways of understanding. Whatever else the family
may be concerned with, it is certainly concerned with parents and children
and the latter part of this chapter focuses more specifically upon these
relationships and how they may have changed. In carrying out this exploration, we shall come across several areas of disagreement and controversy.
Perhaps this should not surprise us. The term 'family' while it seems so very
straightforward at first, turns out upon closer examination to be full of
ambiguities and complexities.

WHAT IS 'THE FAMILY'?

I have in front of me a travel brochure. On the front is a picture of a sun-soaked
beach with a young man and a young woman, together with two children. I
have no difficulty in recognizing this healthy and happy little group as being
a 'family'. How is this?

Partly, I suppose, I know this is a family because I know that the travel
agent is selling 'family holidays' . I also know that this is a family because of

the way in which the adults and children are grouped; they are close to each other, touching each other, looking at each other. They are not, I understand, a set of random individuals. Most of all, I recognize this group as a family without a moment's hesitation because I 'just know' that it is a family, because I have lived and grown up with such representations from my earliest years.

And yet, perhaps, there is something a little odd about the group. Why, I ask, are the children in their early school years rather than infants who require transporting on to the beach with some difficulty or teenagers who would rather be off on their own? Where are the grandparents? Already, in considering this particular everyday image of the family I am contrasting and comparing it with other images that I can bring to mind. Nevertheless, all these images are images of 'the family'.

The term 'family', therefore, while being one of the most readily used words in our language is also a term of some complexity and ambiguity. We can use it in a multitude of different way in different situations, perhaps even within the same conversation. My object here is not so much to provide an authoritative definition of 'the family' but rather to introduce the reader to some of the ways in which the uses of the term may vary. Perhaps this flexibility, the fact that we are able to use the word in such a rich variety of contexts, is one of the most important features of family life in contemporary society.

In order to begin to explore this range of meanings and understandings, let us consider a set of distinctions:

Ideals/realities

1 The family on the travel brochure is clearly presented as a 'happy family'. The reader is encouraged to make a connection between this carefree family and sunshine, fun and freedom. We know, however, that 'normal' families also have quarrels, misfortunes and tragedies and that many families will experience violence or separation.
2 The picture is an ideal representation in a second sense. From a whole range of possible family situations, it highlights one, that of a youngish married couple and their school-age children. This represents just one particular stage in the experience of some families, one set of relationships out of a much wider range of possible relationships.

Family/household

A household, in sociological writings, is a group of people sharing the same dwelling. They will normally (as in some census definitions of the term) share one daily meal together. When we talk of 'families' we are usually talking of a relationship established through parenthood or marriage, however these terms are understood. Households often include family members but they may include others who are not related by either parenthood or marriage; servants or lodgers for example.

More importantly, family relationships extend beyond and between households. Our travel brochure example will probably also constitute a household but it is likely that each adult will also have parents, brothers and sisters, etc. who are living in separate, if similar households.

Nuclear/extended

The group on our travel brochure is sometimes refered to as a 'nuclear family', that is a simple two-generational unit consisting of one set of parents and their biological or adopted children. The term 'extended family' refers to those other relationships that extend outwards from this nuclear unit: grandparents, brothers and sisters, aunts and uncles, cousins and so on. This set of people, potentially very large, is sometimes referred to more popularly as 'relatives' or 'kin' although there is nearly always some kind of distinction between those kin whose existence is merely recognized and those between whom there are some kinds of regular relationships and exchanges. Members of an extended family may sometimes share the same household (as in 'three-generational households'), although statistically this is rare both in our own society and in many other societies.

Structure and process

The travel brochure family is literally a snapshot of a family taken at a particular moment of time. But each of these individuals and their relationships with each other, as it were, frozen in time, have a past and a future. In the not-too-distant-past, the married couple had just one child and before that, they simply constituted a couple each of whom had come from different households. Looking into the future we can see the children getting older, leaving the household at different stages and forming their own households.

Unity/diversity

As we shall see, some argue that it is possible to talk of 'the British family' (or indeed of *the* family) while others argue for a more diverse picture, based upon a variety of family forms. Often, in debates about the nature and future of the family, these differences of approach become confused with our first set of differences, between ideals and realities. Some, therefore, will argue that there is one standard or dominant model of the family (often close to the nuclear family household) and that this is the most desired form of domestic arrangement. Alternatively, others might argue that all different forms of family or household are equally valid and that the nuclear family model should not be privileged over any other chosen form of domestic life.

I shall be considering this debate about unity and diversity at greater length in the next section. What I hope to have shown up to now is that there are a variety of ways in which the family can be understood, and that we must always be sensitive to the various shades of meaning which come into play whenever the term is being used.

THE FAMILY IN BRITAIN TODAY

It should be clear therefore that there is no single way of talking about the family in contemporary Britain. Each approach, each different source of data, can tell us something about contemporary family life while ignoring or obscuring other features.

Households and people in households

Households, it will be remembered, consist of a set of people living under one roof and sharing certain facilities. Much of the statistical data that we have, both for the present and for the past, relate to the composition of households. These statistical data may be analysed in two main ways: we can look at the distribution of different types of households at a particular point in time or we can take individuals and look at the way in which people are distributed across different types of households at a point in time.

Table 1.1 gives us the distribution of *households* by type and shows how this distribution has changed or remained stable over recent years. Note that when the table uses the term 'family' here, it is referring to relationships of marriage and parenthood within the household concerned. The following points emerge from this table:

1 The increase in the percentage of households consisting of one person over the age of retirement. This is one indication of an ageing population although we should not assume from this that these single individuals are necessarily isolated; remember, this table tells us nothing about relationships *between* households.
2 We see a decline in the percentage of households consisting of a married couple with children.
3 Households consisting of two or more families are a very insignificant proportion.
4 Looking at any single year we can see that the percentage of households that conform to the travel brochure image discussed earlier (married couple plus two children) constitute a minority of households, somewhere between a quarter and a third. However, it would be wrong to conclude from this that the nuclear-family-based household is a myth or a minority *experience*.

Table 1.1 *Households by type (Great Britain)*

	1961	1971	1976 (%)	1981	1984	1985
No family						
One person						
Under retirement age	4	6	6	8	9	9
Over retirement age	7	12	15	15	16	15
Two or more people						
One or more over retirement age	3	2	2	2	2	1
All under retirement age	2	2	1	3	2	2
One family						
Married couple only	26	27	27	26	26	27
Married couple with one or two dependent children	30	26	26	25	24	24
Married couple with three or more dependent children	8	9	8	6	5	5
Married couple with independent children only	10	8	7	8	8	8
Lone parent with at least one dependent child	2	3	4	5	4	4
Lone parent with independent child(ren) only	4	4	4	4	4	4
Two or more families	3	1	1	1	1	1

Source: *Social Trends* 17, 1987: 41

This point is illustrated in the same issue of *Social Trends* (from which Table 1.1 is taken) where it is noted:

> Just over three-quarters of people living in private households in 1985 lived in families headed by a married couple, a proportion which had fallen only slightly since 1961. Almost three-fifths of these lived in traditional family group households of a married couple with dependent children . . . Married couples with dependent children accounted for 45 per cent of people in households but only 28 per cent of households.
>
> (*Social Trends* 17, 1987: 43)

This illustrates the point of the importance of looking at both households and persons.

Life cycle and family processes

This kind of statistical material is readily available; data dealing with household composition are routinely collected by censuses and government surveys. Such data tell us more about households than about family relationships, that is, relations between and across households. Further, such statistics tend to provide us with a relatively static picture of the structure of households at one point of time. They do not give us a full account of family processes.

One way of considering family processes is in terms of a 'life cycle'. The idea is straightforward enough. Individuals are seen as moving through a set of stages in the course of which they enter and leave slightly different sets of family and household relationships. In considering life cycles we can focus on individuals (birth, marriage, parenthood, death) or on households (from the formation of a household through marriage to its dissolution through death or separation) or on the shifting patterns of relationships between households over time.

One feature of family life in contemporary Britain is the development of a relatively standardized life cycle:

> In the 1960s and 1970s, a life cycle pattern could be seen in Britain which had a number of clearly demarcated stages through which most of the population passed within a relatively narrow band of ages.
>
> (Anderson 1985: 69)

On average, therefore, most people started work at around the age of 16; married in their late teens or early twenties; left home at or around the same time; if women, completed their child-bearing phase within seven years of marriage; became a grandparent; retired by the age of 65; and often experienced great-grandparenthood. To some extent this is a rather different picture from the one provided by the analysis of household composition. This gives an impression of much greater diversity of household forms while a process or life-cycle analysis suggests that the actual chances of any one individual, experiencing life in a nuclear based household are much greater. It is not surprising, therefore, that one family sociologist should talk of the 'rise of the neo-conventional' family (Chester 1985).

It would seem, therefore, that the travel brochure picture might after all have something to recommend it as a picture of what most people have experienced or might reasonably expect to experience at some stage in their lives. Moreover, other evidence would seem to suggest that this is what a majority of the population expects in their life or sees as desirable. For example, a recent random attitude survey found a high measure of support for the 'conventional' family model (Brown *et al.* 1985: 115–19).

The question of divorce

This apparently rather bland account of the 'neo-conventional' family may run counter to a popular understanding of the modern family as being in a state of crisis, a state largely brought about by the rising rates of divorce:

> divorce has increased significantly so that today somewhere in the region of one in three new marriages will probably end in divorce and it is likely that some one in five newborn children in Britain will have parents who divorce before the children reach the age of 16.
>
> (Wicks 1987)

This is an estimate based upon current trends. It should also be noted that these figures do not necessarily present a serious challenge to the model of the neo-conventional family; it is perfectly possible to state these statistics the other way around so that two in three marriages will *not* end in divorce or that four out of five children will *not* have parents who will divorce.

Opponents of the idea that the contemporary family is undergoing some kind of crisis will also point to statistics dealing with remarriage following divorce. Consider the figures shown in Table 1.2.

Table 1.2 Patterns of remarriage, 1961–84

	1961	1971	1976	1981	1983	1984
Remarriage as a percentage of all marriages	14	20	31	34	35	35
Remarriage of the divorced as a percentage of all marriages	9	15	26	31	32	32

Source: Adapted from *Social Trends* 16, 1986: 37

Table 1.2 shows a marked increase in the percentage of marriages which are remarriages over the period 1961–84 and stresses that this striking increase is almost wholly due to remarriages as a result of the divorce of one or both of the partners. Now something like a third of all marriages are remarriages for at least one of the partners. Supporters of the model of the 'neo-conventional' family will argue that this is a clear indication that, while there have been marked increases in the divorce rates, this has not meant a 'flight from marriage', since individuals seem to be more than willing to 'give it another try'.

However, there is more than one way of looking at this set of facts. The growing percentage of remarriage following divorce, together with the fact that the bulk of divorces will involve children, makes for increasing complexity in family and household processes. While it is true that most people will expect to live in a nuclear-family-based household at some stage in their life, the routes by which they arrive at this stage might be more various. Some of these main routes are:

1 *Standard route*   Marriage followed by parenthood. There are a couple of slight variations on this route: one where pregnancy anticipates marriage and one where cohabitation anticipates marriage and parenthood.
2 *From single-parenthood*   It should be noted that routes into single parenthood are also varied.
3 *Reconstituted families*   Adults may enter into nuclear-family-based households from other nuclear-family-based households (other than their own families of origin) which have been broken by either death or, more likely, divorce.

The routes by which people leave nuclear-family-based households are equally various:

1 *Standard route* Children grow up and leave home, followed at some later stage by the death of one of the partners.
2 *Into single-parenthood* As a result of death, desertion or divorce.
3 *Into other households* (nuclear based or otherwise). One or both of the partners may have to form reconstructed families or households.

A picture of some complexity emerges beneath the surface of the standard life cycle. Individuals may enter and leave the nuclear-family-based household by the standard route or they may enter by the standard route and leave by a non-standard route or vice versa. Of particular importance in modifying any simple picture of a standard life cycle is the process by which families are reconstituted following divorce.

Moreover, if we shift our focus from households to family in the wider sense of a network of relationships established through marriage and parenthood, the impact of divorce and remarriage becomes even more complicated. There is the question (especially where children are involved) of the relationship between the members of the reconstituted household and the partners' previous households prior to divorce. There is the question of their shifting relationships with past and new partners, parents and kin. Put starkly: a man may become an 'ex-husband' through divorce but does he become an 'ex-uncle' as well?

Experiences of family and households

The complexity increases when we begin to explore the more qualitative aspects of family life, how people feel about their family or household situations, whether they experience such relationships as happy or unhappy, as a source of delight and pleasure or as a source of restriction and constraint.

Such qualitative dimensions would seem to be too individual or idiosyncratic to allow for sociological analysis. However, some of these sources of variation can be indicated.

1 Most people, it would seem, do have some sense of family life beyond their immediate household or nuclear family. Janet Finch summarizes a lot of research into family ties beyond the nuclear family in these terms:

> people *do* apparently feel a 'moral imperative' to assist their kin, but how that this actually operates is very variable and not predictable in any simple way.... People are very willing to assist their relatives, but in certain circumstances and of their own volition: we do not like to *have* to do it.
>
> (Finch 1986: 26)

2 An important way in which the experience of family life differs is according
   to gender. Thus the family obligations referred to in the previous paragraph
   are often assumed to be more a matter of concern for women, than for men
   (Finch and Groves 1983); housework continues to be a female responsibility, despite trends in female employment outside the home (Oakley
   1974; Collins 1985) and so on. The survey on family values, quoted earlier,
   hints that men and women may have slightly different perspectives on
   domestic living: married men, for example 'by and large expressed the
   greatest satisfaction with their home life' (Brown *et al*. 1985: 122–3).
3 Another important source of variation is social class. Even relatively
   straightforward distinctions between middle-class and working-class point
   to differences in child-rearing and socialization (Newson and Newson
   1963; 1968), the experience of motherhood (Boulton 1983) and fatherhood
   (Lewis 1986) and the housework (Oakley 1974).
4 Britain is a multi-ethnic society and it is clear that ethnicity is a major
   source of variation in family living and experience. (For one example, see
   Anwar 1985.)

The wider context

There is always the danger of treating the family as 'a thing'. One way of
avoiding this is, as I have done up to now, to emphasize that there are a variety
of different ways in which the family can be understood and studied. Another
way is to stress that the family is not something which stands alone, in
isolation from other trends or processes. In particular it is important to see
the family and household in relation to the economy and to wider patterns
of work and employment.

The conventional model puts the relationship very simply. The nuclear-
family-based household consists of a male breadwinner, who earns to support
his wife and children. The wife's prime responsibility is to run the household.
Put like that, this would seem to be a caricature, although it is surprising to
note how dominant this model (or ideology) remains, in popular understanding (Collins 1985), in social and economic policy (Land, 1978; 1980) and
even in social science (Goldthorpe 1983).

The first way in which this conventional model is undermined is, of
course, through the employment of women, especially married women and
mothers, outside the home. Partly because women are having fewer children
and having them over a shorter period of years, and partly because of the
changing nature of the labour markets, most women are now (as compared
with their equivalents between the wars or in the early part of this century)
more likely to spend a greater proportion of their lives in employment and
a relatively smaller proportion as full-time mothers. While these trends may
not necessarily signify any clear-cut increases in women's sense of independ-

ence they clearly do force a modification of the simple 'male-breadwinner' model.

Another way in which the conventional model of the relationship between home and work is being modified is through the growing impact of unemployment. Clearly the conventional model is affected if the male 'head of household' is not the breadwinner or if this relationship which links the family to the economy via the wage packet is under threat. There may be more complex effects. The standard life cycle, which we explored earlier in this section, assumed an average age of starting work at 16 and an average age of retirement at around 65. This particular interweaving of work and family may require considerable modification if the trends in unemployment continue. For example, children may find themselves dependent upon their parents for longer periods of time and retirement may take place (voluntarily or otherwise) at an earlier age.

More theoretically, the impact of persisting patterns of unemployment have led some sociologists to reformulate our conceptions of the economy and the simple opposition between home and work. Economic activity, it is stressed, is not simply something which takes place at the factory or the office in exchange for a formal wage packet. It also takes place within and between households. The conventionally understood divisions of labour between men and women based upon the opposition between work and home are now shown to conceal much more complex divisions and activities. This was probably always the case; but unemployment together with the greater participation in our times of women in the labour force have highlighted the fact that family and household do not stand apart but are clearly bound up with each other (Pahl 1984).

Thus this section has argued that there are a variety of different ways of viewing the family in contemporary Britain. They all highlight different aspects of a complex reality. Generally, the picture would seem to be one of a fair degree of uniformity in structure and process, but a uniformity which masks a considerable degree of variation in process and experience, variation which increases once you start to consider the family in the wider context of the economy and the class structure.

THE FAMILY IN HISTORICAL PERSPECTIVE: PATTERNS OF CHANGE

It is easy, sometimes, to get a sense of the family as something that has always been more or less the way it is today. We listen to parents or grandparents talking about their families and readily imagine these older generations in the past hearing very similar tales of earlier generations. This preservation of a sense of continuity is particularly important for certain families, members of the landed aristocracy for example, but the interest in establishing and maintaining links with the past seems to be much wider than a particular class or stratu of society.

Yet, at the same time, these same conversations across generations also often convey a sense of change, sometimes even decline. 'We were more caring then', 'children respected their parents more', 'we didn't have the State looking after us from the cradle to the grave'; all these and other similarly general statements are woven into particular accounts of family relationships in past times. More generally still, we are aware of the enormous changes that have taken place in economic and social life since, say the eighteenth century – the Industrial Revolution, developments in transport and communications, and two world wars – and it would seem unlikely that the institution of the family should not be affected in some way and to some degree by these changes. It would seem important, therefore, to fill out and to locate our account of the family in contemporary Britain by providing some kind of historical perspective in order to reach at some kind of overall assessment of the patterns of continuity and change.

In sociological and historical discussions of 'the western family', two major sets of perspectives have emerged.

First, some argue that there has been a decline in the family and its functioning over, roughly, the past two hundred years. The kind of implied contrast is between a wide-ranging, richly textured set of family relationships bound by duties and obligations as against today's much more narrow, more individualistic and more fragile families. In slightly different terms, this argument is sometimes presented as a 'loss of function' on the part of the family. Against this it is sometimes argued that the functions of the family have changed rather than declined and that this change has been in the direction of increasing *specialization*.

In the second place, it has been argued that the nuclear family has become increasingly isolated as an institution, more segregated and distinct from other institutions in society. The image is of 'the Englishman's home as his castle', the home and family as a kind of fortress against the more impersonal worlds of industry, commerce, bureaucracy and politics. Against this it is argued that, on the contrary, the past two hundred years have witnessed a gradual erosion of the boundaries of the family through a variety of interventions from the state and from professionals.

These two debates overlap at certain points. For example, the growth of state education may be seen as entailing a 'loss of functions' on the part of the family as it hands over the responsibilities for educating and socializing the children to specialized schools and school teachers. Similarly, this may be seen as an example of the weakening of the boundaries of the family as professionals co-operate or compete with parents over the education of future generations. Although these two debates do overlap, it does seem to make some sense to distinguish them and to present the relevant historical evidence for each of them in turn.

Loss or specialization?

First, the actual usage of the term 'family' has slowly changed within European society. Usages of the term prior to the eighteenth century were, from a modern perspective, somewhat loose and often included persons who were not necessarily related by marriage or by birth but who were part of, or closely associated with, the household. Present usages, in contrast, may be more limited to immediate legally or socially recognized ties of marriage and parenthood. This shift in terminology could be interpreted as reflecting a shift towards a growing specialization of family functions.

Second, these changes, often subtle, in terms of the usages of the word 'family' should not, however, necessarily lead us to suppose that there has been any significant change in household composition over the centuries. The work of historical demographers (notably Peter Laslett), who have pains-takingly reconstructed earlier households through the use of sources such as parish records, has argued persuasively that the idea of an extended family system existing at some stage in the past is false. The norm before the Industrial Revolution was, as it is now, for a couple to defer marriage until it was possible to set up an independent household. Moreover, this norm – and practice – existed and continued to exist over much of Europe although this pattern was not completely universal. Part of rural Ireland, for example, might be seen as an exception.

The work of Laslett and others, then, called into question the idea that the process of industrialization shattered some pre-existing extended family system, at least in so far as that system might be the basis for the composition of households. Indeed, the early processes of industrialization might have encouraged people, in conditions very close to the margins of poverty, to make use of their family and kinship ties to a much greater extent than was the case either before or in more recent times (Anderson 1971).

It is true, however, that on average households are smaller now than in previous centuries although this change would seem to be fairly recent. A fall from an average of just five children per family to just over two took place during the period 1860 to around the time of the Second World War (Anderson 1985: 73). Moreover, the size of households throughout the nineteenth century was often augmented by the presence of lodgers or servants.

What the historical evidence for household size and composition suggests, therefore, is that the idea of some marked contrast between pre-industrial England and the present, especially the notion of a shift from an extended family system to a nuclear family system has been much exaggerated. Note, however, that Laslett and others were concerned chiefly with households and their composition. Relationships between households are somewhat more difficult to assess.

Third, we have already seen how the family life cycle, as a set of relatively standard experiences through which most people will pass, is something that has developed since the late nineteenth century. This homogenization of the family and individual life cycles is partly a consequence of demographic changes (greater expectancy of life, smaller families and so on) which are, in their turn, the consequence of other economic and technological changes influencing diet, health care, contraception, relative affluence and so on. One consequence of this standardization of the life cycle is that, whether or not we are more caring towards our kin and relatives and whether or not we interact with them more on a day-to-day basis, we certainly have a greater *opportunity* for sustained relationships across the generations.

Fourth, the question of the withdrawal of the family from various other areas of life is more complex. It is possibly clearest in the case of education where the growth of specialized and mandatory systems of education remove the child from the home for part of the day and for most of the year. However, the family continued to provide the first and main set of relationships within which the child learns basic physical and social skills, from the use of language to table manners, from sex roles to notions of personal and private property. If the school undertakes certain specialized educational tasks it also, often at least, makes new demands upon the parents in terms of punctuality, completion of homework or provision of sportswear.

Rather than a loss of functions it is probably more a matter of 'sharing' the processes of socialization between the two institutions. Similarly, we have already seen in the sphere of economic life that it is better to think of a different kind of 'mix' between household and economic activities rather than a radical segregation. In the case of other spheres of life such as leisure or religion, it would seem to be the case that modern society does provide a much greater range of choice in these matters and that worship or recreational activities do not need to be undertaken with other family members. Nevertheless, the separation is hardly complete; most activities conventionally regarded as leisure activities are enjoyed either in the home or with other family members.

It would seem, therefore, that there does not seem to be any evidence for an overall decline in the family in terms of its centrality in the lives of individuals or of its importance in many areas of social life. Further, it does not seem to be particularly helpful to describe such changes as have taken place as a 'loss of functions'. As we shall see, it is possible to talk of a shift in the range of uses to which family relationships are put, with a particular sharper focus on the quality of the material relationship and with the business of childrearing. To this extent the family may be described as a more specialized institution.

Separation or intervention?

Has the family become a more separate, a more private institution or has it become more subject to outside interventions? Again, the historical evidence is by no means straightforward.

First, one of the causes of the already mentioned development of a relatively homogeneous life cycle can be seen as a growing role for the state in matters with direct or indirect consequence for the family. At one end, there is the development of a minimum period of schooling so that it becomes possible to speak of a school-leaving age as a major turning point occurring for nearly all the members of our society at roughly the same stage of life. Similarly, the development of the age of retirement (itself related to the growth of state and private pension schemes) brings about another degree of homogenization at the other end of the life cycle. Much of what appears to be a natural progression through a family life cycle is in fact the consequence of various kinds of state interventions over the centuries.

Second, historical evidence does suggest that the home and the family have become more associated with ideas of privacy. An urban and industrial society certainly facilitates the development of more private relationships between the sexes and between parents and children. In a traditional or rural based community, areas of life which today would be considered private or a matter of personal choice might very often come under the scrutiny of kin or neighbours, sometimes to the extent of informal sanctions being applied against people who depart from accepted norms. Such control is rarely possible in a modern urban or suburban community where there is considerable mobility of population and where there is much greater choice in terms of friends and significant kin.

Industrialization and urbanization may, in some measure, provide some of the conditions for privacy, especially for some of the more affluent sections of the population. (Privacy was hardly something enjoyed by members of the new industrial working class in the overcrowded districts of Manchester or Sheffield, for example.) But it did not necessarily on its own create the idea of privacy as something to be enjoyed and sought after and to be particularly identified with the home and with domestic life. During the early nineteenth century, there was a gradual elaboration of the distinction between the public and the private and the sharper identification of the latter with the home and with women. Religion and ideas of property often underlined this growing development of the middle-class domestic sphere, and the growing idea of the home as a haven from the rigours of business (Davidoff and Hall 1987). During the twentieth century, the domestic ideal spread to other sections of the middle class and the working class.

Third, in the twentieth century in particular, some authors maintain, another important qualitative change in family living took place. This was to do with the relationships between husband and wife within the home and it has been argued that these relationships have become more equal, egalitarian, democratic or symmetrical. The contrast was often made between these emerging family forms and some more patriarchal models, in which the father had a strong measure of control over his wife and children. In terms of a whole host of indicators such as legal status, property rights and opportunities for employment, it cannot be denied that there have been clear moves in this direction. However, it is also true that over the same period, the label 'housewife' (with all its rather limited and negative connotations) became clarified and more firmly attached to women in the home. Certainly, when we look at the actual way in which tasks within the home are divided between husband and wife, there continues to be a tendency for the woman to be responsible for more tasks and to spend a greater proportion of time in these responsibilities than her husband, even where both may be wage earners (Brannen and Wilson 1987).

The relationship between the rather contradictory trends in relation to the balance of power between the sexes in the home and the wider issues of privacy and the separateness of the home need to be elaborated. One way of characterizing the trend in marriage is to argue that it is being increasingly understood as an interpersonal relationship, a relationship which exists not simply for the production of children and not simply as something which is defined by church and state but which is seen increasingly in terms of its importance for the individuals concerned. The stress is on the idea of marriage as something *mutually* fulfilling and it is possible that these expectations may come into conflict with the continuing marked sexual divisions of labour within the home. Nevertheless, in theory at least, there does appear to be a close link to be made between the ideas of privacy, the idea of marriage as an interpersonal relationship to be mutually enjoyed and the idea of marriage as being approximately egalitarian.

Fourth, there is, however, something paradoxical about this notion of privacy, especially as it has become elaborated in the twentieth century. These changing understandings of the nature of marriage have been accompanied by increasing involvements on the part of the state and professionals. Of course, for centuries there have been regulations as to whom one may or may not marry, questions of divorce and remarriage, sexual conduct, and so on. However, it can be argued that there has been a growth of state activities which have an indirect or direct impact upon the family, many of which have been mentioned already (taxation, systems of child benefit, pensions, education, etc.). Legislation dealing with divorce, indeed, has a particular paradoxical feature. While in one sense it can be seen as a liberalization of a willingness to allow partners to determine for themselves whether a marriage has broken down it has also entailed finer legal definitions of marital and parental obligations following divorce procedures.

Moreover, a growing number of experts of varying kinds – health visitors, social workers and family therapists – have increasingly focused their attention upon marriage and the family and, in so doing, have served to sharpen or crystallize the notion of 'the family'. Thus the words 'family' or 'marriage' become attached to particular kinds of professional or near-professional activities: family therapy, marriage guidance, family law and family policy.

To conclude, it would appear that in the debate between those who argue for the isolation and separateness of the family and those who argue for greater external involvement are not necessarily dealing with two opposed perspectives. Rather they are two aspects of the same, if complex, process. There does appear to be some evidence that the family has become particularly associated with notions of privacy and the personal and that to this extent it has developed a kind of relative autonomy. Relationships with kin while they may not necessarily be less frequent have become less obligatory, domestic relationships have become less subject to community scrutiny and the idea of the family today appears to be both more limited and more focused. On the other hand, there have been greater interventions on the part of professionals and the state into family matters and that this has both weakened and strengthened the boundaries of the nuclear-family-based household.

Historical discussion, therefore, can provide a valuable insight into our understanding of the new family today. Such discussion can highlight continuities as well as changes and can remind us of the family as a process, as something which is subject to change over generations as well as within an individual life cycle.

SOCIALIZATION

Three main changes affecting the family of today seem, therefore, to be of particular importance: the development of a more or less standard family life cycle; the growing association of the home and family with ideas of privacy and the growing interest in and intervention into the family on the part of professionals and the state. Taking these and other changes into account, I shall now look more specifically at one aspect of family life: the socialization of young children.

Socialization is a complex term, standing at a point where sociology and psychology meet. Here I am particularly concerned with what is usually described as primary socialization, that is the process whereby children acquire a whole range of skills, norms and values, necessary for their development as social beings in general and as members of a given society or section in particular and where this process takes place largely within the home and in the early years of life.

There are some problems with this approach to socialization, however. In the first place, this approach seems to suggest both too active and too deliberate a role on the part of the socializers (the parents) and too passive a role on the part of the children who are being socialized. Most primary socialization is in fact an *interaction*, not a one-way process, and much of it is unconscious and non-deliberate. Here, as elsewhere, learning 'by example' is probably more important than deliberate instruction. In the second place the simpler models of socialization suggest too straightforward a coincidence between the 'needs' of society and the practices associated with socialization. Apart from anything else, this fails to explain how individuals grow up with views or values which may run counter to some of the dominant values in a given society.

Bearing these difficulties in mind, I shall argue more simply that I am especially concerned with the interaction of adults (usually parents) and children within the home. I shall here look at three aspects of this, placing the discussion in a historical context:

1 Changing conceptions of childhood.
2 Changing conceptions of parenthood.
3 Changing patterns of relationships between parents and children.

Changing conceptions of childhood

In recent years it has been widely argued that the idea of 'the child' is a modern invention. This argument, especially associated with the work of a French historian, Philipe Ariès (1962), claimed that prior to the seventeenth century, European society did not have a clear conception of childhood as a separate stage of human development. After a more or less readily identifiable period of infancy (associated with the actual physical dependence of the baby), there were no clear-cut lines of demarcation between adults and children; they worked together, played together and sometimes were even formally educated together. The notion of childhood as a separate and identifiable stage of development, became elaborated in the intervening centuries between then and now. Some of the factors associated with this growing identification of the child were decreasing rates of child mortality, especially among the upper and middle classes, which meant that more attention and care could be paid to children who were now reasonably expected to survive into adulthood; the development of formal systems of education which in turn became adjusted to the needs of a growing industrial capitalist society; growing humanitarian values and so on.

This remains an interesting argument although it is probably true to say that it is now less widely accepted. For one thing, it has been pointed out that the evidence upon which the original argument was based was somewhat suspect, relating largely to the elite sections of society. Moreover, other evidence has suggested that, at least for Britain and America from the seventeenth century onwards, there have been no clear patterns of development in the conceptualization of 'the child' (Pollock 1983).

However, something of the argument may still remain of importance. It is clear that the actual period which we label 'childhood' is not some fixed entity, that the period which different societies call 'childhood' does vary in duration, and that these variations in the understanding of the length and nature of childhood are related to other changes or patterns within the wider society. For example, compulsory schooling has obviously had a major effect in marking out a period between infancy and adulthood as have, in more recent times, theories of child development which argue for definite states of development and maturation. Additional factors would include restrictions on child employment and the growing elaboration and codification of ages of consent, the age of majority, and so on.

When we switch from talking about the actual period of childhood to considering some of the more qualitative aspects, the picture becomes more complex. There are certainly contrasting, and conflicting, images of childhood as the two similar sounding but very different terms 'childish' and 'childlike' illustrate. The former conveys a somewhat negative view of childhood, as something to be overcome and, in adulthood, willingly put aside. The latter contains a more romantic and positive image of childhood innocence and wonder, a sense which is lost as adulthood approaches. In educational theory, the former encourages the notion of discipline and control, the latter of free expression and exploration. Both these rival perspectives on childhood have been influential among certain sections of the population at different times. What is suggested, however, is that childhood is, and perhaps has increasingly become so, a contested area, one in which a variety of interested and influential adults have conflicting views. Certainly, this sense of childhood as being some kind of battlefield over which adults rage is quite strong; one only has to consider debates about the influence of television or the rights and wrongs of sex education. Thus if it is possible to argue that there has been some kind of elaboration of the *period* of childhood in more qualitative terms, the ways in which childhood has been conceived and understood are much less uniform.

Changing conceptions of parenthood

Generally speaking, a sharper, more focused idea of the nature of childhood also has implications for notions of parental responsibilities to that child. Changing conceptions of parenthood may also be linked to changing definitions in the roles of women and men. The term 'parent' is neutral in gender terms, and to talk of changing definitions of parenthood might conceal quite different trends for mothers and fathers.

The historical evidence would seem to indicate the following themes to be of importance. First, a shift away from a simple 'patriarchal' model whereby the father had in formal legal terms, considerable or absolute power over his wife and children. In cases of dispute over the welfare of the children, the father's claims would be paramount. This was roughly the situation that prevailed at the beginning of the nineteenth century.

In practice, of course, the actual exercise of this patriarchal power must have been more complicated than this simple legal model suggests. However, this nineteenth century situation might be contrasted with the present where, for example, in the cases of custody disputes between estranged mothers and fathers, the majority of verdicts are in favour of the mother.

Second, this legal shift might generally be characterized as a shift away from an emphasis upon the rights and duties, focusing more generally upon parental responsibilities. This is not to say that parents before the nineteenth century did not, as a matter of course, spend time with their children in play, instruction or care. It is rather that parenting increasingly became the subject of specific and explicit guidance. Medicine, child psychology and psycho-analysis focused upon the child in relation to the parents. Together with this elaboration of the craft of parenthood came new understandings of parental responsibilities. This is not simply a matter of seeing that a child is well fed or adequately clothed. A child's delinquency or truancy become accountable in terms of some psychological neglect, some parental failure or some breakdown in the relationships between the two parents.

This has not, of course, been a straightforward progression. There have certainly been, for example, class variations with middle-class parents being more likely to respond to the changing advice offered by child-care experts and working-class parents bringing up their children according to less variable and more traditional understandings. At the upper levels of society, the 'nanny' has not entirely disappeared. It should also be noted that these notions of parental responsibility focus with particular sharpness upon the mother.

Third, the emphasis on the detailed importance of mothering was elabor-ated in the period immediately following the Second World War and particularly influenced by the work of the psychologist John Bowlby (1952). In more recent years there has been a growing focus on a more active understanding of fatherhood. This, in its turn, has led to increasing talk of 'shared parenthood'. Now fathers increasingly wish to be present at the birth of their children. There is some evidence for fathers taking a greater (although rarely equal) role in the routine work associated with childrearing, and there are clear signs of a popular demand for paternity leave, although usually of a modest kind (Bell et al. 1983).

Whether these changes justify a shift in terminology from 'mothers' and 'fathers' to the more gender-neutral term 'parents' is doubtful. Mothers continue to bear the main responsibility for many of the more routine aspects of childrearing (Boulton 1983) such as taking the child to the doctor or bathing the baby, while fathers appear to exercise a greater degree of choice in what aspects of childrearing they might become involved in (Lewis and O'Brien 1987). However, it is not a simple matter of either/or; there are now a wide range of models for fathers and it is likely that more and more couples are feeling their way towards some kind of partnership in parenting, often within the limits imposed by their own employment situation, the expectation of their social circles and the wider culture.

Changing patterns of relationships between parents and children

Much of the discussion here has focused around questions of punishment and disciplining, in particular as to whether parents were more harsh towards their children in the past than they are today. Pollock's study, based upon autobiographies and diaries, suggests that there are no clear patterns to be found in this respect although there is something to suggest an increase in harsh treatment in England during the nineteenth century (Pollock 1983). Pollock also provides plenty of examples of parents expressing concern and distress at the death of a child in past centuries, and this might suggest that higher rates of infant mortality did not necessarily mean that parents were more casual in their attitudes to children.

The main trend would seem to be an elaboration of the apparently contradictory pattern discussed in the previous section. On the one hand it is possible to talk about a *privatization* of relationships between parents and children, that the work of socialization increasingly takes place in private, away from the gaze of neighbours or the immediate community. Even grandparents feel that they should tread carefully in offering advice to parents as to how they should bring up their grandchildren.

At the same time we have seen an increasing *professional* intervention into childrearing and socialization. Birth, as has often been noted, is increasingly and overwhelmingly a hospital and medicalized event, and from the moment of birth, the progress of the child is monitored by health visitors, school teachers and possibly, later, social workers or other specialists. This wider body of expertise is also mediated through to the parents via books on child care or television programmes.

It is important when considering changing patterns of socialization to keep both sets of trends in mind for they help us to account for many of the contradictions and tensions that exist around issues to do with socialization and education and the boundaries between the home and other more formal institutions. On the one hand childrearing has become a major parental *project*, a major source of investment (in time and in money) and involvement for parents. On the other hand as society becomes more complex, as the transitions between home and school and work become more formalized, childrearing becomes a matter of concern for a whole range of others apart from the immediate parents. These others would include teachers, employers, police and magistrates and politicians.

SOCIAL REPRODUCTION

The focus in the previous section was largely on the 'internal' processes and relationships between parents and children that take place within the family, although it became clear that such processes were never just matters of individual concern, that the wider society was always involved, directly or indirectly. In this section, however, the focus is much more explicitly upon the relationships between the family, in all its range of meanings, and the wider society.

One common term to describe this kind of emphasis on the relationships between the family and other social institutions and processes is that of 'reproduction'. Here the term is not simply used in its more generally understood sense of biological reproduction but also, and more significantly, to refer to processes of social and cultural reproduction. In other words, individuals and families do not simply produce new individuals but also, and at the same time, reproduce the wider structure of society. In looking at the processes of social and cultural reproduction we are looking at the ways in which a society persists over time and the role of the family and the household in these processes.

Let us consider a simple example. All societies have certain socially acceptable ways whereby members of that society greet one another. Thus they may shake hands, embrace, kiss on one or both cheeks or simply say 'Hi'. Such routine and everyday practices commonly identify what members of a culture have in common. We know that such practices persist over long periods of time. It is also likely that these practices are learned within the home and through observing the behaviour of parents. In such a way practices are reproduced over time and in so doing the distinctive features of a society or culture are maintained. We can follow the same kind of processes through using much more complex examples to do with the use of language, styles of dress or eating and drinking patterns. Reproduction then is in part a matter of the reproduction of what a culture shares and, to that extent, what that culture *is*.

If these kinds of everyday practices, in which the family and household play an important part and through which it can be said that a culture reproduces itself, identify what a culture shares and has in common, they also identify patterns of difference. These differences occur not only between cultures but also within cultures. To return to the methods we use to greet each other, these also signify gender, age and perhaps also social class differences. The case of gender is perhaps the most obvious; in British society men and women may kiss each other, women may kiss each other but men rarely do so. It is with the processes of the reproduction of differences and inequalities that I shall be chiefly concerned in this section.

Many of the differences already considered – gender, class and ethnicity – are also inequalities, inequalities which appear to be deeply entrenched. I am concerned here with seeking to explain the part played by the family in the social reproduction of these inequalities. Let us consider very briefly two of these: class and gender inequalities. In talking about class differences we are talking about regular patterns of inequality of wealth, income and power and influence which persist over time. There are four key features.

First, patterns of inheritance, that is exchanges that take place between family members across generations, continue to be one of the major ways whereby inequalities persist over time. Wealthy families have developed a variety of strategies whereby wealth is 'kept within the family'.

Second, education continues to be a major factor in understanding class inequalities and their persistence and the family continues to play an important part in influencing educational achievement. It is not possible to go into all the evidence and controversies surrounding social class, family and educational achievement but simply to note that the family plays its part in a variety of ways. It may act directly, where, for example, parents are able to secure advantages for their children through the purchase of private education. This is still an important factor when we consider the backgrounds of many of the top decision-makers in our society. Slightly less directly, upper- and middle-class families have a variety of forms of 'cultural capital' which they are able to hand on to their children; these can range from 'social skills' or a good accent to the ready access to many features of an elite or middle-class culture: books, word processors, sporting or leisure facilities. At an even more fundamental level, all kinds of skills in the use of language, skills which will be especially recognized and approved in schools, will be acquired within the family-based household. The work of Basil Bernstein (1971), although much debated, has been particularly associated with the identification of family, the acquisition of particular linguistic skills and wider patterns of social reproductions.

Third, reference has been made earlier on to the rising patterns of divorce and it is important to note that divorce rates are not spread evenly across the population. Haskey discovered, for example, that divorce rates for unskilled manual workers in 1984 were 30 per 1,000, as compared with 7 per 1,000 for members of the professional classes (quoted by Clark 1987: 114). We should not see these higher rates of divorce as being simply the cause of poverty or social disadvantage; they are more a consequence of these disadvantages. However, we can see them as part of the process whereby social disadvantages (or advantages in the case of the professional groups) are reproduced over generations. Another way of looking at this is to see domestic relationships as a kind of amplifier of various social and economic conditions, both favourable and unfavourable.

Fourth, this understanding of family relationships as an amplifier can be seen clearly in the case of another growing and persisting source of inequality in our society: that between those who experience long periods of un-employment and those who remain in the labour market on a more or less stable basis. There are no simple relationships between long-term un-employment and family breakdown; nevertheless, the study cited earlier showed a divorce rate of 34 per 1,000 for unemployed men (Clark 1987). Another area, at a different stage of the life cycle is to do with youth unemployment. One study of the effect of this, noted:

We also saw a whole continuum of family reactions from parents who sympathized with and supported their offspring to those families where the tensions led to periodic quarrels and on to those where young people left home because they felt the friction had become intolerable. Most families are not, however, easily categorized and parents veered from recriminations to being over-protective.

(Coffield 1987: 92)

Again it is not the case that the family causes unemployment but it is not simply the case either that the family is at the receiving end of such adverse economic conditions.

Turning now to the question of gender inequalities, the issue would seem to be one of explaining why it is that such inequalities persist in spite of, among other things, the extension of the franchise to women and legislation dealing with equal pay and sex discrimination. We have already noted some of those inequalities, ranging from inequalities in the labour market to inequalities in terms of the division of labour in the home.

Two interrelated factors should be stressed in explaining the reproduction of gender inequalities. One is the socialization process. One of the most important features of socialization is in relation to behaviour, responses and activities that are held to be appropriate to woman and to men. These aspects of socialization are rarely specific but are conveyed in all kinds of less deliberate and everyday ways. One example might be the tendency of fathers to engage in more physical forms of play with sons as compared with daughters.

The other aspect is to do with the sexual division in the home. In spite of all the national trends towards female emancipation, it is still clear that people, both women and men, continue to have fairly traditional ideas as to what is appropriate work for each. One respondent to a survey conducted in Middlesborough was quoted as saying 'I basically see that a house is a woman's domain and a woman to look after that. It's not my job to change the baby or do the hoovering or the dusting. I've always felt that way' (Collins 1985: 79). This was a middle-class man speaking, although similar views have been elicited from women, middle-class and working-class. These notions about the appropriate work in the home for men and women are very widespread and are reflected in actual practice. As such, they influence women's ability to compete for work on the labour market, the attitudes of employers towards female employees who are assumed to have a less than whole-hearted commitment to their work and often a woman's assessment of her own educational potential and career aspirations. All these processes interact with each other, the outcome being the continuing reproduction of gender inequalities, an outcome in which the family and household play a major part.

In concluding this section two major points should be made. First, in considering these processes we are never dealing with the family in isolation. It is less than helpful, for example, to isolate the family as a 'cause' of poverty or inequality. Rather we need to understand the family in the context of a wider network of relationships between individuals and between institutions in society.

Second, in both the cases of class and gender inequalities it is important to avoid too deterministic a picture. In the case of class it is important to stress that the class systems of industrial societies such as Britain are fluid and show evidence of social mobility as well as of rigidity. Here, too, the family may play a part in contributing to processes of upward and downward mobility. Similarly, in the case of gender it is important to stress that women and men are not simply passive creatures upon which social institutions such as households or workplaces act. One of the important, but perhaps less widely recognized, effects of the growing self-consciousness on the part of women and men in relation to their marriages and their work as parents may be a greater willingness to seek out alternatives: dual-career or dual-earner families, attempts to rear children in 'non-sexist' ways or role reversals. All these are probably minorities and often limited to particular sections of society. However, it is important to note and explore these exceptions at the very least as an indication of human potentialities and a reminder that individuals are not totally determined by 'roles', 'structure' or 'the culture'.

CONCLUSION

This last point brings us back to our point of departure: the extent to which we can talk about uniformity or diversity in the family. First, as we have seen, this is a matter of definition and it has been suggested that there are a variety of ways in which we understand the term 'family' – household, nuclear family, extended family and so on – and that each usage slightly shifts the focus that we adopt. Second, it is a question of personal or political values; the family and family matters continue to be contested areas and these wider values will, in various ways, affect how individuals see and understand the family.

A third reason for this uncertainty is to do with the level of analysis. In other words, if we are standing back at some distance we can detect fairly uniform patterns, for example fairly stable progressions through particularly identified stages of something which we call a 'life cycle'. As we move in closer, some of the sources of variation become more apparent. In some cases these are to do with culture and it is possible to talk of working-class, middle-class or professional families just as it is possible to talk about Sikh or Cypriot families. In other cases these sources of variation are more individual, reflecting the fact that in a relatively open society there does exist some measure of choice in the way in which people do what might seem, from the outside, very similar things. At the same time we do have and use more general notions of parenting and marriage, general notions which inevitably smooth over some of the finer differences which are experienced on a day-to-day basis.

Perhaps the crucial question is whether a longer historical perspective would discover any significant variations. This, as we have seen, is a difficult matter and some of the earlier certainties which spoke of 'the pre-industrial family' and 'the industrial family' have dissolved. Nevertheless, it is possible to see some broad patterns of change, in terms of the development of a more standardized family life cycle, for example, or the shift to a more focused and 'professional' understanding of parenting. And even if, in some cases, the actual directions of change are not as clear as we would like, there is a growing understanding as to what the crucial variables are: household, family relationships across households, work and employment and gender relationships, seeing all these in terms of a complex and shifting set of interrelationships.

REFERENCES

Anderson, M. (1971) *Family Structure in Nineteenth Century Lancashire*, Cambridge: Cambridge University Press.
—— (1985) 'The emergence of the modern life cycle in Britain', *Social History* 10 (1): 69–87.
Anwar, M. (1985) *Pakistanis in Britain: A Sociological Study*, London: New Century.
Ariès, P. (1962) *Centuries of Childhood*, London: Cape.
Bell, C., McKee, L. and Priestly, K. (1983) *Father, Childbirth and Work*, Manchester: Equal Opportunities Commission.
Bernstein, B. (1971) *Class, Codes and Control, vol. I*, London: Routledge & Kegan Paul.
Boulton, M. G. (1983) *On Being a Mother*, London: Tavistock.
Bowlby, J. (1952) *Maternal Care and Mental Health*, Geneva: World Health Organization.
Brannen, J. and Wilson, G. (eds) (1987) *Give and Take in Families*, London: Allen & Unwin.
Brown, J. *et al.* (1985) 'Marriage and the family' in M. Abrams *et al.* (eds) *Values and Social Change in Britain*, London: Macmillan.
Chester, R. (1985) 'The rise of the neo-conventional family', *New Society* 9 May.
Clark, D. (1987) 'Changing partners: marriage and divorce across the life course', in G. Cohen (ed.) *Social Change and the Life Course*, London: Tavistock.
Coffield, F. (1987) 'From the celebration to the marginalisation of youth', in G. Cohen (ed.) *Social Change and the Life Course*, London: Tavistock.
Collins, R. (1985) '"Horses for courses": ideology and the division of domestic labour', in P. Close and R. Collins (eds) *Family and Economy in Modern Society*, Basingstoke: Macmillan.
Davidoff, L. and Hall, C. (1987) *Family Fortunes*, London: Hutchinson.
Finch, J. (1986) 'Whose responsibility? Women and the future of family care', in I. Allen *et al.*, *The Future of Informal Care*, London: Policy Studies Institute.

Finch, J. and Groves, D. (1983) *Labour of Love*, London: Routledge & Kegan Paul.
Goldthorpe, J. H. (1983) 'Women and class analysis in defence of the conventional view', *Sociology* 17: 465–88.
Land, H. (1978) 'Who cares for the family?', *Journal of Social Policy*, 7 (3): 257–84.
—— (1980) 'The family wage', *Feminist Review* 6: 55–77.
Laslett, P. and Wall, R. (eds) (1972) *Household and Family in Past Time*, Cambridge: Cambridge University Press.
Lewis, C. (1986) *Becoming a Father*, Milton Keynes: Open University Press.
Lewis, C. and O'Brien, M. (eds) (1987) *Reassessing Fatherhood*, London: Sage.
Newson, J. and Newson, E. (1963) *Infant Care in an Urban Community*, London: Allen & Unwin.
—— (1968) *Four Years Old in an Urban Community*, London: Allen & Unwin.
Oakley, A. (1974) *The Sociology of Housework*, Oxford: Martin Robertson.
Pahl, R. (1984) *Divisions of Labour*, Oxford: Blackwell.
Pollock, L. (1983) *Forgotten Children*, Cambridge: Cambridge University Press.
Wicks, M. (1987) 'Family policy: rights and responsibilities', in Family Policy Studies Centre *Family Policy Bulletin 3*.
Wohl A. S. (1978) 'Sex and the single room: incest among the Victorian working classes', in A. S. Wohl (ed.) *The Victorian Family*, London: Croom Helm.

Chapter 2

Nursery school education in Nigeria
Impact on families and society

S. K. Akinsanya

For generations, Nigerian parents have been the principal motivators in determining their children's future. Traditionally, boys followed in their fathers' footsteps; girls became housewives and mothers. With the advent of rapid technological change in the twentieth century and the impact of a formal educational system adapted from western societies, a broader range of occupations was opened to the boys and, to a lesser degree, the girls. However, parents still determined for the most part their child's future occupational career. 'We want Chuka to become a doctor.' Or 'We're preparing Kemi to become a schoolteacher.' No one was concerned about the child's interests. Chuka and Kemi did as they were told and thought what they were taught to think. Up to the present day, Nigerian parents still continue to exhibit a strong degree of control over the preparation of their child's future. With the advent of universal primary education in the 1980s, more children will be able to receive a minimum of a primary school education. Decisions about a child's future may not be shared. The school's influence may exert greater effect on the child than that of the parent. Although parents may continue to believe that they exert the greatest amount of influence, those who continue to dominate their child's acts of decision-making may not only damage their child's chances for independent thinking but also hinder future parent–child relationships.

Changing patterns of parental influence and creating chances for independent thought development are two ways in which education is having an impact on Nigerian society and the Nigerian family. Today we know that if children are allowed to discover their own interests, they tacitly show their parents and teachers what they want their futures to be. When given access to materials and allowed to use them independently, they begin to formulate ideas on their own.

Although we can talk about discovery, independent thinking and exploration in education the Nigerian educational system as it presently exists is not able to meet the most modern advances in child development theory and educational reform. This is not to say, however, that Nigerians must remain innocent in education because we have not put our own house in

order. New knowledge, new methods of detecting and measuring phenom-
ena, and improved communications have made Nigerians aware of the many
ways in which they are influenced by forces surrounding them, within
Nigerian society and throughout the world. In some instances, frustration is
experienced because there are no ready adaptations for the educational
practices deemed important for Nigerian learners. In other instances,
Nigerians have quickly learned how to deal responsively with the problems
that are ever-present.

Since the mid-1970s there have been some dramatic instances of educational
change. The National Policy on Education issued in 1977 and the introduction of universal primary education (UPE) by 1982 are only two examples. We can expect continuous modifications as new knowledge and
changes in basic principles force alterations in Nigerian educational institutions and educative processes not so much from taste and whim but since
awareness requires these changes.

One such area which requires careful study, not only in urban but also in
rural areas, is that of preschool or nursery education, the first environment
that increasing numbers of Nigerian children enter once they leave home.

As a pilot study of nursery education in Lagos State (the most populous
state of Nigeria and the then capital) this study unfolds with an overview of
preschool education in the state and its impact on families and Lagosian
society. Some teachers' views on the purposes and perspectives of preschool
education are then considered. The nursery school environment with a close
look at some classrooms is then depicted.

OVERVIEW OF PRESCHOOL EDUCATION

The impact of social and economic change is readily seen as one drives from
one end of Lagos to the other, whether east or west, north or south. The
garbage heaps, the slums; the high-rise apartment buildings and the newly
renovated industrial sites; the UPE instant schools and the backyard soccer
fields are all seen in the midst of the major expressways. Holes are in the
roads; there is lack of water and inconsistent electricity. Conversations with
residents of the state reveal such critical problems as the rising cost of living
creating hardships, in particular on low- and mid-income families, and the
increasing necessity for mothers of young children to go to work. Families,
who a few decades ago remained in their hometowns in the rural areas, have
moved to the urban centre in hopes of a more affluent lifestyle with better
opportunities for themselves and their children. Families, who once could
afford domestic help, can no longer find domestic workers, especially with
the introduction of universal primary education.

How are families coping with some of these stresses to urban living? One
such coping mechanism is for parents to find assistance for the care of their
children. There has been a rapid growth of various types of pre-primary

institutions in the state. Statistics received from the Lagos State Ministry of Education show that in 1972 there were 43 pre-primary institutions. By 1977 the number had risen to 76; 1979 to 106; 1982 to 212. A 400 per cent increase was seen within a ten-year period. These statistics reflect only the pre-primary institutions that are registered in the Ministry of Education. They do not show the multitude of daycare centres, baby tenders, infant centres and daycare homes that are advertised on almost every major corner or inter-section in Lagos. The environments of these various institutions vary from ideal schools to appalling centres in dirt compounds and makeshift buildings and garages.

As the growth of preschool education continues – almost indiscriminately – in response to the pressing demands of the people for places to keep their children while they work, a major change in the role of the primary caretaker is evident. Rather than the assumed close-knit relationship between mother (or surrogate mother) and child, a more diffuse relationship develops between the 'mommy' teacher and her forty or more children. In order to describe more adequately the nursery school situation in Lagos State, a survey of 156 teachers in twenty-five nursery schools was conducted in 1978–9. The major purpose of the research study was to describe the local nursery school and its environment and to relate this description to teacher attitudes regarding the preferred types of activities for a nursery school programme.

Preschool education is also seen as a means to eliminate some of the inequalities in the present educational system. Primary education has been free and compulsory in Lagos. The majority of the schools are overcrowded, with inadequate facilities and materials and (frequently) untrained teachers. Over 400 makeshift primary schools were built within a six-month period, each including a minimum single-storey block of six classrooms. Upwards of forty children could be found in each classroom with one teacher and no aide. Hence, the attention given to any one child from the age of 6, 7, 8 or even 9, is minimal. Teachers and parents, under the impression that children will be given a head start in the process of schooling if they begin *school* at the age of 3, or even 4, view the nursery school as an initiatory ritual into the competitive nature of the primary school where competition is keen to obtain the first position in the class. Nursery school teachers (88.9 per cent) and parents (92.3 per cent) overwhelmingly agreed with the statement that a child who attends a nursery school stands a better chance of gaining admission into a good primary school and, subsequently, succeeding in that school. Even now with neighbourhood primary schools guaranteeing admission, the nursery school is the first avenue to success in the urban Lagosian schools.

As more nursery schools and daycare centres become available in Lagos State, it is not only the wealthy who are sending their children to the schools. Rising urban middle-class parents see the school as the avenue of success for their child. 'Regardless of what a child learns there is prestige in attending a good nursery school', state 70 per cent of the teachers surveyed. The ones most left out, of course, are the lower-class children – those most likely left to run in the streets or to attend a most unsuitable daycare centre. Although there are a few market nursery schools in the state, the number is surprisingly small for the large number of market-women's children found in the markets. Rising enrolments mean not only an increase in the number of schools, but also that custodial service is provided to more families. As more children are served, parental input into the organization and operation of the schools, by right, must increase.

The National Policy on Education is more theoretical than pragmatic in stating goals for pre-primary education. 'Pre-primary education should lay the foundation for the successful pursuit of general interests and attitudes, so that each child might develop to his full stature as responsible citizens.' Apart from providing adequate custodial care for children, the preschool should perform the functions of helping children to develop to their fullest cognitive, social and emotional potential.

The government has declared that provision for nursery education is to be left in the hands of private individuals. 'The government will encourage private efforts and provision for preprimary education.' This policy again was reiterated by the former head of state, General Obasanjo, in his budget speech (1979–80): 'As the formative years of a child are very crucial, my government sees it as a social responsibility to establish pre-primary and nursery schools.'

Parents, teachers and the government are consistent in their belief that a primary goal for preschool education in Lagos State and in Nigeria as a whole should be the intellectual and social development of the child. Comments such as the following were recorded in both teacher and parent surveys:

I want my daughter to know how to say nursery rhymes and how to write the alphabets and numbers at least from one to ten in order to give her a better start in education.

I want him to have a good academic background.

A child who attends a nursery school will be a better developed social individual than the one who does not.

He will be prepared for his future education with politeness and strong social interaction.

I want him to be socially, mentally, intellectually and morally developed so that in the end he will be a good citizen of his country.

The nursery school will provide the modern teaching of civilization and knowledge for the future.

Goals for Nigerian preschool education, therefore, do not differ substantially from pre-primary educational goals expressed by such historical figures as Rousseau, Pestalozzi, Montessori, Froebel and others who have worked with children and researched the importance of the child's early experiences. The major goal of these pioneers was to create educational centres in which children experience an environment that would promote their social, psychological and intellectual development.

Although the home and the school can provide caregivers that influence the future development of the child's intellectual, social and emotional wellbeing, Lagosian teachers surveyed are uncertain which most greatly influences the early experiences of the child – the home or the school. When that statement is coupled with the fact that 54 per cent of the teachers surveyed believed that a child's ability to learn was primarily based on what a child was born with, or on heredity rather than on the environment, we have a unique contrast in determining just what should be given priority for preschool education in Lagos. If parents more greatly influence a child's experiences and a child's ability to learn is based on heredity, than what is the role of the preschool? The preschool must be seen as an extension of the family, where the Lagosian family unit is highly structured and self-controlled. Therefore, preschool experiences are structured, controlled activities to promote the greatest cognitive growth in a short period of time. The environments reflect this goal.

THE NURSERY SCHOOL ENVIRONMENT

Prior to 1960, preschool education in Lagos State was virtually non-existent although the oldest preschool institution was established in 1941. It is recorded as the first preschool to be licensed by the State Ministry of Education. The majority of the nursery schools in the State have been in existence only since the early 1970s. Nursery schools operate on the same schedule as primary schools: most of the nursery schools are open 4½–5 hours per day from 8 a.m. to 1 p.m. The average enrolment for a nursery school in Lagos State was 205 children in six classrooms or an average class size of 35 children. An average of six teachers per school and one headmistress composed the staff, of whom half were trained (with a minimum of some form of teaching certificate) and half were untrained. Although many parents remarked that they would like to have boarding nursery schools, only one boarding school for nursery age children could be found in the state.

Some nursery schools provide private transportation and buses, but most parents opted to bring their children to school. What does a working mother do when she has to leave her job at 12.30 or 1 p.m. in order to collect her children from the nursery school? In many cases, siblings (an older brother or sister) perform this task. Most nursery schools therefore are attached to primary schools where older brothers and sisters can attend and therefore take care of the younger children at the close of the day.

Of the sample surveyed, only two nursery schools admitted children under the age of 2. The average age of entry was 2½ years; the university nursery school admitted at the age of 3. This has posed another problem for the working mother in that she must find another form of daycare for the child under 2½ years of age. When there is lack of domestic help and when older boys and girls are in primary schools themselves, the mother must find a reliable daycare centre or family home to tend to the baby. Baby-minding is seen as a potentially lucrative economic enterprise and daycare centres and home centres that accommodate children under the age of 2½ have sprung up with alacrity.

With an average class size of thirty-five, the caregiver–child ratio becomes one to thirty-five. This ratio far exceeds any optimum desired by early childhood educators. When the number of children under care is large, class size becomes the major determinant of the activity that can be performed within the classroom. Larger groups not only reduce the frequency of developmentally effective activity but also increase the possibility of children remaining uninvolved or becoming disengaged or caught-up in tangential or unproductive diversions with their age mates. Academic excellence in writing letters and numbers, in reading and in doing simple additions are the main objectives of most headmistresses of these schools. Socialization, play, art, creative activities, outdoor play, music – all assume a minor role in the class scheduling.

CONCLUSION

Nursery school education is making an impact on Lagosian society and its families. Sheer numbers alone support this statement. Over five thousand children enrolled in the twenty-five nursery schools in this study show us the impact that nursery education is having on the society. Parents and teachers alike view the nursery school as a place for intellectual, cognitive development. In addition, having preschools available frees the mother to go out to work and provides an avenue to future enrolment in top primary schools: there is prestige in attending a good nursery school. Even with neighbourhood schools, parents can still find ways to change the primary school allocated to their child. A nursery school education often gives preference to that child when seeking admission to another primary school.

Teachers are uncertain about whether or not parents or schools are prime determinants of the experiences that a child will have; whether or not a child's ability to learn is primarily based on heredity or environment. This uncertainty may be explained by their belief in the legitimate role of parent and family in childrearing. In rapidly developing urban centres, such as Lagos, there seems to be a tendency to maintain strong structured home environments, similar to the classrooms portrayed in this survey. Parental and teacher viewpoints on nursery school education do not conflict, therefore, at least among parents of so-called 'middle-class' homes.

On the other hand, teachers are uncertain about whether or not nursery school education is preferable to in-home early education programmes. Should policies be established to keep mothers at home? This uncertainty may be explained by their strong convictions that nursery school educational programmes are beneficial to a child's cognitive development but not necessarily to a child's social–emotional development. That is the home's responsibility. Teachers are certain that urban families can provide strong supportive environments for the optimum social growth of the child. The nursery school is not needed for this function. Perhaps experience will show that quality nursery school programmes can, and should, offer an environment favouring the development of socialization skills. What role the family will perform in the 1980s and 1990s in providing early educational environments for the young child is a research problem worthy of further investigation. What controls are to be placed on the expansion of preschool programmes in the state? How are the teachers to cope with the stresses and strains that come with the responsibility of thirty to forty children in each classroom? These and other questions will stimulate answers to the educational dilemma – are all our children learning?

Chapter 3

Why nursery education?

C. James

Where does nursery education stand in the whole context of education? Essentially of course, it is 'outside' the system, since the children for whom it caters are below statutory school age. The care and education of children under 5 has been one of the key issues since the mid-1970s. It has been the subject of innumerable national reports, debates and research projects. It has also been the focus of energetic local endeavours on behalf of young children and their families. We are preoccupied with questions of availability and access. What forms of provision are appropriate for young children and their families? On what basis are priorities decided at a time when demand exceeds supply?

Taking the last available statistics from the Office of Population Census, there are 3 million children under 5 whose mothers look after them full-time at home. In contrast, there are 850,000 children in this age group whose mothers undertake some employment outside their homes. Of these, 306,000 have mothers who work for 12 hours or less each week; 372,000 children have mothers who work for more than 12 but less than 30 hours each week. Only 172,000 children have mothers who are at work for more than 30 hours weekly. It is very important to remember that, however it may be made to appear by public figures and the media, most mothers with children under 5 do not go out to work.

The Plowden Report highlighted the educational implications of social background influences on success at school (Central Advisory Council for Education 1967). It also drew attention to the cumulative nature of some children's disadvantage. The report argued that these children are at a twofold disadvantage: they are disadvantaged not only because of the circumstances of their homes, but also because their schools tend to be poorer. The disadvantage is seen to be greatest in inner city areas, where the housing is usually cheaper and of lower standard. The schools tend to be older and to have fewer facilities .

As a first step towards improving educational provision for disadvantaged children, the Plowden Report advocated the designation of Educational Priority Areas (EPAs). Subsequently, schools in these areas were assisted considerably by new buildings and resources, under an Urban Aid Programme, as well as by the action-research projects which were set up under the overall direction of Professor A. H. Halsey in 1967. It soon became apparent that even if the 'quality' of school provision was the same in EPAs as in more advantaged areas, many children would still be at a disadvantage because they had not had the same opportunities for educational experience before reaching school age.

Although superficially (with the benefit of 'positive discrimination'), there may be equality of opportunity for all children to benefit from statutory education, in reality it will be more accessible to some than to others. The children who have had a rich educational experience before they attend primary school, will already have mastered a range of skills which will enable them to benefit more easily and efficiently from the learning experiences provided by the school. For many other children there is a danger that school will consist of frustration and failure from the start, because the children are ill equipped to gain from the experience.

WHAT IS NURSERY EDUCATION?

Nursery education is that particular part of the whole educational system which is seen as being appropriate to the needs of children between the ages of 2 or 3 and 5 years. It can contribute much that is of benefit to the physical well-being, social experience and intellectual development of the child. It is, if it is of a high standard, of value in itself, at the time at which it occurs. In its own special way, nursery education can be seen as an extension of the experiences the child has received at home. It is complementary to everything else that happens to the child.

This provision is specially designed for children who are under statutory school age. It has to be seen as something more than child-minding, however good and caring that might be. It is not merely a preparation for future schooling, either. It is important, though, that the adults working with the children do bear in mind that there will be a time when they do transfer to the infants' school. We have to do all we can to make that transition as painless and as easy as possible for the children and their parents.

An increased interest in the youngest age group no doubt reflects, in part, a general acknowledgement of the importance of early learning. It is also, however, inextricably linked to broader social issues. Such issues involve questions related to the origins of educational inequality, the feasibility of, and the desirability of, compensatory education, the changing character of family and community life, the role of parents in their children's socialization and the equality of employment opportunities for women.

The nursery exists for the benefit of the children and the parents whom it serves. Research findings have influenced our work. The American

'Headstart' programmes radically changed attitudes of parents towards their children's education. Many research projects in the UK were commissioned as a direct response to a White Paper, *Education: Framework for Expansion* (Department of Education and Science 1972). As a result of these projects we now know much more than we did about the organization of pre-statutory school services and about the gaps which exist in our present system. We have learnt much more, too, about the problems of trying to combine and co-ordinate different forms of provision. We are better informed about the families of pre-statutory school children and their environment. We also have a better understanding of what stimulates language development and what adults can do to help this along.

Britain lags behind most other European countries in the provision of daycare for children under 5. There was a time (especially in the 1970s), when nursery education was something of a political football. Many politicians responded to public pressure and included their 'interest' in this area of education in their election manifestos. Now that the desirability of nursery education, and the possibility of a variety of daycare provision have become accepted in principle, there is little 'political' mileage left in it – largely on the grounds of such provision being very expensive.

Nursery education means the provision of a secure and stimulating environment where, under the guidance of trained teachers and nursery nurses, children between the ages of 3 and 5 years old can enjoy themselves in play. In doing so they develop their various skills: physical, intellectual, linguistic, aesthetic, creative, emotional and social. Most children benefit from nursery education. Space and opportunity to play with other children of a similar age are essential to a child's development. For most children, many of the activities provided in the nursery class or school cannot be experienced at their own or in a childminder's home.

Children who are in some way disadvantaged are likely to benefit most from nursery education. While a nursery school or class cannot be expected to put right gross inequalities which stem from basic social and economic problems, it can still play an important part in helping a child's all-round development. As an example, it can be seen that the encouragement of communication and the development of language is a vital benefit of nursery education. It is particularly relevant to the needs of young children who may previously have lacked the opportunity to talk and listen to adults and older children. Even more plainly, this aspect of nursery education is important for the child whose first language is not English.

The link between home, school and community is a perennial educational issue. A variety of studies and research programmes have resulted in a vital interest in improving the links (Smith 1980; Tizard *et al.* 1981). The relationship between children's experience at home and in the school is regarded as important. Home is a constant backcloth against which all of the child's other experiences need to be viewed. The number of hours children actually spend in school is a relatively small proportion of their waking lives. It is arguable that much of their learning does not take place in school at all, but in the home and in other community contexts.

It is widely agreed that the early years of a child's life are crucially important for the child's later development. There is, however, less agreement as to exactly how the well-being of the developing child may be promoted. While there may be general agreement about the 'ends' – the optimum all-round development of the child – differences of opinion exist as to the 'means' of achieving this. So we are inevitably faced with a variety of provision.

There is increasing co-operation now between educational provision and that of the social services, for example in combined nursery centres day nursery provision for children aged 0–3 and nursery school provision for children aged 3–5 are catered for on the same site. The combined centre represents the integration of two different streams of provision for young children (Ferri *et al.* 1981). From an early concentration on the essential health needs of young children, nursery schools developed within the orbit of the education system. Day nurseries were originally provided by the health authorities, and since the early 1970s have become an integral part of the social services provision for families in Britain. The nursery centres represent a way of combining the traditions and philosophies of the two types of provision. In general the nursery school places an emphasis on education. The day nursery concentrates on providing substitute home care, in particular for families where there are exceptional needs.

The proliferation of playgroups of various kinds and the growth of the Pre-School Playgroup Association (PPA), are evidences of the unmet demand by parents for nursery education. Playgroups are not established on the basis of criteria which are nationally recognized and agreed. Not all playgroups are affiliated to the PPA. This results in a haphazard distribution of playgroups, and great differences in the quality of the service they provide and the accommodation in which they function.

The day-to-day running of a playgroup relies heavily on voluntary help. Its particular emphasis on involving interested parents is very well known. Playgroups provide an alternative environment for the child under 5, but are no substitute for well-planned, adequately financed, free nursery education. This should be provided for all children whose parents wish them to have it.

A balanced Nursery education programme, designed to encourage the development of language, perception, social and emotional adjustment, administered by teachers who are trained to use the tools of education in accordance with the particular needs of the child, is required to give all children the right educational start.

(National Union of Teachers 1977)

THE CHILD

All young children, whether they are highly gifted, socially deprived or 'average' have similar basic needs. Rapid emotional, physical, intellectual and social development occurs during the formative years from birth to 5 years. Children need the opportunity to be with other children in small and large groups, as well as alone.

Children are very dependent on adults for the view they have of themselves. They need to be with adults who are interested in them and in a whole range of activities and ideas, and as a result are interesting people themselves. Children need easy and regular contact with living things. They need opportunity to communicate through art, music, drama, role play, etc., not only because these are part of their aesthetic development, but also so that they can engage in the excitement and enjoyment of learning. Children need natural objects and artefacts to handle and explore, as well as space and opportunity for physical activity.

Children need to experience independence, interdependence and dependence. They need to experience success and failure. They need to be able to discriminate at all levels of their activity. They need the opportunity to learn through experience – to acquire concepts through empirical (direct, first-hand activity), as well as through theoretical experience.

The particular nature and needs of children at the nursery age must always be borne in mind. A 3 year old has never been 3 before and will never be 3 again! While a child of 3 or 4 will display many of the same kinds of characteristics as every other 3 or 4 year old, each child is uniquely different, due to the influences of genetic make-up, environmental factors, social class, the childrearing patterns of the parents' family, and so on.

THE FAMILY

Traditionally nursery education focused almost exclusively on the child. The family and home environment were not disregarded, but what was on offer to children in terms of their own personal development within the school setting was paramount. Gradually this view has begun to change. The responsibility for educating the nation's children is seen as a joint enterprise. A growing concern for the family, an increased awareness of social pressures and the need to meet the learning needs of all children, but particularly those in inner city areas, have influenced the provision that is made for young children. There is generally more acceptance of the view that parents should be encouraged to become more actively involved in the education of their children.

The positive and essential contribution to be made by parents is borne out by numerous research findings. Patterns of educational home visiting, the creation of toy libraries, the growth of parent and toddler groups, and so on, have been devised to help parents to enjoy their children and to understand how crucial their contribution is.

An outstanding characteristic of urban society is its rapid rate of change. In general, there has been a steady rise in many people's standard of living. Despite the steep rise in unemployment, there are more opportunities now open to women. Improvements in housing have generally led to more geographical mobility. Families with young children tend to move around; sometimes they live long distances from their relatives.

The 'extended family' is largely non-existent. The nuclear family of parent(s) and children gets much less support from relations and neighbours. In addition there is a great deal of urban development which reduces space and opportunity for play. The increasing volume of traffic makes streets too dangerous for very young children to venture out alone. Many families have no access to gardens or outdoor play space. All these factors inevitably mean that families are isolated. The increasingly high rate of marriage breakdown, the increasing number of single parents (usually women), mean that mothers and children probably spend far more time together than ever before. Very many women with children spend lonely and unhappy lives (Figure 3.1).

We have evidence that this all causes very great strain for many mothers and children. In the mid-1970s research showed that 40 per cent of working-class women with children suffered from clinical depression, anxiety or tension. Agencies working with families are becoming increasingly concerned about children who are in very real danger from non-accidental injury and other forms of child abuse (Rutter 1972).

In other European countries, the proportion of women with young children who work outside the home is much larger than it is in Britain (Van der Eyken 1982). It is not always realized that mothers who go out to work when their children are young are not, as a rule, unskilled and ignorant women. Throughout Europe and in countries like the United States and New Zealand, there is increasing evidence (instanced by the growth of the Women's Movement) that better-educated women, often from the highest social classes, are more likely to seek full-time employment while their children are still very young. It would seem that such women suffer less from severe depression, loneliness, anxiety and feelings of low self-esteem. It is likely too, that if they are able to make satisfactory arrangements for their children during their absence from home, they will make a much better job of parenting, and will enjoy their children.

There can be no doubt that parents (and mothers in particular) would like to have adequate provision for daycare. Although, as has been pointed out, many parents do work and therefore need substitute daycare, many do not. Parents have been, on the whole, very much encouraged to realize the value of the experience of playgroup, nursery class or nursery school for their children. Most parents recognize the value of the social aspects of such experience for their children. Sometimes they perceive it as a valuable

I am in bed and I am dreaming about my dolly Susie who is being naughty.

Figure 3.1 A child's drawing

preparation for the more formally organized experience of the primary school. Certainly the group situation offered in a pre-statutory school setting will go a long way to help a child in the transition from home to school. Echoing Marion Dowling (1978), 'Until individual children have learned to come to terms with their transition to school, their learning development will be arrested or in extreme cases will take a backward step.'

THE TEACHER

Nursery teachers will have undertaken a full teacher's training, with a focus on the early years of childhood. They may have a degree in education or in a special subject area. They will have specialized in the education and care of very young children. The nursery teacher will, in ideal circumstances, have an assistant, usually a trained nursery nurse. Together they will carry out an educational programme and try to give every child all-round care. The nursery teacher is someone who has a deep concern for the nurture, care and safety of young children. The teacher recognizes that they are, in this period of their growth, active, lively and curious. Small children have very little control over their impulses; they have little understanding of potential danger. The school therefore must provide adequate safety measures, and through the teacher contribute to the physical health of the children.

Teachers have knowledge and understanding of child development. They have increasing experience of a large number of children whose ages may be similar, but whose rates of development will have varied considerably. They also have knowledge of learning theory, the emotional needs of children, the development of personality, psychology, teaching methods and what constitutes good practice. The influence of the teacher as a professional is crucial. The attainment of educational objectives at the nursery level is an obvious goal for the teacher. These facets of a teacher's expertise and understanding are essential to the fulfilment of the objectives of supplementing and complementing the work of parents.

Also important is the influence that the teacher has on the structure and exploitation of experiences and interactions for children. The human content of any experience is important. Young children look to their teachers for help and information; the nursery teacher has to be ready, at any moment, to provide this. Children need adults who will encourage but not interfere; who will listen when required; who will explain but not dictate, and who will answer their questions. Such aspects of the child's experiences form appropriate educational foundations upon which this later learning will be built.

The nursery teacher tries to help each child to become increasingly independent and builds upon the experiences that children have had in the home. This is done by helping children to make decisions – choosing for themselves what they will do from a range of possibilities, for instance. Importantly too, the teacher strives to build up children's confidence so that they will tackle new situations and tasks without fear or anxiety. In order to do this, the teacher will show children by the way she or he talks to them and treats them generally how much they are valued as people. Children will be praised and supported in the efforts they make. They will be encouraged to enjoy their successes. They will also be helped to cope positively with frustration and failure, so that they have the confidence to go on.

The role of the teacher in nursery education is crucial. The teacher needs a range of skills and expertise if the enterprise of educating very young children is to be worthwhile and valuable. The teacher is primarily an educator of young children, planning work, organizing the daily programme, keeping careful records, leading supporting staff, developing an appropriate curriculum.

THE CURRICULUM

There are experiences which are appropriate to this age group and level of development which we must try to provide. They represent a sound foundation for learning about life and for learning how to learn. The need is for a stimulating environment and a curriculum that is rich in language and dialogue. Any curriculum is concerned with the acquisition of skills, the development of attitudes and the growth of conceptual understanding. This is as true for nursery education as it is for other phases of schooling.

We have seen that all children come to school with their own unique 'package' of characteristics. This means that each child's viewpoint has to be considered. We can, in the light of experience, make inspired guesses as to what a child's view might be, but we have to be ready to be constantly surprised by the way in which an individual child may see things. All children, therefore, must be accepted for what they are and the possible experiences we plan for them should be built upon those experiences they have already gained. It is at this early stage that attitudes learnt often remain for life, so it is of the utmost importance that thought should be given to fostering attitudes which are appropriate and acceptable in school and in society.

Positive attitudes to children themselves, towards learning, having respect for others, developing awareness and appreciation of the world around them, are aspects we should be trying to promote. Other attitudes and qualities it is desirable to promote in nursery-aged children include enjoyment, enthusiasm, curiosity, wonder, acceptance of challenge, acceptance of change, persistence, and satisfaction. In addition to these, self-confidence, self-control, independence (a willingness to try to cope for themselves), co-operation, sharing, courtesy, care for living creatures and growing things, respect for authority and the care of toys and equipment, all represent a basis for sound development which will enable children to take their place in the world (Figure 3.2).

The teacher's responsibility is to widen and further the child's experience. To this end the nursery curriculum provides motivation, stimulation, continuity and security. It is generally accepted practice that very young children have 'free choice of activities'. Freedom of choice is an important objective; but informed choice is dependent upon knowledge. Children do not have

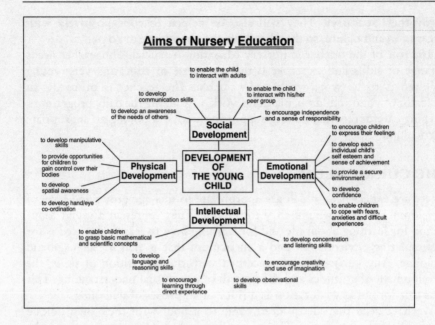

Figure 3.2 Aims of nursery education

freedom of choice if they are unable to cope with the decision-making involved. Such inability may arise because children are unfamiliar with 'choosing'; they may not have experience of a wide range of opportunities to choose from; and they may lack the confidence required to make decisions for themselves. Sometimes it is necessary for an adult to set definite limits for children, so that they are supported in their learning. Within these limits they can make their decisions. The adult will say, for instance, 'You may either do this or that.'

Children who are new to the nursery environment may find the range of activities so bewildering that they are unable to choose for themselves. Guidance for such a child may well be necessary, with perhaps some limitation on what is available to begin with. Once teachers and other adults are aware of the need to provide this kind of support for inexperienced children, they are often surprised at how successfully such children come to terms with the nursery environment. In a very short time, children become more confident, autonomous, competent and excited by the knowledge they are gaining.

From time to time, advocates of nursery education have claimed its value in terms of 'making up deficit'. It should be seen, in my view, as a general enrichment for all children. It should not be looked at merely as a means of compensating children for deprivation, although of course there is an element of this involved, especially if it is seen as trying to meet the needs of individual children. It is not intended to be a substitute for the home. It should be regarded as complementary to everything else that happens to the child. It represents an addition to the child's total educational experience.

WHY NURSERY EDUCATION?

In the present climate, when the public generally is concerned about the cost of education, while nursery education is still outside the statutory sector of provision, and while many members of the public, both inside and outside the teaching profession, generally do not understand the purpose and value of it, it behoves us all as workers in the field to make our aims and objectives clear. We have to provide evidence of children's achievement in their personal development, in their acquisition of skills, knowledge and attitudes, for their time spent in the nursery. If we really do believe that the qualified and experienced teacher is the key factor in the care and education of young children, then we do have to set about providing credible justification for this provision.

The links made between the various forms of early childhood settings are essential. The more people who are working in the field know about each other's expertise (Bruner 1980a; 1980b; Bryant et al. 1980; Garland and White 1980; Sylva et al. 1980; Wood et al. 1980), skills and responsibilities, the more concerted our efforts can be to make the best and most appropriate provision for young children; our knowledge and understanding of family needs will be more precise, too. We must all try to work towards a better articulation of our ideals and aims in early childhood education. We need to be clearer in our own minds about what we are trying to do. We need constantly to check that what we are doing is in fact 'working' – that is, that we are achieving our stated aims.

The implication of this is that teachers of very young children will be increasingly able to convince other people, both inside and outside the profession, that the educational provision we make for children under 5 is tailored to meet their all-round developmental needs. Their pre-statutory (i.e. nursery) experience will set their learning on a firm foundation which will make the task of the infant teacher easier. It will enable children to be agents of their own learning and help them to meet that learning with excitement and enthusiasm. Nursery education which is of a high standard, which meets the various needs of children will help them to take their first steps into school life with positive attitudes and confidence. It will help to prepare children and their families for the wider world of education.

ACKNOWLEDGEMENT

My thanks to Margaret Lālly for Figure 3.2.

REFERENCES

Bruner, J. (ed.) (1980a) *Oxford Preschool Research Project*, London: Grant McIntyre.
—— (1980b) *Under 5 in Britain*, London: Grant McIntyre.
Bryant, B., Harris, M. and Newton, D. (1980) *Children and Minders*, London: Grant McIntyre.
Central Advisory Council for Education (1967) *Children and their Primary Schools*, Plowden Report, London: HMSO.
Department of Education and Science (1972) *Education: A Framework for Expansion*, London: HMSO.
Dowling, M. (1978) *The Modern Nursery*, London: Longman.
Ferri, E., Birchall, D., Gingell, V. and Gipps, C. (1981) *Combined Nursery Centres*, London: Macmillan.
Garland, C. and White, S. (1980) *Children and Day Nurseries*, London: Grant McIntyre.
Jarecki, H. (1975) *Playgroups: A Practical Approach*, London: Faber & Faber.
National Union of Teachers (1977) *The Needs of Under-Fives*, London: NUT.
Rutter, M. (1972) *Maternal Deprivation Reassessed*, Harmondsworth: Penguin.
Smith, T. (1980) *Parents and Preschool*, London: Grant McIntyre.
Sylva, K., Roy, C. and Painter, M. (1980) *Childwatching at Playgroup and Nursery School*, London: Grant McIntyre.
Tizard, B., Mortimore, J. and Burchell, B. (1981) *Involving Parents in Nursery and Infant Schools*, London: Grant McIntyre.
Van der Eyken, W. (1982) *The Education of 3 to 8 Year Olds in Europe in the Eighties*, Windsor: NFER-Nelson.
Wood, D., McMahon, L. and Cranstoun, Y. (1980) *Working with Under Fives*, London: Grant McIntyre.

Chapter 4

Training to work in the early years

A. Curtis and D. Hevey

DEVELOPMENTS IN TEACHER TRAINING

Since the nineteenth century there has been organized training of teachers in England and Wales, set up originally by the voluntary bodies. In 1814 the British Society produced an outline for teacher training in primary schools which remained the model for courses until the early 1970s. It consisted of an academic entry qualification, a concurrent course of general education and professional training, a final examination and a probationary period of teaching, the whole culminating in the award of a teacher's certificate.

In 1960 all teacher training courses were extended from two to three years. Hitherto only the Froebel courses had offered courses of that length. This, and a sharp increase in the birth rate, led to a vast expansion in the number of teachers in training from 18,000 in 1958 to 114,000 by 1969. The next two decades were to see a drastic decline in the numbers, which fell to 46,500 in 1979 and 38,000 in 1989. These rapid changes in student numbers, plus the introduction of the B.Ed degree in the mid-1960s and its subsequent extension to a four-year course granting graduate status to all members of the teaching profession, were to have far-reaching effects upon the training of teachers and on early years courses in particular.

By the mid-1960s there were no longer courses specifically for those wishing to work with the 3–5 age range in nursery school or class. All early years students followed a course of training which covered the age ranges 3–7 years or 3–8 years.

The rapid increase in student numbers followed by an even more rapid decrease led to dramatic changes within teacher training institutions. Colleges were encouraged to broaden their teaching and offered degree courses in the arts and the sciences as well as their traditional education areas. The James Report (Committee of Enquiry 1972) had recommended the ending of monotechnics and with this came the greater differentiation associated with present-day institutes of higher education. In spite of their efforts, many colleges found themselves either overstaffed or with staff inappropriately qualified. However, excellent redundancy terms under the Crombie conditions encouraged many teacher trainers to apply for early retirement and among them were some of our finest trainers of early childhood educators. They were individuals who had been recruited into the colleges in the days when experience was considered more important than academic qualifications. Such tutors found themselves being overshadowed by young new entrants into teacher training, who had not necessarily been classroom teachers but who had the necessary academic status. This was to have an important effect upon early years training in the late 1970s and 1980s.

Having shed staff with early years expertise, colleges were forced either to run their training courses for the infant and nursery years with inappropriately trained staff, or to close their nursery courses. As a result, teachers professionally trained to work with young children were in short supply.

The shortage of early years teachers was further exacerbated by the introduction of the regulations laid down by the Council for the Accreditation of Teacher Education (CATE). The CATE requirement most likely to affect the number of courses offered for the training of early years teachers was the one which stated that all staff working on professional courses with students in initial training should have recent and relevant experience of the age range that they were teaching. Very properly, CATE rejected courses where the school experience of the lecturers was inappropriate and this led to a further decrease in the number of courses covering the 3–5 age range. Currently there are only eighteen institutes of higher education training teachers to work with the 3–8 age range. A further six prepare students for the 4–8 age range and seven others offer 'options' in early years.

Although the institutions offering courses covering the 3–8 age range offer students a substantial amount of preparation for working with the under 5s, it is likely that the courses offering training for 4 to 8 years will be concentrating upon infant education as most of the 4 year olds in educational establishments are in the primary classroom. If we also take into account the requirements of the National Curriculum and the criterion laid down by CATE that all teachers following a B.Ed course must have a subject specialism which accounts for 50 per cent of their study time as well as a specific number of hours for each of the foundation subjects of the National Curriculum (science, mathematics and English), then it is easy to understand why so many young teachers may feel inadequately prepared to cope with the needs of 3–5 year olds.

During the period when comments were invited by the government over the CATE criteria, many early childhood specialists argued that an area of study like 'language and literacy' or 'aesthetic and creative' studies could be made rigorous enough to meet the regulations and yet would be more relevant to meet the needs of early years teachers (those preparing to work with 3–8 year olds). The government would not accept these arguments. Teachers preparing to work in the early years of schooling must have a subject discipline in the same way as those preparing to work with an older age range.

The arguments for this approach are compelling and there is no doubt that we want teachers of the early years to be as well educated as those working with the older age range. The question is, should their training be the same?

There is no doubt that the introduction of the CATE requirements and the changing needs of the schools and early childhood centres have presented a problem to those educating the early childhood educators. How can they best prepare the teachers for the challenging work of the next century, when the needs of young children and their families may not be the same as they are today? Should there be a separate course for teachers working with the under 5s or should we be advocating a situation as in Scotland where teachers working in the nurseries are expected to do a further course of training after gaining their qualifications in primary education?

The European dimension

Although education is not seen as an integral part of the Treaty of Rome, there were modifications during 1991 which will most probably have a bearing upon the training of teachers in the early years. The EC Directive which allowed equivalence in the recognition of qualifications has meant that teachers from other European countries can be employed within the English education sector. So far this has been only with primary-aged children. There are, however, difficulties in accepting that there is equivalence with respect to the teaching of nursery-school-aged children since only in a few countries do teachers have the same level of training as in the UK. Furthermore, although the teachers may have the same length of training, in very few countries are they paid at the same level and nowhere else are teachers able to teach through the 3–11 age range, thus helping to ensure continuity and progression in children's education.

One of the strengths of our current teacher training programmes is that teachers are able to understand the development of children aged 3–11 or 3–9 years and do not see starting statutory schooling as a cut-off point in this process. For example, although it is not standard practice in the UK to teach children to read in the nursery school or class, elsewhere in Europe this is generally frowned upon and is seen as a threat to natural development before the age of 6. Consensus in the UK would suggest that the interest in print shown by many children as a result of the programmes offered should be, and is, encouraged and developed. Therefore, if teachers have had no training in this aspect of education it could be very difficult for them to help children appropriately.

In many parts of the EU there is a clearly defined distinction between care before 6 or 7 years and education thereafter. This militates against the concept of continuity and progression, which is one of the strengths of the British system, made possible by the nature of the training.

Although government responsibility for young children is split between the Department of Health and the Department of Education and Science (DES) there is general agreement among professionals that there should be a greater educational input into all pre-school institutions. As a result, many local authorities are linking care and education in a positive way, or, indeed, placing total responsibility with the education committee.

What makes a good early years teacher?

The Rumbold Report (DES 1990) urged that there should be better quality in all early childhood provision. Before discussing further what constitutes a good early years training course to ensure this quality, it is important to consider what are the attributes we would like an early years teacher to possess.

Definitions of 'quality teaching', like those of 'good practice', are hard to find as most authors tend to be unwilling to commit themselves to state exactly what constitutes a 'good early years teacher'. However, it is essential to attempt this before considering how best to design the ideal training programme.

First of all, teachers are professionals who 'are persons who are able to carry out a complex and socially valued role for which defined expertise is required'. It is only teachers who are competent and qualified and mature who can be allowed 'the widest measure of professional autonomy' (Ward 1986: 9).

Watts (1987) also had some appropriate comments to make on the topic of professionalism stating that

> whatever the future shape and nature of early childhood services, kinder-garten teachers and other staff will continue to serve their clients well if they exemplify in their attitudes and behaviours the hallmarks of pro-fessionalism especially:
>
> - specific expertise and a specialized knowledge base;
> - commitment to continuing enquiry to advance the knowledge base;
> - altruism, service to a public good and assumptions of responsibility for their own continuing professional development.
>
> (Watts 1987: 12)

Ebbeck (1990), speaking at the OMEP World Congress in London in 1989, insisted that the hallmarks of professionalism are very important if we are to improve the status of early childhood educators.

What qualities does an early years teacher require?

These seem to fall naturally into three areas of skills which can be developed with sensitive training: personal/social skills, professional skills and practical skills. There is naturally some overlap between the areas.

Personal/social skills

The early years teacher should be:

1 a well-adjusted person with a positive self-image
2 a well-educated person with wide interests in the arts and an awareness of the physical world
3 aware of and sensitive to the needs of others at all levels, regardless of cultural and social patterns
4 committed, non-judgemental
5 interested in and respectful of the autonomy of the child
6 of an enquiring mind and alert to the need for further personal professional development
7 able to *communicate* by all possible means with colleagues, parents, other agencies and above all with children, irrespective of their culture, religion or gender.

Professional skills

The early years teacher should have:

1 a sound knowledge of child development and educational theory
2 the ability to develop strategies to transmit knowledge to others
3 a deep understanding of the subjects in the early years curriculum and the value of play
4 a knowledge of and respect for cultural and social similarities and differences
5 observational skills and ability to assess and evaluate not only the programmes they offer, and the children's progress, but also themselves
6 a knowledge of the laws relating to families
7 a knowledge of policies and the underlying philosophy
8 the ability to act as an advocate for children.

Practical skills

The early years teacher should be able to:

1 plan programmes which ensure both continuity and progression
2 understand the point of view of others in order to manage the delivery of the programme in various settings with a range of people both professional and non-professional
3 encourage the team of workers to adopt common strategies, which will allow the aims of the pre-school to be met
4 encourage the personal development of team members.

To summarize the adult's role we can do no better than quote Parry and Archer:

A teacher of young children obviously needs to possess certain qualities if she is to face well her responsibilities which are complex in nature and highly demanding of excellence of many kinds. She needs to be someone who is essentially human; someone who likes people, especially children, and is not only full of warmth and goodwill toward them but determined to do right by them. To achieve such ends she needs to be perceptive, sensitive, sympathetic and imaginative. She needs to be highly educated personally and professionally in those areas of knowledge, understanding and skill which she will be conveying to children, albeit indirectly at their stage of development and in those spheres of learning which are essential to her understanding of children and adults and to her skill in dealing with them.

(Parry and Archer 1974: 139)

How do we train teachers?

Are we meeting the training needs of these teachers whom we expect to function in a variety of pre-school settings, not just traditional nursery schools and classes?

The existing teacher training programmes preparing students to work with the 3–8 age range, if they have good selection procedures, should be able to select students with satisfactory personal/social qualities. However, once we move into the areas of professional and practical skills it does not appear that we are offering an appropriate curriculum to achieve the high level of professionalism expected.

Many of the attributes and skills listed are covered in the current syllabuses in training institutions but because of the pressures of the National Curriculum and the emphasis upon subject specialism it is impossible to devote the amount of time to the study of child development and observational skills so vital to our understanding of the growth and development of young children. Few would argue against the need to reform the initial teacher training programmes and to introduce a more rigorous regime, but current research into the way young children's thinking develops should have resulted in a greater, not a lesser, study of child development. At least in former days those preparing to work with children in the early years of schooling were given an understanding of the development of children from birth to 3 years, just as they left college knowing something about the personal and curricular needs of children aged 5–8 years. Furthermore, there was included in most early years courses a compulsory element in which students had to spend time with children of varying ages outside a school setting. For many students this was one of the most rewarding parts of their training. Looking at current syllabuses it seems unlikely that this is now normal practice.

Just as schools are undergoing change so are many of the early childhood establishments where young teachers are finding work. The traditional role of teachers in their own closed domain has to be abandoned in these settings as there is much greater emphasis upon team-work and co-operation. Students fortunate enough to have been trained in the institutes specializing in this age range will find it easier to cope, but even then it is unlikely, with the pressures of the rest of the course, that they will have a real understanding of the needs of workers in many of the family and community centres where teachers are now employed. In these settings where the emphasis is often upon the child *and* the family, teachers need not only management and leadership skills, but also skills to work with parents and professionals from other disciplines. Such a training is not well developed within the current initial training programmes.

In 1988 the government introduced two new school-based schemes for the training of teachers, the Articled Teacher Scheme and the Licensed Teacher Scheme. The success of these schemes will depend to a large extent upon the ability of existing overworked staff to give trainees the support they need to become competent early years teachers.

CURRENT DEVELOPMENTS IN TRAINING FOR CHILDCARE

Estimates vary between 200,000 and 400,000 individuals other than teachers currently involved in work with young children and their families throughout the UK. In England and Wales alone there are roughly 95,000 registered childminders, and probably as many playgroup leaders and assistants in 17,000 playgroups.

Workers with young children and their families are also found in nursery and primary education, crèches, parent and toddler groups, family centres, parent support and home visiting schemes, toy libraries, playbuses and many other types of provision. In fact, some eighty-five distinct job roles were identified by the occupational mapping survey of ten local authority areas undertaken as part of the Working with Under Sevens Project (Hevey and Windle 1990). Further, provision for full daycare, and hence the number of childcare workers, is increasing. In a speech to the Women's National Commission (Bottomley 1991), the Minister for Health reported that between 1988 and 1990 the number of places in registered day nurseries had increased by 60 per cent to 58,000 and that places in nurseries exempt from registration requirements (mainly on health authority premises) had increased by 80 per cent.

The vast majority (97 per cent) of this army of workers with young children are women (Hevey and Windle 1990). Many work part time, some as unpaid volunteers, wages are low and turnover rates are high. According to a report by the European Childcare Network (European Commission 1990), nannies earn just over half the average pay of women workers and childminders less than half. With the exception of full-time workers employed in the public sector, most do not hold any formally recognized qualifications related to their job role.

A small-scale survey in 1986 revealed that the pattern of training and qualifications for work with young children was both confused and confusing (Hevey 1986). There was a burgeoning variety of training courses for childcare, mainly aimed at 16–19 year olds in full-time education or on training schemes, with no way of comparing their content or value for employment purposes. In contrast, the only training opportunities open to the majority of workers – mature women with family responsibilities – were likely to be informal, part time and non-certificated. They varied in duration from as little as one evening a week for six weeks (the typical length of a childminder's pre-registration course) to one day a week for a year (the Foundation Course of the Pre-School Playgroups Association). However, only one-fifth of the respondents to the occupational mapping survey had not taken part in any form of training or induction for their job role, indicating a high degree of take-up of the limited training that was available.

Amazingly, considering the level of responsibility for children's well-being carried by most childcare workers, training has never been a statutory requirement for employment in, or provision of, childcare services. The Children Act 1989 for the first time empowers local authorities to provide training for those engaged in childcare other than its own staff, but it does not require them to do so. The Guidance which accompanies the Act (Department of Health 1991) suggests the personal qualities and experience that might be looked for in childcare personnel but it does not require qualifications nor specify the minimum amount of training and support necessary to enable workers to achieve acceptable standards of care. To have done so would have had large-scale resource implications. More significantly, however, the lack of insistence on qualifications for what are in reality highly responsible roles is underpinned by confused and outmoded public attitudes which deem training unnecessary. The care of young children is often not regarded as 'real' work but as an extension of the mothering role which is assumed to come naturally to women without the need for training. Such attitudes in turn reinforce the low status of childcare work helping to keep pay low and turnover high. Similar sentiments were expressed in the report of the National Child Care Staffing Study carried out in the USA in 1988:

> As a nation we are reluctant to acknowledge child care settings as a work environment for adults, let alone commit resources to improving them. Even though many Americans recognize that child care teachers are underpaid, outdated attitudes about women's work and the family obscure our view of teachers' economic needs and the demands of their work. If a job in child care is seen as an extension of women's familial role of rearing

children, professional preparation and adequate resource compensation seem unnecessary.

(Whitebook *et al.* 1990: 3)

It should be noted that the reference here to 'child care teachers' does not correspond to the British notion of qualified teacher status. In fact, only 31 per cent of the 'child care teachers' who were in charge of classes and centres had a degree or equivalent qualification and only 65 per cent of 'child care teachers' and 57 per cent of aides and assistants had some relevant training in child development. Nevertheless, the survey found that the level of formal education combined with specific training were key predictors of high quality care.

An additional problem both in the UK and in the USA is that up until now, qualifications have not provided a basis for progression or access to higher education and professional training and there has been little incentive through pay or career opportunities for staff to pursue further training.

Radical changes in vocational education and training

In the early 1980s, concerned by low staying-on rates and unfavourable international comparisons of the level of qualifications in the UK workforce, the government commissioned a working group to review the state of vocational education and training across all sectors of industry (MSC and DES 1986). This found a confusing mishmash of qualifications being awarded by a myriad of different awarding bodies with no way of comparing their value, few mechanisms for transferability of credit or credit exemption across related qualifications and no systematic framework through which workers could progress with increasing experience and expertise. Many existing qualifications were criticized for being out of touch with the reality of the workplace and for relying too heavily on knowledge-based assessment. Employers complained that students emerging at the end of training courses might know it all in theory but were ill equipped to do the jobs expected of them in practice and often required considerable on-the-job training before they could function at an acceptable level in the workplace.

The White Paper which followed (Department of Employment and DES 1986) led to the setting up of the National Council for Vocational Qualifications (NCVQ) in the autumn of 1986. The NCVQ was charged with producing a rationalized progressive framework of vocational qualifications across all sectors of industry by 1992.

These new qualifications were to meet certain basic criteria. National Vocational Qualifications (NVQs) were to be based on the notion of occupational competence – the ability to carry out work roles to the standards expected in employment – and assessed by evidence of what candidates could actually do in real work situations rather than on just what they knew (NCVQ 1988; 1989). They were to be modular with provision for credit accumulation and transfer and all unnecessary barriers to access, such as rigid academic entry requirements or time serving, were to be removed. Ideally, candidates would be able to put themselves forward for assessment when they felt ready, regardless of how long or short a time it had taken them to become competent or what mode of study or preparation they had followed. What mattered in the new system was that candidates could actively demonstrate their competence to an assessor in real work settings. This represented a radical shift away from the specification of the 'inputs' of knowledge, skills and experience that a student should be given, and towards a focus on 'outcomes' in terms of the functions a competent worker should be able to perform.

Within the new NCVQ framework, all vocational qualifications were to be slotted into a four-stage ladder from the most basic competences carried out under constant supervision (Level I) to complex, technical and specialized activities carried out with a considerable degree of autonomy and including some managerial functions (Level VI). Each of these levels was to reflect nationally agreed, employment-led standards of occupational competence with agreed routes for progression including access to professional training. Part of the implicit agenda was to ensure that vocational qualifications would be equally valued alongside academic qualifications. Following the White Paper, *Education and Training for the Twenty-First Century* (DES and DE 1991), it is suggested that the parallel ladders can be bridged by the notion of 'core skills' and the introduction of General NVQs as a broad-based preparation for work roles.

The White Paper also expressed the government's commitment to the development of NVQs to cover 80 per cent of the workforce by 1992 and indicated the firm intention to extend the same radical approach to professional qualifications thereafter: 'Once that aim has been achieved, we must secure permanent arrangements to keep NVQs up to date, and to develop them for the remaining 20 per cent of employment, including professional levels' (DES and DE 1991: 17).

Setting standards for work with young children

Because of these wider national reforms, it became imperative to establish a nationally agreed set of occupational standards cutting across the traditional divisions in the field of childcare and education as the basis of new NVQs. This was the task of the 'Working with Under Sevens Project' operating under the auspices of the Care Sector Consortium – the industry-led body which represents all facets of employment interests for social and health care (Hevey 1991a).

It is a basic requirement of the Employment Department, as major funders of development work in this field, that national occupational standards are developed according to a specified methodology and expressed according to strict conventions. Each standard consists of an element of competence describing the functions and activities that a competent worker should be able to do and performance criteria by which an assessor can judge whether the function is being carried out to a level acceptable in employment across a specified range of circumstances. These standards are then grouped together into units (areas of competence that have meaning and value in employment) for assessment purposes.

Applying standards development methodology and conventions to the field of childcare and education was not an easy task because the former are reductionist and product/outcomes oriented whereas the latter is holistic and primarily concerned with process (Hevey 1991b). The sheer diversity of roles and settings caused further problems when attempting to cover all types of workers with young children and their families, regardless of setting or responsible agency or employment status. However, every attempt was made to consult widely and to incorporate those values and principles which have broad-based acceptance in the early years field, such as the integral nature of both 'care' and 'education' functions to the work role, the importance of parent involvement and the need to value and meet the needs of each child as an individual. In fact, more than 3,000 practitioners and managers from across the spectrum of childcare and education settings and from all parts of the UK were involved at some stage in the development of the national standards.

The first batch of National (and Scottish) Vocational Qualifications in Child Care and Education based on those standards were launched in February 1992. The structure of qualifications at Levels II and III is based on a core of units of competence covering the primary functions of promoting the welfare, learning and development of young children (Care Sector Consortium 1991) combined with two or four option units respectively to give the necessary degree of specialization whilst avoiding job or setting specificity. For example, the first three 'endorsements' to be accredited at Level III cover 'Group Care and Education', 'Family Day Care' and 'Pre-school Provision' while in the following two to three years a further four endorsements are anticipated to cover the more specialist areas of 'Family Support', 'Primary Education', 'Special Needs' and 'Hospital Playwork'.

Implications for childcare and education

The advent of National and Scottish Vocational Qualifications in Child Care and Education holds the potential to rationalize and revolutionize training and education and ultimately to improve vastly standards of provision (Messenger and Curtis 1991) through:

1 *improved access* to a nationally recognized, work-related qualification for thousands of women
2 *comparability* with other skilled occupations leading to increased status and recognition (and pay?) for child care work

3 *improved standards* of child care and education based on nationally agreed criteria for worker performance
4 *a framework for progression* within the work role or into higher education and professional training
5 *transferability* of workers across a wide variety of child care and education settings and into related occupations on the basis of generic or core competences
6 *a mechanism for specifying quality* of provision through graded levels of qualification as well as numbers of staff.

This potential has been widely acknowledged and endorsed. The report of the Rumbold Committee stated:

> We welcome the work of the National Council for Vocational Qualifications (NCVQ) towards establishing agreed standards for child care workers, including those in education settings. We believe that, given adequate resourcing, it could bring about significant rationalization of patterns of training. It should also improve the status of early years workers through recognition of the complex range and high level of the skills involved and by opening up prospects for further training.
>
> (DES 1990: para. 176, p. 24)

The EOC stated in their discussion paper and action plan, *The Key to Real Choice*:

> The need in the UK for a professional career structure for child care workers is acute. Work now being done in preparation for National and Scottish Vocational Qualifications in child care may represent an important first step, but will need to be systematically resourced and implemented.
>
> (EOC 1990: para. 2.2.4, p. 4)

However, as these quotes highlight, whether implementation happens on a large enough scale to make a serious impact is dependent on the availability of resources to create and maintain the necessary training and assessment infrastructures.

Particular assumptions of the NCVQ model when combined with characteristics of the early years field make investment of central government resources an essential prerequisite of large-scale implementation. These assumptions stem from the fact that the whole NVQ system is employment based. 'The new model of education and training (or learning) assumes that companies and other employing organizations will become major providers of learning opportunities' (Jessup 1991: 95).

Assessment of competence is assumed to take place largely in the workplace and to be undertaken by extension of the roles of existing line managers and supervisors to include the role of work-based assessor. In large organizations the first tier of standardization and verification is also operated 'in-house' and the awarding bodies merely approve work settings/organizations as assessment centres and provide external verification of assessment. All of this conveniently hides the enormous costs of an individualized, criterion-referenced, competence-based assessment system compared with the traditional model of written examination of thirty or more candidates *en masse* in an examination hall.

The problems with applying this NVQ model to the field of childcare and education are exacerbated by at least three factors. First, with the exception of a hard-pressed public sector for whom services for the youngest children are entirely discretionary, large-scale organizations are notable by their absence. Who then is to provide the training and assessment infrastructures?

Second, childcare workers tend to have a high degree of autonomy and responsibility. Roughly three-quarters of the workforce are not regularly observed and supervised in their work and half are not assessed in any way (Hevey and Windle 1990). How is the competence of unsupervised workers (the majority) to be assessed?

Third, even when a potential work-based assessor is present, ongoing childcare responsibilities within small-scale settings may make it unrealistic for the assessor to carry out detailed observational assessments and questioning of candidates. Who then can fulfil this role?

The only practical solution for large-scale implementation of NVQs in childcare and education would appear to be through the use of qualified and trained peripatetic assessors who visit and assess candidates in their individual workplaces, but this will require the setting up of entirely new training and assessment infrastructures (Wedge 1991) with considerable resource implications (Ross 1990). Unlike other sectors of industry, there simply is no place to hide the costs.

The top of the ladder

Within the NCVQ framework it is assumed that entry into professional training can take place from a relevant 'advanced' NVQ at Level III as an alternative to the traditional A Level route. By implication, those who go on to achieve a 'higher' NVQ at Level IV should have some exemptions from professional training. Level IV, therefore, represents the interface between the vocational and what has traditionally been termed the professional. One problem for childcare and education qualifications is that there are currently not one but at least three interfaces – with teaching, health visiting and social work, and indeed with community work as an additional contender in some cases. The areas of interface and overlap cannot be clearly defined until such time as each of these separate professions undertakes its own functional analysis giving a breakdown of their respective occupational roles in competence terms. However, even when this has been achieved we are left with something of a dilemma. The logical top rung or Level V for a multi-disciplinary ladder is not a single-discipline-based profession!

There is a growing dissatisfaction with the existing discipline-based professional qualifications, such as teaching, as suitable preparation for the sorts of demands imposed by, for example, running a combined centre, a family centre or a community nursery (Calder 1990). The managers of such provision need to be competent in the area of parent support and in the promotion of health and welfare for families with young children but they also critically need competence in curriculum design, evaluation and management if the educational needs of the children are not to take a back seat. The ultimate question then becomes, can existing professional qualifications be adapted to accommodate this range of competences or should we be talking about a new breed of multidisciplinary early childhood professionals?

REFERENCES

Bottomley, V. (1991) Text of speech given at Women's National Commission: Seminar on Child Care, 12 June 1991.

Calder, P. (1990) 'The training of nursery workers: the need for a new approach', *Children and Society* 4(3): 251–60.

Care Sector Consortium (1991) *National Occupational Standards for Work with Young Children and their Families*, available from the National Children's Bureau.

Committee of Enquiry (1972) *Teacher Education and Teacher Training*, Report of a Committee of Enquiry under the Chairmanship of Lord James of Rusholme, London: HMSO.

Department of Education and Science (1990) *Starting with Quality: Report of the Committee of Inquiry into the Educational Experiences Offered to Three-and-Four-Year-Olds*, Rumbold Report, London: HMSO.

Department of Education and Science and Department of Employment (1991) *Education and Training for the Twenty-First Century*, Cmnd 9823, London: HMSO.

Department of Employment and Department of Education and Science (1986) *Working Together: Education and Training*, Cmnd 9823, London: HMSO.

Department of Health (1991) *The Children Act 1989 Guidance and Regulations, Vol. 2: Family Support Day Care and Educational Provision for Young Children*, London: HMSO.

Ebbeck, M. (1990) 'Preparing early childhood personnel to be pro-active policy working professionals', *Early Child Development and Care* 58: 87–96.

Equal Opportunities Commission (1990) *The Key to Real Choice*, Manchester: EOC.

European Commission (1990) *Childcare in the European Communities, 1985–1990*, Brussels: European Commission.

Hevey, D. (1986) *The Continuing Under Fives Training Muddle*, London: VOLCUF.

—— (1991a) *Final Report of the Working with Under Sevens Project*, Presented to the Care Sector Consortium, September.

—— (1991b) 'Not child's play: developing occupational standards for workers with under sevens and their families', *Competence and Assessment* 15: 11–14.

Hevey, D. and Windle, K. (1990) Unpublished report of Working with Under Sevens Project Occupational Mapping Survey.

Jessup, G. (1991) *Outcomes: NVQs and the Emerging Model of Education and Training*, Lewes: Falmer.

Messenger, K. and Curtis, C. (eds) (1991) *NVQ: The Workplace Revolution* Luton: Local Management Board.

MSC and DES (1986) *Review of Vocational Qualifications in England and Wales*, London: HMSO.

NCVQ (1988) *Assessment in National Vocational Qualifications*, NCVQ Information Note No. 4, London: NCVQ.

—— (1989) *The NVQ Criteria and Related Guidance*, London: NCVQ.

Parry, M. and Archer, H. (1979) *Pre-School Education*, London: Schools Council/ Macmillan Educational.

Ross, D. (1990) *Costs of Implementing National Vocational Qualifications*, Papers 1, 2, and 3, CCETSW/Local Government Training Board in conjunction with the ADSS North West Regional Training Unit.

Ward, E. (1986) 'Sound policies promote effective programmes for young children', in *Children Are Worth the Effort: Today, Tomorrow and Beyond: A Memorial to Evangeline Ward 1920–85*, Australian Early Childhood Association, Canberra.

Watts, B. N. (1987) 'Changing families: changing children's services', *Australian Journal of Early Childhood Education* 12 (3): 4–12.

Wedge, D. (1991) 'Building a consortium', in K. Messenger and C. Curtis (eds) *NVQ: The Workplace Revolution*, Luton: Local Management Board.

Whitebook, M., Howes, C. and Phillips, (1990) *Who Cares: Child Care Teachers and the Quality of Care in America*, Executive summary of the National Child Care Staffing Study, Berkeley, CA: Child Care Employee Project.

Chapter 5

Parents and professionals

A. Edwards and P. Knight

WHERE THE POWER LIES

There are enormous and important differences in the relationships between home and school when we compare the statutory and non-statutory phases of early years provision. Once children are in school, teachers as key holders to publicly codified knowledge assume a powerful position *vis-à-vis* parents, although, as we shall see, the parent as consumer can challenge that assumption. The under 5s field is, however, as complex as the purposes and forms of provision available. Some parents will find themselves powerless as their 'at-risk' children are given mandatory places in daycare centres which may or may not have overtly educational aims. Other parents may have more choice about their children's attendance but will be relatively powerless because of the counter-demands made by their own socio-economic, emotional and educational needs. Others will choose to use available provision as a service, which releases them for paid work or time to be spent on other interests or responsibilities. Others will be involved powerfully and actively as members of, for example, management committees.

Pugh (1987) provided a 'five-fold dimension' of parental involvement in preschool centres. The five major elements in her analysis are: non-participation, support, participation, partnership and control. Three of these elements have further sub-categories. For example, participation is subdivided into 'parents as helpers' and 'parents as learners'. These five elements will have different definitions attached to them when they are applied to infant school settings or to nursery classes. But they do provide a useful framework for an examination of possible forms of home–school relations in the early years of education. A comparison of statutory and non-statutory provision reveals that although parental control of statutory provision may have increased through the enhancement of the powers and responsibilities of governing bodies, it is unlikely to ever equate with the degree of parental control evident in a management committee of a preschool playgroup. Equally, non-participation is more likely to be an accepted feature of most parents' relationships with schools, while participation is likely to be a desired feature of nursery provision in, for example, family centres.

The major demarcation in the balance of power that exists between home and educational settings lies in the extent to which the professionals concerned are ultimately responsible for managing the institution. Power will lie with those who are responsible. What then determines the nature of the relationship between professionals and parents is the mission or aims of the institution. Parental involvement is, as a consequence, harnessed to institutional policy and is shaped by it.

Consequently, it is usually an oversimplification to see the importance of good relationships between professionals and parents simply in terms of creating a bridge for the child between home and school in order to ease the transition into school. Most early years specialists in both under-5s and over-5s educational settings see their work with adults as a long-term investment. Dividends are claimed by practitioners as children proceed through their education with informed and trained supportive parents or caregivers. There is also the possibility of additional rewards as these parents or caregivers will work with younger family members. That so many early years practitioners give so much energy to work with parents suggests that there is a consensus that it is a valuable activity. Large-scale evaluation is unfortunately difficult because control and experimental groups are impossible to establish for sound comparisons between different types of involvement and non-involvement. For important ethical reasons, practitioners have to rely on their own observations and compile case studies of small-scale successes.

Because evaluation of the subtle long-term processes and aims of work with parents has to be complex and takes more time than can usually be paid for, it has been difficult to prove successfully that parental involvement programmes are beneficial. None the less, Hannon (1989) argues that parental involvement, in the teaching of reading, at least, is unstoppable. The function of evaluation is therefore to steer those engaged in the activity away from any possible pitfalls. Our own experience of evaluation in this field over an extensive period has identified some pitfalls. Some of these we will discuss in the sections that follow.

Most studies of parental involvement suggest that practitioners involve parents in the work that they do for educational reasons. Parents and caregivers are enrolled to support, in a variety of ways, the educational purposes of the educational institution. This may be a personally empowering experience for the parent or caregiver, but if the development of parents is an aim, it is desired with the educational needs of the child in mind. The prime source of power in most institutions therefore lies with the professional practitioners as decision-makers. This assertion leads us to consider in more detail why practitioners make the decision to collaborate with those who also care for the children they teach.

PARENTAL INVOLVEMENT AND EQUALITY OF OPPORTUNITY

Any attempt at justifying strengthening the links between home and school raises the ideological questions which can more easily be avoided when one thinks simply about how to enhance children's learning. Once nurseries and schools are forced to look at their educational aims, so that they can share them with parents in their parental involvement programmes, the values that are inherent in the narrow entitled curriculum can become apparent. The elevation of one set of standards over another, whether it is standard English over dialect or academic performance over craft skills, gives an indication of what is narrowly regarded as a successful citizen. The hierarchy of standards that is implicit in any national curriculum is certain to mirror those of some social groups and not others. Parental involvement is often pursued under the banner of providing equality of learning opportunities for children. However, unless it is carefully managed, it can become a vehicle for undermining the value systems of some social groups through implicit criticism of what these groups hold dear, whether dialect or craft skills.

A view of educationally oriented parental involvement as a goal that is so worthy that it is beyond critique can prevent even the most reflective teachers from considering their own value positions and those embodied by the curriculum they are operating. We are suggesting that before parental involvement is tackled as a priority in early years educational provision, considerable soul-searching is essential. This examination should include a questioning of what is to be shared with parents and why it is to be shared. Questions about how should arise when the what and the why have been clarified. Later in this chapter, we shall argue that soul-searching and resulting policy decisions cannot be undertaken effectively unless all staff, both teaching and non-teaching, are involved.

Attempts at answering the why and the what questions in order to find a rationale for parental involvement or improved links with children's homes and their community may not always produce comfortable answers. Tizard *et al.* (1981) traced the origins of the interest in the early 1980s in parental involvement in nursery and infant schools. The major threads in their analysis were the relatively new understanding of social influences on child development and a simplified view of working-class environment as contexts that were deficient and less effective in the preparation of children for academic success. The two sets of beliefs combined in the 1970s to encourage a deficit model of working-class parenting which might be improved by increasing contact between home and school. This deficit model can still be heard in current discussions about home–school links in the early years. In the 1970s, it was informed by the work of Bernstein (1971), Blank (1973) and Tough (1976), and the emphasis was on the development of complex forms of language use and as a consequence on the intellectual functioning of children in the family.

Tizard's later work (Tizard and Hughes 1984), which drew on detailed analysis of girls' interactions at home and in preschool settings, showed that the girls in the study received more cognitive challenge at home than at school. These findings led to a reassessment of the assumptions that the experiences of working-class children were richer in school-type settings than they were at home. Stereotypical notions of working-class life were at last damaged.

It could be said that the attempts of the 1970s at encouraging parental involvement because of perceived deficits in the home environment rested on a set of assumptions about the supremacy of middle-class attitudes and values. An unkinder argument would be the suggestion that early years practitioners as a group were struggling to be recognized as professionals and were therefore willing to take on parental involvement schemes, as these schemes in fact depended on the maintenance of a distance between the competent professional practitioner and the underperforming parent.

Professional distancing may also have occurred as a totally understandable reaction to the 1980s assumption that parents and practitioners might be equal partners in the education of young children. This assumption undermined the specialist and professional status of practitioners. Practitioner action research studies of parental involvement programmes consistently demonstrated that, in fact, even the most open-minded staff had cut-off points beyond which they would brook no collaboration with parents. While the most resistant staff used increased distance as their coping strategy, the assumption that parallel involvement necessarily decreases professional distance has not always been confirmed.

In the 1980s, the intellectual inadequacies of a 1970s deficit/compensatory education justification for parental involvement gave way to a rationale that appeared more optimistic and, as we have said, more clearly based on the notion of parents as partners in the education of their children. During this period, we observed programmes of parental involvement in home–school reading partnerships (Topping and Wolfendale 1985) and in mathematics schemes (Merttens and Vass 1990). Yet behind this curriculum aim, a deficit model of parents still lurked. Parents might be harnessed to curricular demands, but the training that they received in how to teach their children as a by-product of involvement was also considered an important feature and parental deficit was assumed. Parental diligence in the tasks set for them was monitored by the need for them to communicate, often in pleasant jokey letter formats, with teachers. Teachers' own evaluations of the success of curriculum partnership projects would depend extensively on parental participation rates and the assumption that parents were unwilling educators.

When we examine concerns that dominate in the 1990s, we can see that although a working-class deficit model in all its 1970s simplicity has been laid to rest, other forms of deficit, operating under the guise of difference, are currently apparent. Teachers who are responsible for the delivery of a national curriculum have little choice over the broad principles of involving parents from homes where, for example, English is the second language. Teachers pass on to parents school information, curriculum content and other key features of school and associated culture. This information-giving is a corollary to giving pupils access to an agreed curriculum. But unless difficult questions about cultural supremacy are addressed by staff groups, the ways in which these issues are passed on may resonate of colonization and ultimately lead to alienation rather than collaboration or co-operation.

These are difficult topics without easy answers, but we suggest that they need to be discussed among practitioners before they invest the considerable energy required by a programme of encouraging home–school links or enhanced parental involvement.

TYPICAL PARENTS?

Any examination of why a nursery or school might wish to undertake a programme of encouraging links with the families of the children they teach will have to take into account their potential collaborators. Parental expectations and needs will create the possibilities for teacher action.

Some parental expectations present few difficulties for practitioners. The non-participating parents who are also supportive rarely express any difficulties. The disaffected non-participants are a challenge and some may belong to the group we shall call 'needy parents', whom we discuss in some detail later. Participating parents, as Pugh (1987) has already indicated, may be learners or helpers: the helpers are often a godsend, the learners we will discuss as needy parents. Though we recognize that not all learners are needy and that helpers find that they too are learning and developing valuable confidence and skills which may contribute to their own personal or career development. Pugh's final categories of partnership and control can, as we have already indicated, present some problems for practitioners, the most recent manifestation of which is the parent as consumer. We shall therefore attend to needy parents and parents as consumers as examples of extreme sets of demands that might be made by parents on those nurseries and schools that decide to interact more openly with parents. These issues apply to a lesser degree to the voluntary sector, but some key features remain constant across settings.

Needy parents whose own economic, emotional and/or educational deficiencies potentially inhibit the educational support they might give their children can consume enormous amounts of teacher time. They can present problems that schools are unable to address and ultimately demand that schools begin to operate as referral agencies. They are not a responsibility that can simply be handed to reception class teachers as part of their home–school liaison duties. These parents will move on through the school, and unless they continue to receive support the efforts of the reception class teacher may be wasted as parental disappointment sets in.

The management and support of these parents can be a full-time and exhausting job and carried more easily by a team than an individual. Nursery workers will be more used to multidisciplinary teams than education specialists. But an increasing number of the schools which are operating in the field are discovering the advantages of directly involving community workers and adult education specialists in their work with parents. An added advantage of this kind of co-operation is access to the funding which is available to these partners but not directly to schools, for example from local initiatives or adult education funding. Our own experience of evaluating work in this field since the late 1970s would lead us to suggest that work with needy parents is not to be undertaken lightly and is certainly a route which has to have the commitment of the whole staff.

Needy parents can be seen as clients of caring professionals rather than as potential partners. Parents as consumers are a distinctly different client group but are equally unlikely to be seen as partners. They are a product of a categorization of social roles which encourages professionals in the caring professions to see clients as customers with associated rights. Interestingly Tizard *et al.*, writing in the early 1980s, note the growth of parent consumer groups in the 1960s, of which the Advisory Centre for Education (ACE) was one of the first, as an influence on the tendency to involve parents in the work of nurseries and infant schools. The challenges that these relatively small pressure groups made to the teaching profession formed part of a climate in which education itself became the subject of major national debate and a topic that could be publicly negotiated and discussed. This grassroots movement has, in some ways, been supported by legislation which has encouraged a consumer view of the Welfare State in general and of education provision in particular. This is evident in the publication of a *Parents' Charter* and the idea of 'customers' rights' in education.

In the 1990s, we find ourselves with a curriculum which is not negotiated, with indeed a relatively fixed menu for children. The role of parents of children after 5 as consumers is now not so much to negotiate that menu in public discussion, but to demand that it is delivered effectively. Their function is to remind practitioners, in the statutory sector at least, of their accountability. Vincent (1993) examined these contradictions and found what can be described as bounded consumerism in her exploration of parental participation in a city's education service through the work of a city Parents' Centre. Her analysis of the themes at work in the centre summarize the points we have been raising. She emphasizes the illusory nature of participation, the hidden agenda and the push away from partnership to individual consumer-based relations:

firstly ... apparent attempts to increase participation may well prove illusory in substance; secondly, that moves to introduce participating processes are often motivated by a wish to legitimate the more general action of the institution concerned; and finally ... the dominant political ideology shuns the ethos of collective citizen participation, preferring instead an emphasis on the role of the individual consumer.

(Vincent 1993: 231)

The parent as consumer is a notion that may be premised in part at least on a view of teaching as a technical operation rather than a complex profession. It implies that market forces can shape education. Co-operative partnership with parents is unlikely if a purchaser–provider, parent-as-consumer model of education holds sway. In this context, closer co-operation with parents can degenerate into public relations exercises in which schools' images are packaged. Interestingly, Hughes *et al.* (1993), in their study of parental attitudes to school, found that the majority of parents did not see themselves as consumers who were able to make consumer choices and almost half were puzzled by the term. It seems that this definition has yet to direct the way that parents see themselves in relation to schools.

The parent as consumer is a different form of client from the parent as deficient educator. The former definition springs from a notion of client as customer, whereas the latter has its origins in education as a caring profession. Neither may provide a particularly useful premise for all forms of parental involvement in school. Consequently, in a climate in which parents are being encouraged to see themselves as consumers, nurseries and schools may find that a discussion of parental involvement might benefit from an analysis of parents as clients and the possible advantages that might be derived from moving towards closer partnership with them. Close partnership with a sharing of aims may prevent the final emergence of parent as consumer.

WAYS AND MEANS

Our discussion of parental involvement has so far been cautionary. The intention has not been to deter but to encourage lengthy consideration of the purposes of involvement and some associated misapprehensions. We feel that this period of soul-searching is essential as clear identification of the aims of a parental involvement will give direction to the extent and limits of the activities that will be undertaken. Early years practitioners cannot work miracles and most already find themselves under immense curricular pressure.

Figure 5.1 places forms of parental involvement on a continuum which runs from a view of parent as client to one of parent as partner. It also allows us to distinguish between activities that take place during the working day in the school or nursery and those that can be described as extramural and occurring either in homes or at other sites outside the main educational setting.

The categorization of ways of involving parents is useful because it forces us to consider a number of issues. First, it allows us to see that parental

Parent on the premises

	Use a room for own social or educational purposes	Attend concerts and information evenings	Run toy and book libraries and help with concerts	Regularly help on mundane tasks, e.g. cleaning paint pots	Regularly supervise children's activities, e.g. cutting and pasting	Regularly lead children's activities, e.g. baking, reading	
Parents as clients							Parents as partners
	Attend sports days and fund raising activities	Help children to make things at home	Raise funds and make costumes	Help on school trips and with sports activities	Reinforce learning started with practitioners, e.g. listening to reading	Teach their children on structured schemes	

Parent off the premises

Figure 5.1 Types of parental involvement

involvement is a developmental process. If the intention is to move parents into closer partnership, practitioners need to place the parents they are targeting on this continuum and consider what is possible. We would argue that it is overly ambitious to attempt to shift parents from being concert attenders to becoming teachers on structured home learning schemes without considerable bridge-building.

The developmental element of this continuum is not simple because it does not only depend on the growing skills and confidence of some parents. In some cases, it will depend on the willingness of teachers to blur the boundaries between the work of teachers and parents. Parents who work closely with children in educational settings then become adults whose work has to be managed by the practitioners who have ultimate responsibility for provision for their children. In addition, the need to defend professional status can come into play and make partnership an unlikely option.

A large number of the activities shown in Figure 5.1 represent work that parents do to improve the resources available to their children. These resources include not only the library books or computers bought with Parent Teacher Association funds, but also teacher time which is released from the more mundane tasks that are all too essential to classroom management. This form of involvement is widely available and much appreciated but brings us back to the purposes of parental involvement.

Parents will not become better teachers of their children if they spend their time with other parents in their own workroom repairing the spines on library books or cutting out crowns for the nativity play. But by undertaking these mundane tasks they release teacher time. They may be useful monitors of children as the children cut and stick jewels on to the crowns, but one has to query the educational purpose of such an activity without the presence of a trained practitioner able to exploit it for a discussion of colour, pattern and shape. It has to be at least questioned whether they have the ability to lead activities which might maximize the learning that can occur for a group of children, for example engaged in a baking activity, without training in group management, the conceptual structure of the subjects being covered and the language formats that might be reinforced. Loenen (1989) reported an evaluation of a school-based volunteer reading programme with junior school children and found considerable discrepancies between the approach recommended by the volunteers and their actual practice. This was particularly evident in the areas of reading for meaning and talking with the children. She concludes that more professional help for the volunteers might improve their effectiveness. Parents might be good educators of their own children at home, but despite the domestication of much early years provision, educational settings are different.

Our own work with practitioners has indicated that most parental involvement initiatives have not been premised on any analysis of the cycle of children's learning, or analysis of the types of tasks that are given to parents to undertake with their children, and the interrelationship of these two elements. One has to ask: 'Participation for what?'

Teachers are well aware of these issues. We have frequently observed the contradiction that schools justify their considerable efforts in the field of parental involvement in parental deficit and equal opportunities terms but operate systems which are geared at releasing teachers from mundane work. The decision to keep parents away from children may have been wisely taken given our concerns with the purpose and quality of conversations in learning environments, but may sit oddly with the espoused aims of the programme.

These concerns lead us to consider parents as partners in educational settings within a wider political framework. Underfunding of early years provision has led to the use of an untrained, unpaid, largely female workforce to sustain attempts at achieving what is described as good practice in early years provision. This has to be a topic that is at least discussed when schools undertake and evaluate their work with parents.

Other topics for discussion that arise from an examination of the purposes and processes of parental involvement include the role boundaries of practitioners and parents, the rights and responsibilities of each in the use of the premises and resources, and above all the educational purpose of each action that is undertaken. Practitioners take it as given that their actions have to be justified in relation to children's learning. It may be more difficult to keep parents to such a tight agenda. Once practitioners lose control of the agenda that determines the range and style of involvement, the aims and nature of the school or nursery may themselves shift. We have been warning throughout that although parental involvement may be a worthwhile venture, it is not without its risks.

PARENTAL INVOLVEMENT AND WHOLE-SCHOOL POLICIES

Mead's (1934) notion of symbolic interaction is helpful in understanding how children learn to categorize their social worlds and themselves within them. This notion can begin to explain the distinctiveness of subjects and the need to get inside a subject so that one might operate with it. We shall now refer to symbolic interactionism in order to reinforce the claims we have been making for the importance of a whole-school policy if parental involvement programmes are to be effective in achieving their aims. The sharing of meanings between staff is an obvious first step.

Perhaps more than any other institutional policy, parental involvement requires that as many members of staff as possible are engaged from the first flickering of an idea. This will ensure that time can be given to soul-searching and careful examination of the purposes of involvement. During this period, the language used to justify involvement can be clarified and what is important to the school and its community can be made explicit. In addition, attention to the beliefs and feelings of staff at an early stage may mean that some of the contradictions we have discussed in this chapter can be avoided as differences are opened up and faced and meaning ultimately shared.

Once policy aims have been agreed, strategies can be selected. Our advice here is to be incremental and not over-ambitious in what you set out to achieve. Again the maximum involvement of staff is crucial and individual staff will have to feel comfortable with the actions they will undertake and be aware of their meanings and implications. If discomfort occurs, role boundaries will harden and professional resistance to involvement will result.

The selection of strategies needs to be followed up by in-house staff development during the period in which initial action is being prepared. This staff development needs to be related to the aims and strategies to be employed. In the best examples training involves domestic staff and non-teaching assistants. If parents are to be encouraged to fulfil roles available to them in the involvement scheme, the messages they receive from all the adults in the educational setting must be consistent. Here an understanding of symbolic interactionism helps us to see the importance of a consistent and coherent behaviour of all staff towards parents or caregivers. As staff chat to parents when they collect children or telephone with a query, a sense of parental rights and responsibilities within the school is conveyed and a set of expectations of parent as client or as partner is established in the language used and the tone of the interactions.

The extent to which parents themselves might be involved in the development of policy and selection of strategies needs to be considered. Yet again this is not any easy issue: the typical parent does not exist. One or two parents at the policy-making stage may exert unwarranted influence. It may, however, be possible to check the policy with existing groups of parents associated with the school. It would certainly be expected that the governing body might have a view on this policy. As strategies will stem from policies and be limited by resourcing and staff readiness for involvement, the role of any existing parental group might be as limited as to receiving information and comment if it wishes to.

The development of policy and selection of strategies might usefully be informed by other professionals involved in work with local families. We have sometimes observed overlap between the activities of home–school liaison teachers and community workers. We have already indicated that other professional groups might have access to other strategies and additional funding. They may also offer insights into work with families that cannot be found in the training that education specialists receive. They will certainly alert education practitioners to additional pitfalls to be avoided.

Funding is another important reason why parental involvement needs to be taken seriously, as a matter that affects the whole school or nursery. Parental involvement activities can be expensive. This is particularly the case if home visits are involved or if staff time is spent in supporting parents as they prepare to work at home with their children. Decision making about funding staff work with parents is yet another reason to put parental involvement programmes at the centre of school management concerns.

THE OPEN LEARNING ENVIRONMENT

We have so far discussed links between professionals and parents largely in terms of parental involvement initiatives. Yet many of the types of parental involvement shown in Figure 5.1 are common occurrences in schools and nurseries which would not regard themselves as overtly operating a parental involvement policy. A common quality in these environments is an openness to others which is clearly evident to any symbolic interactionist. Children tend to move freely to and from main resource or teaching bases; a visiting adult causes no disruption; and the curriculum is enriched not only by constant interplay with the immediate nursery or school environment, but also by bringing the wider world into the learning situation, whether it be through a bunch of bud-laden twigs or a visit by a local firefighter.

Open institutions create situations in which a relaxed dialogue with parents can take place. This is imperative if discipline issues are to be tackled before they develop, if children with both major and minor special needs are to be accommodated, and if parents and practitioners are to share their understandings of what motivates or deters the children.

Openness of this kind implies a respect for parents as informed carers with a part to play in the education of their children. One problem with overt parental involvement initiatives identified by Brown (1993) is that they tend to establish models of ideal parenting against which parents are judged and usually found wanting. Public scrutiny – for the first time in some cases – of the products of their child-rearing can be stressful. To add to this a direct assessment of themselves as participating parents can be unnerving. A relaxed climate of mutual respect which is consciously supported by all members of staff may be the context in which the most useful and meaningful of conversations between practitioners and parents may occur.

Creating a climate for dialogue is not easy as both practitioner and parental attitudes can prevent this. Hannon and James (1990), in their exploration of parents' and teachers' perspectives on the development of preschool literacy, observed that only five of the forty highly concerned parents they studied actually talked to nursery staff about how they might work with their children at home! This was despite the majority belief that nursery teachers would be able to help them. Twenty-two of the forty parents felt that nursery education did help in the acquisition of literacy but were vague about how. Hannon and James also accuse nursery staff of vagueness. Interestingly, they comment that: 'In order for nursery teachers to communicate effectively with parents they need to be sure of what constitutes the nursery curriculum' (Hannon and James 1990: 269).

An open learning context depends on clarity of purpose and strategies if chaos is not to ensue. The school or nursery that can afford to take the risks involved in being open and maintaining permeable boundaries with the local community is usually the establishment where goals are clear, relate to children's learning and can be made explicit whenever necessary. In this way, spontaneity can be checked against children's learning needs and the best of both the worlds of home and school can be seen in action.

REFERENCES

Bernstein, B. (1971) *Class, Codes and Control, vol. 1*, London: Routledge & Kegan Paul.

Blank, M. (1973) *Teaching and Learning in the Preschool*, Columbus, OH: Charles E. Merrill.

Brown, A. (1993) 'Participation, dialogue and the reproduction of social inequalities', in R. Merttens and J. Vass (eds) *Partnerships in Maths: Parents and Schools*, London: Falmer.

Hannon, P. (1989) 'How should parental involvement in the teaching of reading be evaluated?', *British Journal of Educational Research* 15(10): 33–40.

Hannon, P. and James, S. (1990) 'Parents' and teachers' perceptives on preschool literacy development', *British Educational Research Journal* 16(3): 259–72.

Hughes, M., Wikely, F. and Nash, T. (1993) 'Parents in the new era: myth and reality', in R. Merttens and J. Vass (eds) *Partnerships in Maths: Parents and Schools*, London: Falmer.

Loenen, A. (1989) 'The effectiveness of volunteer reading help and the nature of the reading help provided', *British Journal of Education Research* 15(3): 297–316.

Mead, G. H. (1934) *Mind, Self and Society*, Chicago: University of Chicago Press.

Merttens, R. and Vass, J. (1990) *Bringing School Home: Children and Parents Learning Together*, London: Hodder & Stoughton.

Pugh, G. (1987) 'Introduction', in G. Pugh, G. Aplin, E. De'Ath and M. Moxon, *Partnerships in Action, vol. 1*, London: National Children's Bureau.

Tizard, B. and Hughes, M. (1984) *Young Children Learning: Talking and Thinking at Home and at School*, London: Fontana.

Tizard, B., Mortimore, J. and Burchell, B. (1981) *Involving Parents in Nursery and Infant Schools*, London: Grant McIntyre.

Topping, K. and Wolfendale, S. (eds) (1985) *Parental Involvement in Children's Reading*, London: Croom Helm.

Tough, J. (1976) *The Development of Meaning: A Study of Children's Use of Language*, London: Allen & Unwin.

Vincent, C. (1993) 'Community participation? The establishment of a "City Parents' Centre"', *British Educational Research Journal* 19(3): 227–41.

Chapter 6

Learning begins at home

Implications for a learning society

T. Alexander

Imagine an education system where none of the educators is trained, indeed, where training is seen as a sign of weakness. There is no curriculum, but the amount to be learnt is vast and it is assumed everyone knows what it is. There is no assessment, but if people fail, the penalties are severe. This is not any old education system, but the foundation for every course, job and profession in the UK. It is, of course, the family. Parents are the most important educators in any person's life, yet they get most of the blame when things go wrong and the least support and training to ensure that all children get the best possible start in life.

As knowledge skills and interpersonal competence become increasingly important for employment and other opportunities throughout life, so the importance of this foundation course in life is likely to grow. Thus concern for equality of opportunity as well as attainment demands that the education system takes account of children's different starting points and home circumstances.

It would be quite wrong to 'professionalize' parenting through training, assessment and qualifications and thus increase the pressures on parents. But the formal education system needs to do much more to recognize and support families' fundamental role as the foundation for all learning.

Learning within the family is more lasting and influential than any other. Values, attitudes, behaviour, language and a vast range of skills are learnt or shaped at home. Family life can be a source of inspiration and personal growth, stimulating learning throughout life. But family experiences can – and often do – also cause stress, distress and even illness, damaging personal development and inhibiting learning.

Experiences within the family have a profound influence on people's learning and life chances. Many studies show that home background is the most single significant factor in educational achievement at school and in later life (e.g. Bloom 1985). Poor parenting is associated with low achievement and even criminality in later life (Utting 1995). Where there is abuse, conflict or neglect, or parents/carers are stressed, depressed and unable to cope, family life can cause terrible suffering, permanent damage and long-term disadvantage.

So family life is not a happy experience for many people. A survey by NCH Action for Children suggests that at least 750,000 children in Britain suffer long-term trauma as a result of domestic violence (NCH Action for Children 1994). Over 36,000 children are on the Child Protection Register. Over 7,000 cases of sexual abuse were reported in 1992. It is estimated that one in eight adults were beaten or abused as children. The numbers who suffered from constant criticism or emotional neglect are much greater. Millions of people seek help from counsellors, therapists or the Samaritans, or suffer from mental illness, often tracing their distress to experiences within the family. Virtually all parents want the very best for their children, and indeed do their best. But when abuse, neglect or even just a lack of love is their only education in family life, the best they can offer their own children may not be enough.

Raising children is an act of love and a source of joy. Most families are 'good enough'. But the pressures on parents have certainly increased since the early 1970s, family patterns have changed significantly and past experience is no longer an adequate guide to the future. On present trends, one-quarter of children born in the mid-1990s will see their parents divorce before they are 16 years old. Although eight out of ten families with dependent children have two parents, some 8 per cent of children have a step-parent and one fifth of all families are headed by a lone parent, usually the mother. Two-thirds of all mothers have jobs and families are increasingly divided between 'dual-earner' families and homes where nobody has a paid job (Utting 1995). Families are also much more mobile and less likely to live close to relatives. Britain is also more ethnically diverse, with a greater variety of home languages, faiths, cultures and family patterns. The amount of information and entertainment available in many homes through the media and computer technologies has increased enormously. At the same time, the divide between families has also grown wider in both material and educational resources.

An early challenge facing any new parent is learning to deal with a bewildering patchwork of provision, from antenatal services and health visitors to an ever-changing voluntary sector of playgroups, one-o'clock clubs, toy libraries and the arcane enrolment criteria of different nurseries. This experience rarely inspires people in their own competence. It usually generates anxiety, defensiveness or sheer exhaustion. And in the middle of all this, people somehow learn to be parents, the most important job in the world.

Families experiencing difficulties often do not know where to turn. Asking for help sounds like failure, an admission that you cannot cope. Many are afraid of interfering officialdom and the risk that their child may be taken away. Parents brave – or desperate – enough to overcome these fears must find their way round a maze of services lacking coherence and co-ordination. Agencies like health and social services and the police are also beginning to recognize the need to work together in dealing with family problems although most are far from doing so. According to a 1994 Audit Commission report, agencies set up to support children and families, which cost £2 billion a year are badly co-ordinated, poorly focused and did not involve parents sufficiently (Audit Commission 1994).

The education system is the biggest warren in this maze. It has little to offer people as parents. A lucky few discussed relationships and parenthood, awkwardly perhaps, on the fringes of sex education. Then there may be a part-time playgroup or nursery as the child grows. But no opportunities for the adult to come to terms with the experience of becoming a parent. And when nursery or school begins, however friendly and welcoming, the over-whelming emphasis is on the parent as a vehicle for the child and on maintaining the institutional routine.

Growing numbers of schools recognize the value of working in partnership with parents, which in practice usually means the mother. But most of the emphasis is on involving parents in school, in teaching parents to extend school work. Home-learning schemes, like PACT (reading) and IMPACT (maths), are about taking school home. Relatively little attention has been given to bringing experience from home and community into school, or using the school as a resource centre for supporting the home as a place of learning.

It would be more productive if schools and other services saw their main job as providing professional support for families and the community to solve problems themselves in order to prevent them from becoming crises. This would mean designing services round families' needs for learning and support, rather than expecting families to fit in with the institutional needs of education and the caring professions. We need to turn schools round, in terms of not only the kind of activity and curriculum offered, but also who schools are for. Much more emphasis needs to be put on giving parents opportunities to learn, with their children as well as in their own right.

I want to suggest that the education system can become learner centred only by fully recognizing that the home is the most significant place of learning in people's lives. Teachers, schools, libraries and other services provide vital resources to children and families, but the way in which they are provided makes all the difference. Our failure to do this means that most educational resources, including teachers' time, are probably wasted.

THE WASTING EDUCATION SYSTEM

Most educational provision is wasted because it is not organized to support learning as and when the learner is best able to make use of it, but to a predetermined pattern based on historical habit more than a conscious design for learning. This pattern includes long summer holidays so that children can help their parents bring in the harvest. The school year starts in the autumn with exams in the summer, like an old-fashioned assembly line, although we know that this disadvantages children born at the 'wrong' time of year. Class sizes remain remarkably constant throughout the day and over a year, although we know that learning needs everything from one-to-one coaching to very large groups, as well as work in pairs and groups without a teacher. School buildings are closed to learning for more than three-quarters of the time. Of course there are exceptions, particularly in community schools, but this ancient pattern is the basis of all funding, training and administration for education in the twenty-first century.

We know that educational resources are being wasted because young people, endowed with an innate capacity to learn, achieve far less than their full potential by the time they leave school. We know from our own experience, if not from school inspections, that almost one-third of all lessons are unsatisfactory. That is an awful lot of wasted time for pupils, teachers and educational plant. Most lessons are satisfactory, but few are memorable moments of learning. We know that even children who appear to do well at school are simply learning to survive and play the school game successfully and cannot apply what they appear to know to their own lives because it is divorced from their lives. It is, therefore, not surprising that so many young people go on to further education without really knowing what they want to do. Many leave courses before finishing them or choose qualifications and careers they later regret.

This wastage is compounded by the high cost of juvenile crime, children in care and other services needed to cope with the large numbers of people who leave school ill equipped to lead satisfying, healthy lives and get involved with crime, drugs or other forms of abuse. Crime alone costs the UK over £18 billion a year, more than enough to double spending on education. Poverty and lack of opportunities for young people leaving school are significant factors in these problems, but they are not the cause. Many children from poor and deprived homes do not commit crime or become abusive adults. We know that the quality of relationships within the home is one of the biggest influences on people's ability to make the most of whatever circumstances they face in life and to overcome poverty and deprivation. This is the experience of many immigrant families, into Britain, the United States and other countries, who arrived with nothing.

Educational resources are wasted, above all, because they do not acknowledge or support the vast range of independent learning that goes on at home and in the community. Children are in school for only a small proportion of waking time between birth and the age of 16 – less than 15 per cent. Yet educational provision is planned as if it alone were the source of all knowledge. Relatively little attention is paid to the vast range of abilities among children when they come to school, even though we know that range of ability remains unchanged unless the less able get extra help as early as possible. In most schools there is very little constructive communication between teachers and the most important educators in a child's life, their parents. Most direct communication between home and school concerns administrative matters or instructions from the school to parents, about what they should do, about how the school sees their child and about things that have gone wrong.

This waste of educational resources is endemic and systemic. It is not the fault of individual teachers or even schools. Although many schools and teachers could improve their contribution to learning, even the most ambitious, well-financed school improvement programme cannot address the chronic weakness of our educational system until it stops neglecting its foundations: families as places of learning.

EFFECTIVE FAMILIES ARE FUN

'It takes a whole village to educate a child' goes the African proverb. This is still true in the fast moving world of a global village, where events in Guangdong, Seattle or Wall Street can have more impact on our lives than our neighbourhood, town hall or even Parliament. Multimedia, television and computer technologies can bring more information and knowledge into people's homes today than most universities held in the past. But what they do not bring is the guide, the skilled facilitator and teacher which enables people to direct their learning and create their own coherent understanding of the world.

Instead, children learn to live in a fragmented world of separate realities among fleeting television characters, heroes of the football pitch, the strange order of school and jumble of home life. Families are so very varied it is difficult to generalize, but whether a child's family is chaotic and dangerous or loving and safe, it is the most constant reality for almost all children. Even a child that is moved incessantly between relatives, childminders and a series of temporary homes, including council care, usually has a mother, grandmother or other family figure holding some kind of thread more lasting than any school.

Family experience. however secure or disturbed, is the foundation of a child's learning throughout life. Many studies have shown the contribution parents make to children's learning (e.g. Minns 1990; Hancock 1995; Hannon et al. 1995). In The Meaning Makers, Gordon Wells shows 'the very strong relationship between knowledge of literacy at age five and all later assessments of school achievement' (Wells 1986). Barbara Tizard and Martin Hughes's study of 4-year-old girls at home and in school showed that the home provides a very powerful learning environment covering a very wide range of topics (Tizard and Hughes 1984). From their detailed observations, it was clear that interactions between mothers and children at home were richer learning experiences than those with teachers. The nursery school usually offered more resources, opportunities to play with other children and other activities which provided different learning experiences not available at home, so the authors did not argue that schools were unnecessary, but that they should take account of home learning and the gap between home and school. Their study also highlighted important differences in the way in which working- and middle-class children interacted with school, and the extent to which working-class parents undervalued their contribution to their child's learning.

Tizard and Hughes conclude by summarizing five factors which make the home such a varied and effective learning context. These are:

1 the extensive range of activities within or from home, links with the wider world through parents' work, shopping and other activities, and the models of adults engaged with life
2 the vast body of shared experience which enables the parent, usually the mother, to help the child make sense of experience and put it into a framework of knowledge
3 the opportunities for sustained one-to-one conversations and undivided attention are much greater where the ratio of adults to children is so much smaller than in school
4 learning is embedded in contexts of great meaning, where the outcome has emotional and practical importance
5 the intimacy and intensity of home can give children greater freedom and safety to pursue questions, while the mother's concern for the child means she will put whatever energy she has into pursuing her educational expectations for her child.

It is this parental concern that 'converts the potential advantages of the home into actual advantages', the authors continue. 'The learning potential of the home is not a necessary attribute of all family settings' (Tizard and Hughes 1984).

The authors criticize home-visiting schemes and most parent education courses, questioning 'the assumption that professionals know how parents should interact with, and educate, their children'. They conclude that there is a 'useful role for parents' groups, and for advice and information centres which respond to these needs [for sharing experiences, support and learning], but none for attempts by professionals to alter the way in which parents carry out their educational role'. 'Indeed, in our opinion, it is time to shift the emphasis away from what parents should learn from professionals and towards what professionals can learn from studying parents and children at home' (Tizard and Hughes 1984).

There is little evidence that schools and professionals have made a significant shift towards learning from parents and children at home. The development of home–school links (see e.g. Bastiani 1996; RSA 1993), shows that recognition of the importance of parents is widespread, but the full implications of this and other studies have not been assimilated by the education system or policy-makers.

Yet there has been growth in different kinds of parenting education in response to parents' needs. These courses or parents' groups provide opportunities to share experiences and learn practical strategies for dealing with everyday problems. Programmes like *Parent Link* and *Veritas* are not run by professional agencies, but by parents or volunteers who have trained to use parents' own experiences and a package of materials with groups. Unlike the professional parent education courses criticized by Tizard and Hughes, which are mainly targeted at parents considered 'deprived' or 'inadequate', these courses are more available in middle-class areas where parents can afford to pay. These parents see the value of improving parenting and are less likely to fear intervention by social services or other professionals than in many poor areas. But many of these materials are also being used successfully by working-class, African, Caribbean and bilingual Asian parents, as in the London Borough of Waltham Forest.

The National Children's Bureau's comprehensive survey of policy and practice in parent education in 1994 listed the main features of these programmes (Pugh *et al.* 1994). This describes an emerging 'pedagogy of family' which is also relevant to schools. Among the key points are:

1 a belief that 'good enough' parents are responsible, authoritative, assertive, positive, democratic and consistent
2 they are not autocratic, authoritarian or permissive
3 parents' strengths should be reaffirmed, building on confidence and self-esteem
4 experience, feelings and relationships are as important as knowledge, with the emphasis on understanding and enjoyment.

This pedagogy is consistent with over a decade of research into well-motivated high achievers from low-income backgrounds in the United States, from which Reginald Clark (1983; 1987) concluded that 'effective families' had made the biggest difference in children's lives:

> Like effective schools, effective families have a set of easy-to-identify characteristics. These cut across family income, education, and ethnic background. They remain true for single- and two-parent households and for families with working and non-working mothers. Effective families display a number of positive attitudes and behaviors towards their children which help them to succeed in school and in life.
>
> (Clark 1983; 1987)

The characteristics of effective families also describe a pedagogy of family learning from which educational professionals could also learn:

1 *A feeling of control in their lives:* parents believe they can make a positive difference in their children's lives and do not feel overwhelmed by circumstances. Their homes are a safe place for children to find support and understanding.

2 *Frequent communication of high expectations.*
3 *A family dream of success for the future:* parents have a vision of success for each child and talk with their children about the steps to realize them.
4 *A view of hard work as a key to success.*
5 *An active lifestyle:* parents encourage children to use out-of-school activities and community resources, they know where their children are, who they are with, and encourage them to associate with children who have similar values regarding work and school.
6 *25 to 35 home-centred learning hours a week:* including homework, reading, hobbies, household chores, family outings and youth programmes.
7 *The family as a mutual support system* in which parents give children some appropriate responsibilities from an early age and children realize they are needed and contribute to family life.
8 *Clearly understood household rules consistently enforced,* with the emphasis on acceptance and responsibility rather than punishment.
9 *Frequent contact with teachers* and involvement in school life.
10 *Emphasis on spiritual growth* encouraging children to find inner peace and love.

The most significant feature of these ten points is that they are based on a study of successful young adults from poor, black families. They bear the hallmarks of their particular culture and society, but many are relevant to the British education system.

The central point is that we know many of the features which contribute to family failure, we know the general characteristics of effective families, and we know what kind of education and support for parents can make a positive contribution to their role as educators, yet none of this is recognized in the education system.

It has been said that, on average, people learn half of everything they are taught during their lives during the first five years. It is probably impossible to quantify and compare learning in this way, but it is certain that we could not do without everything we learn by the age of 5, and those skills, knowledge and abilities we acquire by the age of 6 make all the difference to all subsequent learning. It would therefore make sense to secure adequate resources and support for those vital early years. What might this mean in practice?

A VISION OF A LEARNING SOCIETY

First, a learning society would be one in which, above all else, parents and other family members had time to spend with children. Work, wages and welfare would be structured in such a way that parents could choose to spend significant amounts of time with their children, particularly in the early years, without being penalized financially. Family income support, maternity/

paternity leave and services for people with dependent children would be recognized as an investment in education, not a cost to be cut by getting parents into employment as quickly as possible. Increased opportunities for women to work would be matched by more opportunities for fathers to spend time with their children. Family-friendly policies by employers are not only good personnel practice, but also a vital part of training and staff development for future generations.

Second, families would have a wide choice of affordable activities, courses and provision to support and extend learning in the home, starting with antenatal classes and continuing through to intergenerational activities with older people and bereavement counselling. Parenting education would be a small but significant part of total provision, and most parents would expect to participate in some kind of support group, parenting programme or activity to develop their abilities as parents. It would be quite normal and easy for parents to seek advice and support for any concerns when they arise.

Third, every school and public library would be a community education centre, open every day for most of the year, providing resources and support for learning to all family members, as and when they wanted to learn. Grandparents and other adults would be actively involved. School premises would be a focus for community celebrations and neighbourhood democracy as well as places of learning.

The process of attending school would be turned inside out, as is beginning in a very few places. There would be huge encouragement and incentives for parents and children to participate in activities and a nursery or playgroup before school age. Children would start classes at school when they were ready and able to learn in class. School would start with parents, teacher and child making a joint assessment of what the child could do and what the child could best learn next. The exercise would be repeated every term. A group of children would spend much of the time together as a class with a teacher, but the variety of activities and adults in class would be greater. The ratio of children to a class teacher would rise from about eight to one in infant school to twenty to one in secondary, but there would be more variety in group sizes for different activities and specialist subjects. The average ratio across the school system might even be similar to now, but there would be many more teachers in early years and more self-directed study groups and projects at secondary level. Lessons would draw on children's experience and activities outside school much more, including television, film, hobbies and excursions. Young people would take work home to apply and practise what they have learnt in school, and bring experiences into school in order to understand and engage with the world in which they are growing up.

Teachers and parents would meet at least once every half term in a class meeting to discuss the curriculum, progress and anything affecting the class as a whole. All parents would meet the teacher for an in-depth discussion at least once every term. Many parents, family members and other adults would spend more time in school, sharing their experience and knowledge, helping out and learning themselves. Continuity of experience between home and school would flow both ways, with school more like the intimate, interactive meaningful personal learning that takes place in most homes, while the range of knowledge, skills and issues developed at home would deepen.

The functions of home and school would still be distinct, perhaps even more so than today. With a clear partnership between home and school, teachers of skills and knowledge could be confident that child and parents will expect to learn at home. Whole-class teaching might be more widespread than now, because lessons would be focused on what participants were ready and willing to learn and there would be a lot more small-group learning in people's lives beyond the classroom.

School would not be seen as the source or store of knowledge, but a place where people could develop their skills and deepen their understanding of the knowledge that is all around them. Children and parents would bring questions and problems to learn about in school, and all would work together at the frontiers of knowledge in the twenty-first century.

Schools cannot make this transformation alone. Children and parents already bring many problems to school which act as a block to learning. In order to create a learning society we need to recognize and transform the educational role of *every* agency that works with families.

LEARNING BEYOND SCHOOL

Recognizing that home is the centre of life and learning also means re-organizing the way in which many public services are provided. From the public's point of view, services for families and children are a bewildering maze. Finding the help or advice you need can be a hazardous voyage of chance and frustration. Trying to influence service providers is even more difficult, since they are answerable to different branches of government or voluntary organization, each pursuing a different agenda according to different timetables. Getting agencies to develop a comprehensive strategy together is extremely difficult.

There are few examples where agencies have really transformed the way they work together to put families first. In many areas early years networks link playgroup workers, nursery nurses, teachers, education visitors and others at a local level. They are often informal, meeting in lunch breaks to share information and support. The Children Act 1989 has increased co-ordination of provision for under-8s, with some joint planning between education, social services, health and sometimes other agencies. But joint planning is still subject to departmental priorities. Since every department has different priorities and different funding criteria, progress is slow and is just as likely to be in reverse as moving forward.

The only example I know of a serious attempt to co-ordinate family services is in Washington State, USA. The legislature has set up a statewide Family Policy Council on which all agencies that work with families are represented, from education and health to the juvenile justice system, together with elected representatives. This structure is reproduced at local level. Every county of about 40,000 people has a Community Network of twenty-three people, ten from the different agencies and thirteen representing different community interests. The Council and each Network has a responsibility to plan provision for the area. They have powers to vary departmental funding criteria, so that funds can be allocated flexibly to meet specific needs of the area. The Family Policy Council and Networks were set up as a preventive strategy in response to rising juvenile crime, drug use and children at risk, but their scope is wide, including recreation and creativity. These 'policy-focused networks' aim to cut across departmental boundaries and develop joint strategies for all agencies which work with families, and to give users more direct access to strategic decision-making (Figure 6.1). Breaking down the hierarchies and functional barriers between institutions set up to serve families is as important as turning schools inside out.

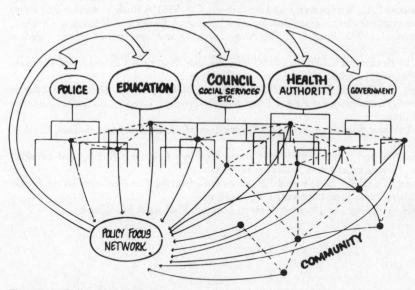

Figure 6.1 Policy focus network

Schools are a vital element of this strategy, as a community focus in contact with most families and young people in the neighbourhood. Schools bring together people from different faiths, denominations and, quite often, different social backgrounds and ethnic origins. Schools are potential successors to places of worship as a focus for community life, in which community values, experience and knowledge can be shared. The emphasis on parental choice and competition between schools increases community fragmentation, valuing division over cohesion. The potential of schools as a meeting place for shared learning as well as social events and political action remains a vital part of the vision. But at its centre are families as the foundation for learning throughout life. We ignore the enduring centrality of home at our peril. Home is, in every sense, the very heart of learning.

REFERENCES

Audit Commission (1994) *Seen But Not Heard: Co-ordinating Community Child Health and Social Services for Children in Need*, London: HMSO.

Bastiani, J. (ed.) (1996) *Home–School Work in Britain: Review, Reflection and Development*, London: David Fulton.

Bloom, B. S.(1985) *Developing Talent in Young People*, New York: Ballantine.

Clark, R. M. (1983) *Family Life and School Achievement: Why Poor Black Children Succeed or Fail*, Chicago: University of Chicago Press.

—— (1987) 'Effective families help children succeed in school', *Network for Public Schools* 1. Columbia, NY: National Committee for Citizens in Education.

Hancock, R. (1995) 'Family literacy: a French connection', *Primary Teaching Studies* 1, spring.

Hannon. F. L., Weinberger, J. and Nutbrown, C. (1995) 'A study of work with parents to promote early literacy development', *Research Papers in Education* 6: 77–97.

Minns, H. (1990) *Read It To Me Now! Learning at Home and at School*, London: Virago.

NCH Action for Children (1994) *The Hidden Victims – Children and Domestic Violence*, London: NCH Action for Children.

Pugh, G.. De'Ath, E. and Smith, C. (1994) *Confident Parents, Confident Children: Policy and Practice in Parent Education and Support*, London: National Children's Bureau.

RSA (Royal Society of Arts) (1993) *Directory of Home–School Initiatives*, London: RSA.

Tizard, B. and Hughes, M. (1984) *Young Children Learning: Talking and Thinking at Home and at School*, London: Fontana.

Utting, D. (1995) *Family and Parenthood: Supporting Families, Preventing Breakdown*, York: Joseph Rowntree Foundation.

Wells, G. (1986) *The Meaning Makers*, London: Hodder & Stoughton.

Chapter 7

Special needs

Personal trouble or public issue?

L. Barton and M. Oliver

With the introduction of the Education Reform Act 1988 the question of special needs became a more urgent and serious topic in Britain. One reason for this is due to the issue of entitlement and the National Curriculum. This legal right covers all pupils. The extent to which it is being implemented, therefore, raises questions of equity and social justice. The impact of the publishing of results, open enrolment and the local management of schools will also be significant in relation to the allocation of monies, support services, statementing and the role of local education authorities (LEAs) in special needs provision.

This chapter is concerned with providing an overview of the main characteristics and developments of sociological approaches to the issue of special needs. The analysis is set within the context of the centrality of equal opportunities and social justice.

SOCIOLOGY OF EDUCATION

Research, fundamentally influenced by structural functionalism, was particularly influential in the initial development of the discipline (Floud *et al.* 1956; Glass 1954; Banks 1955). This work was restricted to a specific set of concerns, including the issue of achievement and social mobility. Investigations examined input–output measures and the findings supported the view that there was a serious wastage of working-class ability (Jackson and Marsden 1962; Jackson 1964; Douglas 1964).

The interest in the social determinants of educability led to the highlighting of a depressing picture of the extent and stubbornness of inequalities. These were in terms of access, duration and outcomes of educational opportunity and experience. Such inequalities were depicted as both unjust and the expression of an inefficient system of provision.

More recent work, critical of many of the presuppositions and explanations of earlier analyses, while confirming the centrality of inequality as a socially divisive issue, identified, for example, the complex ways in which race and gender factors compounded social divisions (Arnot 1981; Davies 1984;

Weiner 1986; Carrington 1986). This form of analysis encouraged a greater interest in the politics of social reproduction and equal opportunities. Anti-sexism and anti-racism became crucial issues of concern. New research topics, questions and explanations began to be established (Williams 1986; David 1986; Gillborn 1988; Demaine 1989).

However, while such analyses focused on the situation of working-class girls and minority groups, hardly any consideration was given to the question of disabled people or special educational needs. A number of reasons can be identified for this omission. By focusing on the task of demonstrating the nature and extent of inequalities of selection by 'brightness' or 'ability', sociologists of education have given little consideration to the relationship between the ordinary and special school systems. Also, studies concerned with deviancy have tended to focus on the more 'exotic' forms of pupil life and behaviour, thereby failing to consider deviancy in terms of those who have been identified as having 'special needs' (Quicke 1986). The dominance of medicine was also significant in powerfully characterizing the notion of 'special needs' in terms of illness or individual pathology (Bart 1984). Finally children in special settings were assumed to be politically insignificant and thus not a powerful force, in terms of enhancing the more general interest in the sorts of comprehensive changes that sociologists were advocating. His-torically, therefore, the nature and functions of the special educational system have been essentially invisible as far as sociological analysis is concerned.

Medical and psychological perspectives have been extremely powerful in shaping the definitions, policies and practices of special education. Stigmat-izing labels have been applied to those individuals deemed in need of such provision. Thus, 'children are viewed as possessing a handicap, a learning difficulty, an emotional disturbance' (Dessent 1988: 5).

This form of exclusive discourse has legitimized qualitative distinctions between 'special' and 'normal' as well as contributing to the belief in the necessity of experts. Their task has been to identify and treat such individuals. The priorities and values of these approaches have also given legitimation to the establishment of segregated settings (Wolfensberger 1975; Ryan and Thomas 1980; Scull 1982).

Both the grounds for, and the difficulties of, providing a sociological analysis can, therefore, be summarized in the following way. First, special education has been dominated by a form of reductionism which gives a privileged status to individualistic explanations. Within-the-child factors are emphasized, encouraging 'special needs' to be viewed as a personal trouble and not a public issue (Mills 1970). This has had the effect of de-politicizing the issues involved. Second, given the restrictive nature of this viewpoint, attempts to introduce complex questions of class, gender and race into the analysis will be seen as unnecessary and unhelpful. This will be particularly so, where the 'special' quality of such provision is justified on the grounds that all children are treated equally. Lastly, the strong tradition that professionals involved with 'special needs' are caring, patient and loving makes it difficult to raise questions, for example, about low expectations, patronizing and over-protective practices and stigmatizing labels. However, sociologists are concerned with the ways in which society deals with 'deviant' groups or individuals. Where discrimination and oppression exists then the interest will be on how this occurs and under what conditions (Fulcher 1989).

DEVELOPING INTERESTS

Within Britain, therefore, sociological analysis of special education is a relatively new development. An important basis for such work is that an understanding of the plight of marginalized groups gives us some crucial insights into the nature of society. Part of the growing sociological interest has been in identifying and critiquing such individualistic and deficit views of disability (Barton and Tomlinson 1981; 1984; Barton 1988). This has involved examining the ways in which legislation, policy and practice contributed to the legitimation of key assumptions and categories. Analysis has focused on the centrality of power, control and vested interests with the intent to generate a more adequate understanding and explanation of the complex issues involved (Barton and Smith 1989; Tomlinson 1982; 1985; 1988).

New questions and topics for examination have been generated including, for example, the social construction of categories; the ways in which definitions are shaped by economic and political factors; the role of professional groups in the development and legitimation of disablist practices; the relationship between 'normal' and special schooling; the role of ideology; and the ways in which disabled people make sense of their world. Historical and comparative material has also been an important feature of the application of the sociological imagination to this field of study (Scull 1982; Ford *et al.* 1982; Barton and Tomlinson 1984; Fulcher 1989; Barton 1989).

One of the most important and influential contributions to a sociology of special education has been made by Tomlinson. Strongly influenced by Weberian ideas, she is particularly interested in the issue of the vested interests of professionals. Analysis is made of professional ideologies and practices in relation to how they both define and implement definitions of 'need'. Labels are seen as social constructions and therefore as problematic. The nature of 'special provision' is seen as a social process in which questions of context and relations are crucial.

Critical of those justifications for professional involvement based on claims of benevolent humanitarianism, Tomlinson maintains that the issues of power and control must be seen as essential features of a critical analysis. Using historical material and insights from research, including a three-year study of her own of children moving into a particular form of special education (1981), she argues that individuals placed within such provision are mainly the unwanted, objectionable and difficult pupils. They are largely from lower socio-economic backgrounds and black children are over-represented among them. These individuals are of low status, relatively powerless and vulnerable. Indeed she argues that 'to be categorised out of "normal" education represents the ultimate in non-achievement in terms of ordinary educational goals' (Tomlinson 1982: 6). This procedure has served an important social function, that of enabling the mainstream to run more smoothly and be more effective.

A key feature of her analysis is the distinction drawn between normative and non-normative categories. In the former, there is some agreement between professionals and lay-people about those categories which are 'defined as a medical sphere of competence' (p. 65). These include the blind, epileptic and those with speech defects. However, Tomlinson contends that: 'On the other hand the categories of feeble-minded, educationally subnormal, maladjusted and disruptive are not, and never will be, normative categories' (Tomlinson 1982: 65).

This provides the basis for dispute between interested parties over the nature of such categories. The power-struggles involved in the construction of categories are seen as significant in this analysis. These often have little, if anything, to do with the personal qualities of the children concerned.

Tomlinson believes that part of a sociological approach is to encourage new ways of thinking about the issues. In special education this means moving away from clinical definitions and establishing a different agenda. This involves raising key questions such as:

> In whose interests did special education actually develop? Do the social origins lie more in the interests of ordinary education?
>
> How is the system of administration of special education linked to the use of professional expertise? And are the vested interests of expanding groups of professionals and practitioners served by the discovery of more and more children with 'special needs'?
>
> Are some types of special schooling more a form of control for particular groups of children?
>
> (Tomlinson 1982: 18–19)

It also means establishing relationships between the processes and politics of interaction and the structural conditions of society. By this means, Tomlinson maintains, it is possible to see the discourse of special needs as a form of 'ideological rationalization' in which the crucial political and economic needs being served by the increased provision of special education are hidden (Tomlinson 1985).

Tomlinson's work has made an original contribution to the development of a sociological approach to special education, providing a vital stimulus to many of the debates within the literature.

Another particularly significant development has been the more recent contributions made by disabled sociologists to the establishment of a political and social theory of disability. These analysts share a number of basic ideas with Tomlinson, including a critical approach to questions of professional involvement, social control and the negative features of segregated provision. However, in contrast, they also offer a much stronger commitment to a class analysis and to the centrality of politics in this process. They are critical of 'personal-tragedy' models of disability. For them, the difficulties of participating in society are not due to personal limitations, but arise from the prejudices, discriminatory policies and practices and social restrictions of an unadaptive society. Disability is a fundamentally political, social issue, which is a form of oppression. Through the process of social engagement, particularly those of an institutional and professional nature, disabled people are encouraged to view themselves as helpless and dependent. Oliver (1990) expresses this position in the following manner:

> All disabled people experience disability, as social restrictions, whether these restrictions occur as a consequence of inaccessible built environments, questionable notions of intelligence and social competence, the inability of the general public to use sign language, the lack of reading material in braille, or hostile public attitudes to people with non-visible disabilities.
>
> (Oliver 1990: xiv)

Disabled people within such conditions and relationships are often treated in a patronizing and dehumanizing manner. Although age, race, gender and class will have an impact on the nature and degree of these experiences, people's perceptions are a common source of distress and offence in the everyday encounters of disabled people.

Advocating the social nature of oppression implies that disabled people are viewed as inferior to other people because they are disabled and Abberley (1987) also notes:

> It is also to argue that these disadvantages are dialectically related to an ideology or group of ideologies which justify and perpetuate this situation. Beyond that it is to make the claim that such disadvantages and their supporting ideologies are neither natural nor inevitable. Finally, it involves the identification of some beneficiary of this state of affairs.
>
> (Abberley 1987: 7)

Recognizing the importance and exploring the origins of differences in the lives of disabled people compared to the rest of the community are thus fundamental elements in a social theory of disability. Capitalism is seen as significant in this process through the prominence it gives to work and the distinction it encourages between productive and non-productive people. This legitimizes a form of social relations in which disabled people are viewed in terms of what they cannot do. The problem is thus individualized.

Spurious forms of empathy, in which the desire to be 'normal' is emphasized, are challenged and viewed as counter-productive to the best interests of disabled people. The lack of a coherent and rigorous understanding of the social and political nature of disability is evident in these positions. The role of the disability movement as a vehicle for change and mutual support is depicted as central to the struggle against disablist policies and practices. Thus, the voice of disabled people needs to be heard if they are to realize a greater control over their own lives, including the services they need and how they are delivered. This inevitably involves a political process in which questions of choice, power and change are central to the agenda.

Disabled sociologists have been instrumental in providing a stimulus to ensuring that 'disability' is seen as a serious topic of investigation. They have brought a fresh vigour, vitality and urgency to the analyses (Abberley 1987; 1989; Oliver 1985; 1989; 1990; Barnes 1990).

THE WARNOCK REPORT

The Warnock Report on the Enquiry into the Education of Handicapped Children and Young People (Department of Education and Science (DES) 1978) and the Education Act 1981 (the legislation based on it) are viewed by many commentators as landmarks in the history of special education.

The Warnock Report provided a challenge to orthodox models based on the identification of defects. The Report emphasized the importance of context and resources and proposed a service model based on delivering the goods. It introduced:

> a new conceptual framework within which special educational provision should be made. This entails a continuum of special educational need rather than discrete categories of handicaps. It embraces children with significant learning difficulties as well as those with disabilities of mind or body.
>
> (DES 1978: 327)

The notion of 'special educational need' applied to more than the 2 per cent of children within special schools. According to Warnock, it related to approximately 20 per cent of all children at school. One in five school children would, from this perspective, have special needs at some time in their school career.

The committee sought to focus positive attention, not on defects, but on what children need if they are going to benefit from education. A clear commitment to the principle that the purpose and goals of education are the same for all children is stated in the opening pages of the Report. Education is 'a good, and a specifically human goal, to which all human beings are entitled' (p. 6). This is not a question of charity, but a matter of right in order that their real potential be developed to the full.

Several criticisms have been made about different aspects of the Warnock

Report. Lewis and Vulliamy (1981) are critical of the significance given to psychological presuppositions and categories, of the emphasis on administrative systems and the creation of an elaborate bureaucracy staffed by more 'experts'. They believe that the Committee largely neglected the issue of social factors in the creation of learning difficulties. Kirp (1983), in a comparison of British and US special education, maintains that the Warnock Committee was dominated by professional groups. This is compared unfavourably with the United States in which the rights of consumers are viewed as essential. This led, in the British case, to the importance of benign professional discretion in discussions relating to children or parents. Finally, Fulcher (1989) is critical of the limited consideration given to curriculum issues. This reflected a conservative and politically expedient view of integration and questions which Fulcher believes should inform discussions about integration were not raised. This included the question 'why do children fail in school?'

However, the definition of special educational needs which Warnock advocated was seen by many professionals and parents as a major advancement in terms of removing deficit views of the child. For Pumfrey and Mittler (1990) the concept has been powerful as a tool for consciousness-raising and uniting pressure groups in their demands for greater resources. Several questions have been raised over the value of the concept and how it means different things to different people. Also, the word 'special' has certain connotations relating to difference in a negative sense. It is a divisive word, one which has been said to separate and segregate pupils from pupils. An individual identified as being outside of the range of acceptability is thus defined as special. The notion of 'need' is also problematic in that, for example, the tacit meaning implies being needy, thus, helpless, powerless and to be controlled (Freeman and Gray 1989). Also, the use of this term 'need' tends to obfuscate the question of power-relations between professionals and clients, and, importantly, the disagreements between professionals over what constitutes the 'needs' of a particular child (Baldwin 1986).

Mary Warnock (1982), in a re-evaluation of the concept 'special needs' several years after the publication of the Warnock Report, acknowledges some of the precarious assumptions underpinning the committee's position, yet still maintains that:

> I still see that there was a kind of simplicity in the concept which made it attractive; and it was useful, insofar as it at least departed from the medical model based on diagnosis of defects, and turned attention to a service model, based on delivering the goods. And it might have worn better, this smart little number, if it hadn't been for the recession.
>
> (Warnock 1982: 57)

While it is important to see reference being made to economic factors and their influence on the implementation of policy, the weakness in the position of Warnock is the apparent inability to recognize the structural conditions of schooling and the ways in which the concept, expressed within such conditions could be used to serve interests other than those of the individual.

A system of education based on selection and competition gives priority to particular conceptions of 'ability' and 'disability'. Hargreaves (1982) captures some of the basic factors involved in his discussion of the nature of secondary education, in which he argues that

> The more profound and disturbing message is that the very concept of ability becomes closely tied to the intellectual–cognitive domain. 'Intelligence' becomes defined as the ability to master cognitive–intellectual aspects of school subjects. Pupils who experience difficulty in so doing are labelled with the euphemism of the 'less able' or even the overly insulting epithet of 'the thickies'.
>
> (Hargreaves 1982: 60)

Ability labels under such a system are seen as 'generalized judgements' and Hargreaves continues:

> The 'less able' understand that they lack the very quality on which the school sets most store; a sense of failure tends to permeate the whole personality leaving a residue of powerlessness and helplessness.
>
> (Hargreaves 1982: 63)

Thus decisions about people's needs and abilities involve value-judgements and power-relations. The notion of 'special educational needs' has been applied to increasing numbers of pupils, many of whom are not statemented, and thus it serves the purpose of controlling difficult, objectionable and problem pupils. These pupils are deemed unable to meet the standards by which the system measures success. However, by emphasizing the pupils' failure, the fundamental issue of the system's failure to meet the needs of all pupils is marked.

In a school system dominated by selection, competition and academic success, the notion of 'special educational needs' can be viewed as a euphemism for pupil failure at an individual level.

CONCLUSION

We believe that sociological research in this particular area is both important and urgent. However, it is essential that those involved in such work take seriously Becker's fundamental question, 'Whose side are you on?' The book in which he posed the question was called *Outsiders* (1963). This is an apt term in relation to the subjects of such research, in that they constitute the vulnerable, marginalized and discriminated groups within society. It is necessary, therefore, for researchers not only to clarify their value-positions, but also to examine the extent to which involvement in the research process, including the outcomes, can be *enabling*. Questions of social justice, equity, power and control will be perennial concerns in this field of human enquiry. Part of the sociological task will be to contribute to the establishment and maintenance of special needs as a key equal opportunities issue. This is necessary because it will provide a basis for the identification of those features of the existing society, policy and practice that are unacceptable and offensive and need to be challenged and changed. Also, through this approach any attempts to redirect resources in order to provide opportunities for the most marginalized, disadvantaged and discriminated people in society cannot pretend to be apolitical. It also provides stimulus for the crucial task of establishing connections between other discriminated groups in order that attempts can be made to engage in common struggles (Roaf and Bines 1989; Rieser and Mason 1990). This inevitably necessitates a socio-political perspective which challenges individualized and social pathology explanations. However, there are difficulties in taking this position in that equal opportunities policies at both LEA and school levels are overwhelmingly concerned with issues of race and gender. In many instances disability is merely a bolt-on tokenistic gesture (Leach 1989). Also the possibility of the incorporation of equal opportunities concerns within the dominant hegemony of new right ideas, is one to be constantly aware of and to struggle against.

One of the dangers of living in a period of extensive educational and social change is that it tends to anaesthetize the mind with regard to the importance of the past. In a discussion of teacher evaluation Grace (1978) advocates the necessity of a historically located inquiry because:

> it has the advantage of sensitising us to the principles and procedures which have been dominant in the past so that we are alert to the mode of their reproduction, reconstitution or change. It has the advantage also of concretely exemplifying and making visible the relations between educational structures and processes and wider structures of power, economy and control in particular periods of social change.
>
> (Grace 1978: 4)

The importance of such an approach is essential in relation to the issues we have outlined in this chapter. What historical analysis does exist seriously neglects questions of ideology and politics in the accounts offered (Pritchard 1963; Cole 1990). The discourse of special needs has encouraged an individualized perspective. By examining the relationship between special schools, school provision generally and the socio-economic order, we can begin to unpack complex relationships and contradictory factors. Also, we can explore the extent to which such discourse and practices have served social, political and ideological factors in particular historical periods. While policy analysis which focuses on specific practical issues can be viewed as attractive and cost-effective, it is important to recognize the complex and contentious notion of policy. Thus, as Grace (1990) also argues, conflicts and struggles are endemic to the policy-making process and historical studies raise questions about the power-relations which influence the nature of education policy. This is particularly applicable to special needs provision.

Disability is a social construct and sociological research needs to address the development of a social theory of disability in which issues of power, oppression and politics are carefully worked through. Documenting and evaluating the institutional form of discriminatory practices and disablist images will be necessary if the cycle of dependency-creating pressures is to be challenged and changed. We have no serious ethnography in education of special needs policy and practice. An urgent research task is to carefully explore, in given social contexts, how disablist ideas get constituted and re-constituted through the minutiae of daily interactions. The role of professionals in this process will be crucial. How disabled people make sense of their world and struggle within oppressive conditions and social relations needs to be seriously examined. The divisive impact of a market-led system makes this research task absolutely essential. The question of labelling and its effects on both the labelled and the labeller is a significant one. Removing a label does not mean that the values and expectations associated with it become moribund. Professionals are adept at creating new labels. The notion of the 'Level-One Child' is a classic example. How identities are constructed therefore is a topic which future research needs to address. Given the over-representation of black pupils in certain forms of special provision such work will also involve confronting the issue of racism and racial stereotyping (Coard 1971; ILEA 1985). The politics of difference is thus an urgent task for sociological enquiry.

In the beginning of this chapter we raised the crucial issues of the publishing of test results, the local management of schools and the contentious question of LEA formulae funding. These provide significant topics and opportunities for sociological research, and in particular, the effects of these developments within school. A number of serious questions arise which need to be explored. For example, how far will these factors lead to an increase in ghettoized or segregated forms of provision within the inner cities? Will the pupil make-up of such provision be overly representative of children and young people from particular socio-economic and racial backgrounds? To what extent will the distribution of resources be shaped by subject-specific concerns to the neglect, or reduction, of support services for special educational needs? Within a period of such extensive and rapid change how far will teachers be able and/or willing to express a strong commitment to questions of entitlement and the rights of disabled pupils? Finally, how far do the social relations and practices within school legitimize particular power-relations, which result in the marginalization of pupils who are seen as different?

The aforementioned topics are not exhaustive of the areas of investigation sociologists can undertake. In the struggle for change, we must not underestimate the demanding issues which have to be engaged with. The process will be difficult but absolutely necessary if special needs provision and practice are not to lead to the creation of an underclass.

ACKNOWLEDGEMENTS

We are grateful to Madeleine Arnot and Jenny Corbett for their helpful comments on earlier drafts of this chapter.

REFERENCES

Abberley, P. (1987) 'The concept oppression and the social theory of disability', *Disability, Handicap and Society* 2: 5–19.

—— (1989) 'Disabled people, normality and social work', in L. Barton (ed.) *Disability and Dependency*, Lewes: Falmer.

Arnot, M. (1981) 'Culture and political economy: dual perspectives in the sociology of women's education', in B. Davies (ed.) *Educational Analysis* 3: 97–116.

Baldwin, S. (1986) 'Problem with needs – where theory meets practice', *Disability, Handicap and Society* 1: 139–46.

Banks, O. (1955) *Parity and Prestige in English Secondary Education*, London: Routledge.

Barnes, C. (1990) *Cabbage Syndrome*, Lewes: Falmer.

Bart, D. (1984) 'The differential diagnosis of special education: managing social pathology as individual disability', in L. Barton and S. Tomlinson (eds) *Special Education and Social Interests*, London: Croom Helm.

Barton, L. (ed.) (1988) *The Politics of Special Educational Needs*, Lewes: Falmer.

—— (ed.) (1989) *Integration: Myth or Reality?* Lewes: Falmer.

Barton, L. and Smith, M. (1989) 'Equality, rights and primary education', in C. Roaf and H. Bines (eds) *Needs, Rights and Opportunities*, Lewes: Falmer.

Barton, L. and Tomlinson, S. (eds) (1981) *Special Education: Policy, Practices and Social Issues*, London: Harper & Row.

—— (1984) *Special Education and Social Interests*, London: Croom Helm.

Becker, H. (1963) *Outsiders: Studies in the Sociology of Deviance*, New York: Free Press.

Carrington, B. (1986) 'Social mobility, ethnicity and sport', *British Journal of Sociology of Education* 7: 3–18.

Coard, B. (1971) *How the West Indian Child is Made Educationally Subnormal in the British School System: The Scandal of the Black Child in Schools in Britain*, London: Beacon.

Cole, T. (1990) *Apart or A Part? In Integration and the Growth of British Special Education*, Milton Keynes: Open University Press.

David, M. (1986) 'Teaching family matters', *British Journal of Sociology of Education* 7: 35–58.

Davies, L. (1984) *Pupil Power: Deviance and Gender in School*, Lewes: Falmer.

Demaine, J. (1989) 'Race, categorisation and educational achievement', *British Journal of Sociology of Education* 10: 195–214.

Department of Education and Science (1978) *Special Educational Needs*, Warnock Report, London: HMSO.

Dessent, T. (1988) *Making Ordinary Schools Special*, Lewes: Falmer.

Douglas, J. W. B. (1964) *The Home and the School*, London: Panther.

Floud, J., Halsey, A. H. and Martin, F. M. (1956) *Social Class and Educational Opportunity*, London: Heinemann.

Ford, J., Mongon, D. and Whelan, M. (1982) *Special Education and Social Control: Invisible Disasters*, London: Routledge.

Freeman, A. and Gray, H. (1989) *Organising Special Educational Needs: A Critical Approach*, London: Paul Chapman.

Fulcher, G. (1989) *Disabling Policies? A Comparative Approach to Education Policy and Disability*, Lewes: Falmer.

Gillborn, D. (1988) 'Ethnicity and educational opportunity: case studies of West Indian male–white teacher relationships', *British Journal of Sociology of Education* 9: 371–86.

Glass, D. V. (1954) *Social Mobility in Britain*, London: Routledge & Kegan Paul.

Grace, G. (1978) *Teachers, Ideology and Control: A Study in Urban Education*, London: Routledge & Kegan Paul.

—— (1990) 'Labour and education: the crisis and settlements of education policy', in M. Holland and J. Boston (eds) *The Fourth Labour Government*, Auckland: Oxford University Press.

Hargreaves, D. (1982) *Challenge to the Comprehensive School*, London: Routledge & Kegan Paul.

ILEA (1985) *Educational Opportunities for All?*, Fish Report, London: ILEA.

Jackson, B. (1964) *Streaming: An Education System in Miniature*, London: Routledge & Kegan Paul.

Jackson, B. and Marsden, D. (1962) *Education and the Working Class*, Harmondsworth: Penguin.

Kirp, D. (1983) 'Professionalisation as a policy choice: British special education in comparative perspective', in J. Chambers and W. Hartman (eds) *Special Education Policies: Their History, Implementation and Finance*, Philadelphia, PA: Temple University Press.

Leach, B. (1989) 'Disabled people and the implementation of local authorities' equal opportunities policies', *Public Administration* 67: 65–77.

Lewis, I. and Vulliamy, G. (1981) 'The social context of educational practice: the case of special education', in L. Barton and S. Tomlinson (eds) *Special Education: Policy, Practices and Social Issues*, London: Harper & Row.

Mills, C. W. (1970) *The Sociological Imagination*, Harmondsworth: Penguin.

Oliver, M. (1985) 'The integration–segregation debate: some sociological considerations', *British Journal of Sociology of Education* 6: 75–92.

—— (1989) 'Disability and dependency: a creation of industrial societies', in L. Barton (ed.) *Disability and Dependency*, Lewes: Falmer.

—— (1990) *The Politics of Disablement*, London: Macmillan.

Pritchard, O. (1963) *Education and the Handicapped, 1760–1960*, London: Routledge & Kegan Paul.

Pumfrey, P. and Mittler, P. (1990) 'Peeling off the label', *The Times Educational Supplement* 29–30.

Quicke, J. (1986) 'A case of paradigmatic mentality? A reply to Mike Oliver', *British Journal of Sociology of Education* 7: 81–6.

Rieser, R. and Mason, M. (1990) *Disability Equality in the Classroom: A Human Rights Issue*, London: ILEA.

Roaf, C. and Bines, H. (eds) (1989) *Needs, Rights and Opportunities*, Lewes: Falmer.

Ryan, J. and Thomas, F. (1980) *The Politics of Mental Handicap*, Harmondsworth: Penguin.

Scull, A. T. (1982) *Museums of Madness: The Social Organisation of Insanity in Nineteenth Century England*, Harmondsworth: Penguin.

Tomlinson, S. (1982) *A Sociology of Special Education*, London: Routledge & Kegan Paul.

—— (1985) 'The experience of special education', *Oxford Review of Education* 11: 157–65.

—— (1988) 'Why Johnny can't read: critical theory and special education', *European Journal of Special Needs Education* 3: 45–58.

Warnock, M. (1982) 'Children with special needs in ordinary schools: integration revisited', *Education Today* 32 (3): 56–62.

Weiner, G. (1986) 'Feminist education and equal opportunities: unity or discord?', *British Journal of Sociology of Education* 7: 265–74.

Williams, J. (1986) 'Education and race: the racialisation of class inequalities?', *British Journal of Sociology of Education* 7: 135–54.

Wolfensberger, W. (1975) *The Origins and Nature of our Institutional Models*, Syracuse, NY: Human Policy Press.

Chapter 8

Educational inequality as a social problem

The case of England

M. Hammersley

The study of social problems is a major focus for sociological research. This field of inquiry has usually been defined as consisting of those issues that are publicly identified as matters of concern, and which it is widely believed ought to be the target of state policy. As might be expected, research in this field has generally been concerned with the causes of social problems and with how they can be remedied. However, in recent years there has been a shift, often labelled as social constructionism towards taking account of the processes by which particular issues come to be recognized as social problems, and how they are formulated as problematic (Holstein and Miller 1993). In other words, it is argued that social scientists need to give attention to the political campaigns by which issues get put on, or moved up, government and other agendas; along with the rhetorical formulations of the nature of the problem that form part of these campaigns. One of the most striking implications of this change in focus is that research on social problems of the earlier kind now itself comes under investigation, since it has often played an important role in the construction and promotion of the problems it studies.

Educational inequality has long been recognized as an important social issue, and there is a considerable amount of research dealing with it. However, as yet, the social constructionist approach outlined above has not been applied.[1] This chapter is intended as a contribution towards remedying this situation. It sketches the conditions under which educational inequality came to be recognized as a social problem, and how its character has been formulated and reformulated, focusing particularly on the role that educational researchers have played in this. It is primarily concerned with developments in England, but the story told has wider relevance.

THE EMERGENCE OF THE PROBLEM

There was a time in western societies when neither educational inequality, nor any other kind of inequality, was widely regarded as a social problem or as amenable to change; and this was probably the view not just of members of the upper classes but even of many of 'the lower orders' themselves. In the

Middle Ages, for example, differences in social status, wealth and power, and the inheritance of these, were generally treated as facts of life and/or as part of a natural and divinely ordained social order. As Coleman (1968) has pointed out, this was not just a matter of ideology, material factors were important too; notably, the all-encompassing role played by the family (on which see Laslett 1971). It was only from the seventeenth century onwards that inequality began to be recognized as a public issue, partly as a result of the gradual spread of the idea that all human beings are born equal, and that they should enjoy opportunities to rise (and fall) in the social order according to talent.[2] This change was particularly associated with the emergence of the commercial, urban middle classes, and was accelerated by the industrial and political revolutions associated with them (Hobsbawm 1962).

Educational inequality started to become recognized as a social problem in the nineteenth century. At that time, the class structure was still widely regarded as static, and as properly so. What social mobility occurred was viewed as individuals 'bettering themselves', so that promoting such move-ment was not generally regarded as an appropriate task for public policy. In this context, different social classes were believed to require different sorts of education. Indeed, at the beginning of the nineteenth century it was still widely assumed that the lower classes did not need any formal schooling at all, and that giving them it could be dangerous. It was quite late on in that century before the state took direct responsibility for providing universal elementary education. And, even by the beginning of the twentieth century, access to secondary education was very restricted on the part of the working class; indeed, this came to be the central issue for campaigns against educational inequality.[3]

The roots of the problem of educational inequality stretch further back than the nineteenth century, however. There seem to have been at least two conditions associated with its emergence. One was the widening influence of the idea that to be truly human is to be educated. The Renaissance was of particular importance here, with its expansion of the scope of secular learning and knowledge; while the Reformation had the effect of promoting literacy in vernacular languages and thereby further weakening priestly control of knowledge. On top of this, the scientific revolution of the seventeenth century presented knowledge as something that could be acquired by anyone who was prepared to adopt rational methods: it did not demand a level of classical erudition that was only available to those with the money and leisure to access the literature of the ancient world, nor did it require religious virtue or perhaps even intellectual genius. These various ideas were combined by the Enlightenment thinkers of the eighteenth century, many of whom placed scientific investigation and education at the centre of social reform. And, in the nineteenth and early twentieth centuries, we find education treated as essential to human life, both by those who stressed science as the spearhead of modernity, and therefore campaigned for scientific and technical education, and by those who saw the humanities as the true source of human knowledge, emphasizing personal and cultural development. Moreover, once education had come to be regarded as constitutive of true humanity, calls for equal access to it followed almost automatically, given the growing influence of egalitarian arguments generally.

The second condition that encouraged the emergence of educational inequality as a social problem was the increasing role of literacy and numeracy in a variety of social spheres over the course of the eighteenth, nineteenth and twentieth centuries in the growing activities of the state, in the running of economic organizations that were getting larger and more complex, and in the widening realm of political and cultural activities. As a result, schools became important as providers of literacy and numeracy skills, these being essential in many new and expanding occupations. And later, with the greater importance of standard qualifications in occupational recruitment, schools began to prepare candidates for examinations of various types and levels. In this way, schooling came to take on an increasing role in the process of occupational recruitment. As a result, educational inequalities were linked with social inequalities; remedying the former came to be seen as a means of remedying the latter.

CHANGING CONCEPTIONS OF EDUCATIONAL INEQUALITY IN THE TWENTIETH CENTURY

In the first half of the twentieth century it was widely believed that intelligence is genetically determined, with the different social classes varying in average intelligence, members of the lower classes having the lowest. This view was given scientific support by the emerging discipline of psychology and its development of intelligence tests. However, while research in this discipline reinforced ideas about social class differences in intelligence, it also highlighted the possibility of individual mismatches between intelligence and social class background. Intelligence testing came to be regarded as necessary in order to identify the kind of education appropriate to each child, though the amount of educational inequality that existed was generally assumed to be relatively small overall.

Within the education system more attention than before began to be given to identifying individual working-class children who showed exceptional ability, and to providing them with the opportunity to develop their talents. This was achieved through increasing the provision of free places, creating a 'ladder of opportunity' from elementary into secondary schools.[4] In this way, it was believed, not only would the system be made fairer but also the nation could capitalize upon more of its talent.

The numbers of free places available for secondary education grew dramatically in the early twentieth century. Places were filled on the basis of competitive examinations (oral and/or written), teachers' reports, and/or intelligence test results. However, while this increased the number of working-class students in secondary schools, there was more and more criticism of the free place system as inadequate, both because many places were taken by middle-class children and because the number of academically able working-class children came to be seen as greater than had previously been thought (see Floud *et al.* 1956: 139–49).

Political pressure to recognize social class inequalities in access to secondary education as a social problem requiring action came initially from the labour movement, but later gained broader support, particularly as a result of the change in political climate produced by the Second World War.[5] The Education Act 1944, which was the product of this pressure, was an attempt to open up educational opportunity to all working-class children, though it was still based on the idea that an academic secondary education should be available only to those with a high level of inherent ability.

In the 1950s and 1960s there was widespread questioning of some of the basic assumptions of this first stage in the development of the problem of educational inequality. The claim that intelligence was largely inherited came to be challenged, and greater emphasis was placed on the effects of social environment (Simon 1953; Vernon 1969; see also Vernon 1979). Earlier psychologists had not denied the role of the environment; indeed, the provision of increased access to secondary education had been motivated in part to facilitate realization of the intellectual potential of able working-class children by countering the effects of their home backgrounds. But built into this point of view had been the idea that there is a definite limit to the number of academically able working-class children. This was enshrined in the Norwood Report, where three types of child were identified: what might be referred to as the academic, the technical, and the practical (Committee of the Secondary School Examinations Council 1943: ch. 1). This influenced the implementation in England and Wales of the 1944 Act, resulting in the prevalence of the tripartite system, composed of grammar, technical, and secondary modern schools (though in most places it became a bipartite system, technical schools being rare).[6]

However, with growing doubts about the heritability of intelligence, and greater emphasis on the role of the environment, differences in home background came to be seen by many commentators as the major factor behind variation in school achievement. The focus of much research became 'the social determinants of educability' (Floud and Halsey 1958: 181–5); and, in the wake of this, the concept of cultural deprivation was imported from the United States and became influential in explanations for the differential school achievement of the social classes (see, for example, Schools Council 1970). Thus, the relative failure of working-class children in schools, compared to middle-class children, began to be explained by many in terms of the effects of culturally deficient home backgrounds that failed to provide the cognitive and attitudinal socialization believed to be a prerequisite for academic success.[7] This explanation stimulated proposals that there should be direct intervention by schools, in the form of compensatory education (Halsey 1972), and calls for stronger links between home and school (Craft *et al.* 1972).

These changes in view about the nature and origin of academic ability, along with doubts about the capacity of intelligence tests to measure it in a culture-fair way, also led to pressure for comprehensive secondary schooling. It was argued that to select at 11+ inevitably denied a large number of intelligent working-class children access to a grammar school education who could have benefited from one. Many working-class children failed the 11+, it was suggested, because they had had insufficient time in school to 'catch up' with their middle-class peers. In 1956 Floud, Halsey and Martin pointed out that 'the likelihood that a working class boy will reach a grammar school is not notably greater today, despite all the changes, than it was before 1945' (Floud *et al.* 1956: 33). Furthermore, Douglas's (1964) work suggested that even where measured ability was equal, social class differences in obtaining grammar school places persisted. Of considerable political significance at this time was the fact that, as a result of the post-war baby boom, a substantial proportion of children of middle-class parents found themselves in non-selective education. One consequence of this was that a growing number of secondary modern schools started to offer an academic education to top-stream students, leading to their entry for GCE examinations. This had the effect of revealing the extent to which the 11+ had consigned academically capable students to non-selective schools. Another result was the expansion of local experiments with comprehensive schooling and pressure at national level for comprehensivization, culminating in Circular 10/65, in which the Department of Education and Science invited local education authorities to submit schemes for comprehensive secondary education (Rubinstein and Simon 1969).

In this context, there was also criticism of the effects of streaming in schools. A major charge against the 11+ had been that it had a backwash effect: encouraging streaming in the later years of primary schooling and thereby effectively pushing the point of selection even earlier (Douglas 1964; Jackson 1964; Barker Lunn 1970). Equally, though, attention came to be given to streaming in secondary schools. The argument here was not just that such internal selection reinforced differences in home background that did not reflect educational potential, but also that these processes had consequences which increased social class disparities in academic achievement. It was claimed that streaming, and the differentiation of students on academic-behavioural grounds generally, served to depress the academic performance of those ranked lowest, through generating negative attitudes towards school. Moreover, since a higher proportion of working-class children found themselves in low streams, this exacerbated social class differences in educational achievement and led to a very high proportion of working-class children leaving school at the earliest opportunity with no qualifications (D. H. Hargreaves 1967; Lacey 1970).

Here, then, the emphasis in the explanation of educational inequalities started to move away from the personal characteristics and social backgrounds of students back to processes of selection within the education system. This fed into the promotion of comprehensive schooling, suggesting that the new schools should be organized on the basis of mixed ability teaching groups.[8] At the same time, these arguments about the effects of streaming and other forms of academic differentiation provided a bridge to the more radical sociological arguments about educational inequality, and about the role of schooling in society, which were to follow.

THE NEW SOCIOLOGY OF EDUCATION

Crucial to these subsequent developments was the emergence of what came to be called 'the new sociology of education' (Young 1971; Gorbutt 1972). This shifted the focus of debate dramatically. As we have seen, most previous discussion of educational inequality had been concerned with working-class children's access to secondary education, or with what needed to be done to facilitate their capacity to benefit from it. Now, however, attention started to be given to the nature of the education that was on offer, to the sort of academic ability on which school achievement depends, and to the kind of learning schools fostered.

In some respects these preoccupations were a development of earlier themes (see Williamson 1974; Bernbaum 1977). Within the campaign for comprehensive education, the grammar school curriculum had often been dismissed as too narrow, and intelligence and achievement tests had been criticized for being subject to middle-class bias. However, the new sociologists pursued a much more radical line in relation to these issues, drawing on the arguments of radical educators and deschoolers which were influential in the late 1960s and early 1970s (see Hargreaves 1974). They began to challenge the whole nature of the education provided in schools. This was itself now seen as a barrier to the achievement of educational (and social) equality. One aspect of this was the argument that the knowledge and skills purveyed, or at least those accorded high status, stemmed from the culture of dominant social groups. In other words, it was suggested that the very knowledge that schools offer reflects the unequal social structure of the wider society. As a result, sociological attention started to be given to how and why particular forms of knowledge had come to be included in the curriculum, this no longer being regarded as explainable in terms of their intrinsic validity (Young 1971; Pring 1972; White and Young 1975; Whitty 1985).

In this way, schooling began to be seen as involving the imposition of a dominant, middle-class culture on subordinate groups. Previously, a distinction had been drawn between educational and social selection, between selection on the basis of relevant abilities and attitudes, on the one hand, and selection by social class characteristics which had become spuriously associated with ability, on the other. Now, by means of a theoretical 'stepping back', the whole notion of academic ability came to be bracketed and treated as a socio-historical construction, rather than as something that could be taken for granted (Hudson 1970; Squibb 1973).

The new sociology of education completed the shift begun by Hargreaves, Lacey and others from explanations of educational inequalities in terms of the individual and social characteristics of students to explanations that emphasized the role of the education system. From now on, any attempt to explain differences in educational achievement in terms of students' differential abilities, or of the effects of their home background on their motivation and capacity to learn, was challenged on the grounds that it took for granted the education system's definition of what counted as knowledge, learning, ability, and motivation: definitions which reflected the dominant culture and were discrepant with working-class culture. The central issue for the new sociologists became the inequality of power between the social classes in their capacity to define what counts as education. And the remedy recommended, or at least implied, was a transformation of society as a whole.

What emerges here is a conception of the problem of educational inequality as in large part the product of an education system that constructs a conception of knowledge and ability which discriminates against working-class children. Marxist accounts became influential that portrayed the whole structure and content of education systems in modern societies as functionally tuned to reproduce social inequality: in providing recruits of appropriate kinds for different levels of the social structure, by legitimizing this inequality through transmitting ideological accounts of why society must be like it is, and through ensuring that for the most part children ended up in social class positions that were much the same as those of their parents (Althusser 1971; Bowles and Gintis 1976). From this point of view, 'ability' became little more than an ideological cipher for the characteristics or interests of the dominant classes, and/or for the capacities needed to function in capitalist society.

This view subsequently came to be modified, not least because it failed to recognize any scope for resistance on the part of students and teachers, and thereby ruled out any prospect of change (see Arnot and Whitty 1982). However, the Marxist framework was still retained by many researchers, with capitalism treated as the determinant in the last instance: even though emphasis was now placed on the relative autonomy of the education system, and of the state generally, from the economy (see A. Hargreaves 1982; Harris 1992).

The 'new sociology' differed from earlier work, then, both in its definition of the problem of educational inequality, and in how inequality was to be explained. Where previously the failure of working-class children to achieve at the same level as middle-class children had been accounted for, to a large extent, in terms of features of their home backgrounds, now this failure was reinterpreted as a product of the school system. Moreover, it was treated as just one part of the process by which capitalist society reproduces itself. The criteria of assessment, and the whole manner in which schooling is organized, were now seen as functioning to bring about that failure.

AFTER THE NEW SOCIOLOGY OF EDUCATION

In the late 1970s and 1980s, the sociology of education developed against the background of a movement to the Right in British politics, and a consequent shift in the political agenda towards a concern with educational standards and what was seen as the failure of education to contribute to economic growth. Moreover, the sociology of education was itself in the firing line, as one of the main sources of the progressivism and educational radicalism that had allegedly deformed teacher education and resulted in the decline of standards and the transmission of anti-capitalist ideology in schools.

Even so, concern with educational inequality did not disappear completely in national and local politics, and it continued to be central to much educational research. Furthermore, that concern came to be widened to include other social divisions than class. Important factors here were the spreading influence of feminism, and of multiculturalism and anti-racism. In political terms, campaigns against 'racial' and sexual discrimination resulted in the passing of the Race Relations and Sex Discrimination Acts (in 1975 and 1976, respectively), and the establishment of the Commission for Racial Equality and the Equal Opportunities Commission. Moreover, local authorities became increasingly involved in monitoring and seeking to remedy sexual and 'racial' inequalities in schools (on these developments see Arnot 1985).

This was associated with a shift within educational research away from the previously dominant preoccupation with the fate of white, working-class boys towards an interest in the educational experiences and fortunes of girls and of ethnic minority (especially Afro-Caribbean and Asian) students. Researchers continued to draw on many of the same theoretical resources employed in the identification of educational inequalities between the social classes. Thus, it was claimed that the capabilities of girls had been systematically underestimated by schools and teachers, especially in science and mathematics. It was also argued that their access to some courses had been restricted by the assumption that they would not go on to higher education, or take up employment requiring high-level academic knowledge, but choose marriage and a family instead. In addition, though, it was claimed that the nature of school knowledge reflects patriarchal assumptions, with the result that it either demotivates girls or socializes them into forms of knowledge and learning that are alien to them. Indeed, schools came to be seen by many feminists as institutions that inculcate traditional conceptions of masculinity and femininity, directly and indirectly, thereby reproducing patriarchy (Deem 1978; 1980; Stanworth 1983: Arnot and Weiner 1987; Weiner and Arnot 1987; Measor and Sikes 1992).

In a similar way, it was argued that ethnic minority students suffer substantial discrimination in schools: that teachers tend to view Asian children as suffering from language problems and as having cultural backgrounds that disadvantage them, while Afro-Caribbean students (particularly boys) are regarded as highly disruptive. These stereotypes were seen as informing both the treatment of students in classrooms and their allocation to bands and sets in secondary schools. Furthermore, it has been suggested that much the same consequences follow from this for ethnic minority students as for white working-class ones: in the case of Afro-Caribbean students, in particular, it leads to the development of anti-school subcultures, which increase their antagonism to teachers and depress their academic performance. Moreover, discrimination against black students in schools has been seen as arising not merely from prejudice on the part of teachers, but as reflecting the fundamentally racist character of the whole society. Thus, much of what is valued in schools, both in terms of curriculum and behavioural norms, is criticized as based on 'white culture' (Wright 1986; 1992a; 1992b; Mac an Ghaill 1988; Gillborn 1990; Mirza 1992).

As with the earlier work on social class, this research presented educational inequality as a problem requiring political intervention. Some formulations of sexual and racial inequalities took a less radical position than the new sociologists had done, focusing on unequal access to, and unequal opportunity to benefit from, what was offered by schools. To a large extent this constituted an internal critique of the education system for not achieving its own ideal of equality of opportunity, albeit now sometimes interpreted in terms of equality of outcome.[9] However, there was also a more radical response present from the beginning, influenced by developments within feminism and by the black power movement in the United States, as well as by the new sociology; and this became more prominent as work in these fields developed.[10] This research provided an important background resource for local struggles over sexism and racism within the education system.

In the late 1980s and early 1990s government emphasis on the issue of standards came to be embodied in a spate of legislation instituting major reforms, not least the introduction and subsequent modifications of the National Curriculum. While welcomed in some respects by those campaigning for educational inequality, the overall effect was to shift the focus of public debate about education and to marginalize the issue of equality still further (Flude and Hammer 1990). Moreover, the substantial reduction in the role of local education authorities affected their work in relation to educational inequalities, and selection started to be reintroduced into recruitment to state secondary schools. Against this background, the focus of educational research has changed somewhat, considerable research effort being devoted to examining the impact of the reforms and to addressing issues of school effectiveness, though a preoccupation with educational equality still underpins much of this work.

CONCLUSION

As I noted at the beginning of this article, most research concerned with educational inequality has focused on the causes of the problem, and remedies for it. Here, instead, I have adopted a social constructionist approach, examining the development of educational inequality as a recognized social problem, and tracing changes in the formulation of that problem over time. I identified its historical roots as lying in egalitarian ideas stimulated by the rise of the urban middle classes, and subsequently developed by political movements drawing on the working class, as well as in the increased importance given to education, not least because of growing occupational demands for literacy and numeracy. However, I particularly emphasized the role that educational research has played in later reconceptualizations of the problem, in which what counted as equal opportunity and what were identified as the causes of inequality changed dramatically. As we saw, initially, the primary focus of concern was on social class inequalities in access to elementary and secondary education. Later, the formulation of educational inequality as a social problem widened to include sexual and 'racial' inequalities.[11]

I have only been able to sketch what a constructionist account of educational inequality as a social problem might look like here. But there is one particularly important point that arises from my account. This is that educational inequality is a concept that is open to multiple interpretations. It can be, and has been, defined in diverse ways. This is not a novel point to make (see, for example, Williams 1962; Ennis 1978), but it is one that has been neglected by much empirical research concerned with educational inequalities. There has been a tendency to treat these as if they were simple matters of fact, whereas what counts as a significant inequality depends on how one interprets the values of social justice and education. It is in this sense, above all, that the problem of educational inequality is socially constructed.

ACKNOWLEDGEMENTS

This article draws on material from Foster, Gomm and Hammersley (1996: ch. 1).

NOTES

1 Social constructionist ideas have been used in looking at the nature of school knowledge and learning, academic ability, etc., but they have not been applied to

educational inequality. This is not to say that there have been no accounts of the development of policy in relation to educational inequality and of the role of research in relation to this; indeed, I have drawn on some of these. See, for example, Silver (1973) and Rubinstein (1984).

2 On the idea of equality and its development, see Abernethy (1959), Lakoff (1964) and S. I. Benn (1967).

3 Within each social class, of course, educational opportunity was more restricted for females than for males; and, where education *was* provided for girls and young women, it was generally designed to prepare them for marriage and the domestic sphere (see Purvis 1991).

4 While originally intended as free places for which candidates merely had to qualify, these were, in effect, competitive scholarships (Gordon 1980: ch. 8).

5 On the politics of reform in the interwar period, see Simon (1974). Silver (1973) provides a brief overview, along with extracts from some of the key documents.

6 Similar changes were instituted in Scotland and in Northern Ireland by specific legislation, in 1945 and 1947 respectively.

7 It was argued that whereas in the past the material circumstances of their homes disadvantaged working-class children, by the middle of the century this was no longer a key factor, hence the emphasis on cultural factors. See Banks (1971: ch. 4) for a review of research in this area. See also Craft (1970).

8 In fact, only a minority of comprehensives adopted this policy across all subjects and students, even in the initial years of secondary education: see C. Benn and Simon (1972: ch. 10).

9 See, for example, Byrne (1978). Equality of outcome requires that similar proportions of students from different categories (for example, male/female, white/black) reach any given level of educational achievement.

10 For discussions of the diversity of orientations to be found amongst educational researchers working in the fields of gender and 'race' see Weiner (1985) and Troyna (1987), respectively.

11 There has also been political campaigning and research focusing on inequalities relating to the treatment of children defined as having special educational needs (see, for example, Barton and Oliver 1992), and, more recently, with inequalities arising from the failure to recognize homosexuality as an issue in schools (Epstein 1994; Mac an Ghaill 1995).

REFERENCES

Abernethy, G. L. (1959) *The Idea of Equality: An Anthology*, Richmond, VA: John Knox Press.

Althusser, L. (1971) 'Ideology and ideological state apparatuses', in L. Althusser, *Lenin and Philosophy and Other Essays*, London: New Left Books.

Arnot, M. (ed.) (1985) *Race and Gender: Equal Opportunities Policies in Education*, Oxford: Pergamon.

Arnot, M. and Weiner, G. (eds) (1987) *Gender and the Politics of Schooling*, London: Hutchinson.

Arnot, M. and Whitty, G. (1982) 'From reproduction to transformation: recent radical perspectives on the curriculum from the USA', *British Journal of Sociology of Education* 3: 93–103.

Banks, O. (1955) *Parity and Prestige in English Secondary Education*, London: Routledge & Kegan Paul.

—— (1971) *The Sociology of Education*, 2nd edn, London: Batsford.

—— (1982) 'The sociology of education 1952–1982', *British Journal of Educational Studies*, 30 (1): 18–31.

Barker Lunn, J. (1970) *Streaming in the Primary School*, Slough: NFER.

Barton, L. and Oliver, M. (1992) 'Special needs: private trouble or public issue?', in L. Barton and M. Arnot (eds) *Voicing Concerns: Sociological Perspectives on Contemporary Education Reforms*, Wallingford, Oxon: Triangle. See also Chapter 7.

Benn, C. and Simon, B. (1972) *Half Way There: Report on the British Comprehensive-School Reform*, 2nd edn, Harmondsworth: Penguin.

Benn, S. I. (1967) 'Equality, moral and social', in P. Edwards (ed.) *The Encyclopedia of Philosophy*, New York: Macmillan.

Bernbaum, G. (1977) *Knowledge and Ideology in the Sociology of Education*, London: Macmillan.

Bowles, S. and Gintis, H. (1976) *Schooling in Capitalist America*, London: Routledge & Kegan Paul.

Coleman, J. (1968) 'The concept of equality of educational opportunity', *Harvard Educational Review*, 38 (1): 7–22.

Committee of the Secondary School Examinations Council (1943) *Curriculum and Examinations in Secondary Schools*, Norwood Report, London: HMSO.

Craft, M. (ed.) (1970) *Family, Class and Education*, London: Longman.

Craft, M., Raynor, J. and Cohen, J. (1972) *Linking Home and School*, 2nd edn, London: Longman.

Deem, R. (1978) *Women and Schooling*, London: Routledge & Kegan Paul.

—— (ed.) (1980) *Schooling for Women's Work*, London: Routledge.

Douglas, J. W. B. (1964) *The Home and the School*, London: MacGibbon & Kee.

Ennis, R. (1978) 'Equality of educational opportunity', in K. A. Strike and K. Egan (eds) *Ethics and Educational Policy*, London: Routledge & Kegan Paul.

Epstein, D. (ed.) (1994) *Challenging Gay and Lesbian Inequalities in Education*, Buckingham: Open University Press.

Floud, J. and Halsey, A. H. (1958) 'The sociology of education: a trend report', *Current Sociology* 7 (3): 165–235.

Floud, J., Halsey, A. H. and Martin, F. M. (1956) *Social Class and Educational Opportunity*, London: Heinemann.

Flude, M. and Hammer, M. (1990) *The Education Reform Act 1988: Its Origins and Implications*, London: Falmer.

Foster, P., Gomm, R. and Hammersley, M. (1996) *Constructing Educational Inequality: An Assessment of Research on School Processes*, London: Falmer.

Gillborn, D (1990) *'Race', Ethnicity and Education*, London: Unwin Hyman.

Gorbutt D. (1972) 'The "new" sociology of education', *Education for Teaching* 89 (Autumn).

Gordon, P. (1980) *Selection for Secondary Education*, London: Woburn.

Halsey, A. H. (ed.) (1972) *Educational Priority*, London: HMSO.

Hargreaves, A. (1982) 'Resistance and relative autonomy theories: problems of distortion and incoherence in recent Marxist theories of education', *British Journal of Sociology of Education* 3 (2) 107–26.

Hargreaves, D. H. (1967) *Social Relations in a Secondary School*, London: Routledge & Kegan Paul.

—— (1974) 'Deschooling and the New Romantics', in M. Flude and J. Ahier (eds) *Educability, Schools and Ideology*, London: Croom Helm.

Harris, D. (1992) *From Class Struggle to the Politics of Pleasure: The Effects of Gramscianism on Cultural Studies*, London: Routledge.

Hobsbawm, E. (1962) *The Age of Revolution 1789–1848*, London: Weidenfeld & Nicolson.

Holstein, J. A. and Miller, G. (eds) (1993) *Reconsidering Social Constructionism: Debates in Social Problems Theory*, New York: Aldine de Gruyter.

Hudson, L. (ed.) (1970) *The Ecology of Human Intelligence*, Harmondsworth: Penguin.

Jackson, B. (1964) *Streaming: An Education System in Miniature*, London: Routledge & Kegan Paul.

Lacey, C. (1970) *Hightown Grammar*, Manchester: Manchester University Press.

Lakoff, S. A. (1964) *Equality in Political Philosophy*, Cambridge, MA: Harvard University Press.

Laslett, P. (1971) *The World We Have Lost*, London: Methuen.

Mac an Ghaill, M. (1988) *Young, Gifted and Black*, Milton Keynes: Open University Press.

—— (1995) *The Making of Men: Masculinities, Sexualities and Schooling*, Buckingham: Open University Press.

Measor, L. and Sikes, P. J. (1992) *Gender and Schools*, London: Cassell.

Mirza, H. S. (1992) *Young, Female and Black*, London: Routledge.

Pring, R. (1972) 'Knowledge out of control', *Education for Teaching* 89: 19–28.

Purvis, J. (1991) *A History of Women's Education in England*, Milton Keynes: Open University Press.

Rubinstein, D. (1984) Unit 6 Equal Educational Opportunity, Open University Course E205, *Conflict and Change in Education: A Sociological Introduction*, Milton Keynes: The Open University.

Rubinstein, D. and Simon, B. (1969) *The Evolution of the Comprehensive School, 1926–1966*, London: Routledge & Kegan Paul.

Schools Council (1970) *'Cross'd with Adversity': The Education of Socially Disadvantaged Children in Secondary Schools*, London: Evans/Methuen Educational.

Silver, H. (ed.) (1973) *Equal Opportunity in Education: A Reader in Social Class and Educational Opportunity*, London: Methuen.

Simon, B. (1953) *Intelligence, Psychology and Education: A Marxist Critique*, London: Lawrence & Wishart.

—— (1974) *The Politics of Educational Reform 1920–1940*, London: Lawrence & Wishart.

Squibb, P. (1973) 'The concept of intelligence: a sociological perspective', *Sociological Review* 21 (1): 57–75

Stanworth, M. (1983) *Gender and Schooling: A Study of Sexual Divisions in the Classroom*, London: Hutchinson (originally published 1981, London: Women's Research and Resources Centre).

Troyna, B. (1987) 'A conceptual overview of strategies to combat racial inequality in education: introductory essay', in B.Troyna (ed.) *Racial Inequality in Education*, London: Routledge.

Vernon, P. (1969) *Intelligence and Cultural Environment*, London: Methuen.

—— (1979) 'Intelligence testing and the nature/nurture debate 1928–78: what next?', *British Journal of Educational Psychology* 49: 1–14.

Weiner, G. (1985) 'Equal opportunities, feminism and girls' education: introduction', in G.Weiner (ed.) *Just a Bunch of Girls: Feminist Approaches to Schooling*, Milton Keynes: Open University Press.

Weiner, G. and Arnot, M. (eds) (1987) *Gender under Scrutiny*, London: Hutchinson.

White, J. and Young, M. F. D. (1975) 'The sociology of knowledge', *Education for Teaching* 98: 4–13.

Whitty, G. (1985) *Sociology and School Knowledge: Curriculum Theory, Research and Politics*, London: Methuen.

Whitty, G. and Young, M. F. D. (eds) (1976) *Explorations in the Politics of School Knowledge*, Driffield: Nafferton.

Williams, B. (1962) 'The idea of equality', in P. Laslett and W. G. Runciman (eds) *Politics, Philosophy and Society*, 2nd series, Oxford: Blackwell.

Williamson, B. (1974) 'Continuities and discontinuities in the sociology of education', in M. Flude and J. Ahier (eds) *Educability, Schools, and Ideology*, New York: Wiley.

Wright, C. (1986) 'School processes: an ethnographic study', in J. Eggleston, D. Dunn and M. Anjali (eds) *Education for Some: The Educational and Vocational Experiences of 15–18 Year Old Members of Minority Ethnic Groups*, Stoke-on-Trent: Trentham.

—— (1992a) 'Early education: multiracial primary school classrooms', in D. Gill, B. Mayor and M. Blair (eds) *Racism and Education: Structures and Strategies*, London: Sage.

—— (1992b) *Race Relations in the Primary School*, London: David Fulton.

Young, M. F. D. (1971) 'Introduction: knowledge and control', in M. F. D. Young (ed.) *Knowledge and Control*, London, Collier-Macmillan.

Chapter 9

Is Britain a meritocracy?

P. Saunders

In the week of the 3rd to the 9th March, 1958, 17,414 births throughout Britain were recorded and logged as part of a huge and unique research project designed to collect information about the children's health, education and development. The researchers have tried their best to stay in contact with all of these children ever since, and on five occasions they have revisited them (and, where appropriate, their parents, their schools and their eventual partners) and further documented the development of their lives. The last time they were interviewed was in 1991, when they were aged 33, and by then there were still 11,397 of the original panel of individuals on whom at least some information was obtained.

This National Child Development Study (NCDS) can provide us with an invaluable source of information on social mobility patterns in Britain in the recent period. Since 1958, it has recorded information on the occupations of the parents of panel members, these parents' behaviour and attitudes in relation to their children as they were raising them, the housing conditions in which the children were raised, their schooling and examination records, their measured ability at 7, 11 and 16, the employment histories of the panel members since leaving school, their attitudes to work and employment, their aspirations through childhood and adulthood, and so on. It therefore enables us to evaluate what I have called the *SAD hypothesis* (that social advantages and disadvantages determine where people end up in the class system) against the *meritocracy hypothesis* (that individual ability plus effort are the key determinants of occupational success or failure), for it includes robust and reliable information on virtually all the relevant factors entailed in each of these theories.

Because it targeted every child born in that one week in 1958, the NCDS provides us with a reliable and fairly representative survey of this age cohort. Panel 'wastage' has reduced the total size of the sample substantially, and proportionately more individuals from lower-class origins have dropped out, thereby skewing the sample towards the middle-class both in terms of class origins and class destinations.[1] The surviving NCDS panel in 1991 is, therefore, no longer fully representative of all 33-year-olds in Britain, but there are still sufficient cases remaining in all classes to enable us to analyse the factors driving upward and downward social mobility. Furthermore, now that panel members have reached age 33, it is possible for the first time to take their current class position as a reasonable indicator of their eventual class of destination, although some movement between classes will obviously continue to take place in the future.

Many of the surviving panel members were not in full-time employment in 1991. These people will be omitted from the analysis which follows because they cannot be allocated to a particular social class position on the basis of their own current occupation. Dropping these cases, most of whom are part-time employees (45 per cent), 'housewives' (37 per cent) or unemployed (10 per cent), leaves us with 6,795 individuals, 85 per cent of whom are employees and 15 per cent self-employed. Because more women than men are to be found in part-time employment or in full-time housework, a disproportionate number of women have been dropped from the analysis, and this final sample consists of 70 per cent males and 30 per cent females.

All of these individuals can be classified to a 'social class' position using the system of classification developed by the Office of Population Censuses and Surveys (OPCS). For the purposes of this analysis, we shall divide them between three principal classes which we shall term the 'middle-class' (classes I and II, comprising professionals, managers, administrators and employers), the 'lower working-class' (classes IV and V, comprising semi- and unskilled manual workers), and the 'intermediate classes' (classes IIIN and IIIM, comprising mainly routine white-collar and skilled manual workers).

On this three-class schema, 52 per cent of the NCDS panel had been intergenerationally mobile (i.e. they occupied a different class position in 1991 than the one occupied by their parents in 1974 when the panel members reached the legal working age of 16). This figure is the same whether we compare the social class they had achieved by age 33 with the social class of the fathers, or with the higher social class of either the mother or the father. Table 9.1 shows that over one-third of middle-class children had been downwardly mobile, most of them into class III. Among lower working-class children, one-quarter had been upwardly mobile into the middle-class while half had moved into class III. Less than half of those achieving middle-class entry had come from middle-class origins, and less than one-third of those entering class IV/V had started out there. These *absolute* patterns are broadly consistent with those reported in previous British studies of social mobility, including Goldthorpe's which similarly found that around half of the population had undergone social mobility.

The NCDS data appear rather less consistent with Goldthorpe's results, however, when we consider *relative* measures of social mobility. Goldthorpe, it will be recalled, recorded disparity ratios in favour of middle-class children of between 3:1 and 4:1, but Table 9.2 shows that, in the NCDS sample, children born to middle-class fathers were only about twice as likely to have

Table 9.1 Intergenerational social mobility rates based on father's class (higher class of either father or mother in brackets)

(a) Percentage from different class origins arriving at each class destination (read across):

Class origin	Child's class age 33		
	I/II	III	IV/V
I/II	63(59)	31(33)	7(8)
III	37(37)	49(49)	14(15)
IV/V	28(27)	49(51)	23(22)

(b) Percentage in each class from different class origins (read down):

Class origin	Child's class age 33		
	I/II	III	IV/V
I/II	42(46)	20(25)	14(21)
III	46(44)	60(57)	56(55)
IV/V	12(10)	20(17)	30(24)

achieved middle-class positions by the age of 33 as compared with children born to fathers in semi- or unskilled occupations. Does this mean that the class system has become more fluid since Goldthorpe did his research?

We need to be cautious about this. One problem is that Goldthorpe's social class categories are defined rather differently from the OPCS class categories. His definition of what he calls the 'service class' does not coincide exactly with classes I and II in the OPCS schema, and his definition of the 'working-class' is much broader than (though certainly encompasses) OPCS classes IV and V. This means that Goldthorpe's results cannot be directly compared with the NCDS findings. Furthermore, although the disparity ratio in the NCDS data is much lower than Goldthorpe's as regards children's relative chances of achieving a middle-class position, it is broadly similar to Goldthorpe's as regards relative chances of avoiding a lower class position (around 3.5:1). If fluidity has increased, it seems that top positions have become more open but that middle-class chances of dramatic failure have not risen. We also need to remember that Goldthorpe's study focused solely on men whereas the data in Table 9.2 include both men and women. When women are excluded from these calculations, the advantage for middle-class children in getting into class I/II is stretched somewhat to 2.6:1, and their advantage in avoiding class IV/V also increases slightly to 3.8, thus bringing the results somewhat closer to Goldthorpe's.

Bearing all these points in mind, it is nevertheless striking that the disparity ratios for the NCDS sample are so small (particularly given our tight definition of the 'working-class' as comprising only semi- and unskilled manual workers). It will be remembered that Goldthorpe's 1972 data gave

Table 9.2 Social mobility disparity ratios (NCDS data)

Father class	Relative chances of being in:	
	Class I/II	Class IV/V
I/II	2.21	set at 1
III	1.29	2.18
IV/V	set at 1	3.47

disparity ratios of around 4:1 while his 1983 data gave disparity ratios of nearer 3:1. It is not unreasonable to suggest that the NCDS disparity ratio of little more than 2:1 indicates that this trend towards greater fluidity has continued. Of particular relevance here is the fact that everybody in the NCDS sample is the same age (33 in 1991) whereas both of Goldthorpe's earlier samples were of mixed age groups. What NCDS gives us is a panel of young Britons all born and raised in the post-war years, whereas Goldthorpe's samples included men who grew up before the war. If the class system has become more fluid, we should expect this to show up particularly sharply in the NCDS sample, as indeed it does. For all these reasons, we may tentatively conclude that the increased social fluidity discovered by John Goldthorpe between 1972 and 1983 has continued to rise into the 1990s.

At ages 7, 11 and 16, the children in the NCDS survey all sat maths and English tests, and at 11 they also took a (non-standardized) general ability test consisting of eighty verbal and non-verbal items. Analysis of scores on this general ability test reveals two important findings (Table 9.3). First, the children's scores reflected to some extent the social class of their parents. We can see that there was a clear and consistent gradient in mean (i.e. average) test scores between those with fathers or mothers in class I/II and those whose parents were in classes IV and V. We also see that parental class and children's test scores correlate with a coefficient (r) of 0.24. The strength of association between two variables can be expressed on a scale from 0, which indicates no association, to 1, which indicates that the first variable totally predicts the second. A correlation coefficient of 0.24 therefore indicates that the parents' class and the children's test scores are related, though not particularly strongly.

Table 9.3 Mean ability scores by class of origin (higher parental class) and class of destination

Class of origin	Mean test score	Std deviation	Class of destination	Mean test score	Std deviation
I/II	50.6	14.3	I/II	51.6	13.7
III	44.0	15.0	III	42.2	14.7
IV/V	40.2	15.3	IV/V	36.3	14.8

$r = 0.24$ ($N = 5565$, missing = 1230) $\qquad$ $r = 0.37$ ($N = 5826$, missing = 969)
(Mean test score for total sample = 45.4 on 80 items, standard deviation = 14.3)

Both the SAD and the meritocracy hypotheses would expect to discover a correlation like this. For the former, it is the result of social advantages which enable middle-class children to 'over-achieve' on ability tests. For the latter, it is evidence that bright middle-class parents tend to produce and raise bright children while less bright working-class parents tend to produce and raise children of lower average ability.

The second key finding is that test scores correlate much more strongly ($r = 0.37$) with the social class achieved by the children twenty-two years after taking the test, than with the class of their parents around the time that they sat it. Again, there is a clear gradient in scores ranging from those entering class I/II to those entering class IV/V, but the higher correlation is due mainly to a much more marked association between ability and class of destination at the lower end of the class hierarchy.

This result is consistent with the meritocracy thesis, but not with the SAD thesis. In a meritocratic class system we would expect bright parents often to produce bright children, but we know (and can calculate from regression to the mean) that some bright parents will produce dull children just as some dull parents will produce bright ones. Because a meritocratic class system will select able children for higher positions regardless of their social background, the association between class of origin and ability should be weaker than that between ability and class of destination, and this is indeed what we find. The particularly strong association between low ability and low class destinations indicates that bright children are tending to avoid class IV/V entry and are to some extent being selected for higher positions. The SAD hypothesis, by contrast, would predict associations of equal strength since ability is seen merely as a correlate of class background and should not itself contribute to the determination of class of destination.

It seems that ability does play some part in influencing class destinations. But could social class differences in ability alone account for the disparity ratios found in mobility tables in both the Goldthorpe and the NCDS data?

By age 33, 43 per cent of the NCDS sample were in class I/II occupations. The score achieved on the ability test by the top 43 per cent of children was 49 or above. If class positions achieved by age 33 simply reflected ability as measured at age 11, then we would expect all those achieving class I/II positions to have scored 49 or better on the ability test.

Taking an ability score of 49 as the threshold for class I/II entry, we actually find that only 62 per cent of those entering class I/II scored this highly. Put crudely, 38 per cent of those arriving in class I/II were not bright enough to be there! Here we have the first indication that class destinations have to be explained by something more than just ability. Focusing on the less able entrants to class I/II (i.e. those scoring less than 49), we find that twice as many (32 per cent) came from class I/II backgrounds as from class IV/V backgrounds (17 per cent). Looking at the data in a different way, and focusing on the lowest quartile of ability across the whole sample, we find that 41 per cent of low ability children from class I/II origins still managed to gain entry to class I/II as compared with 21 per cent of low ability children from class IV/V origins. Low ability middle-class children are therefore twice as likely to succeed as low ability children from semi- and unskilled manual worker homes, although even among the latter, around one-fifth still arrive in the middle-class despite low ability scores at age 11. It is clear from this that low ability is not necessarily a barrier to later occupational success. Conversely, high ability does appear to offer a reasonable guarantee against failure, for only 5 per cent of children in the top ability quartile ended up in class IV/V while 65 per cent of them made it to class I/II.

Ability, then, is part of the explanation for why middle-class children are more successful than working-class children, but it is not the full story. We can gauge how important it is by calculating a modified set of disparity ratios dividing the sample into those with an ability score high enough to warrant entry to class I/II and those scoring below this threshold point (Table 9.4). The first part of Table 9.4 shows (first cell) that the relative advantage enjoyed by class I/II children over class IV/V children in achieving a middle-class destination is reduced to just 1.7:1 once we control for ability. The second part of Table 9.4 shows (last cell) that middle-class children reduce their relative chances of avoiding class IV/V from 3.5:1 to 2.3:1 once we control for ability. Summarizing all this, it seems that differences in average ability levels between children of different classes explain anything up to a half of the disparity in their relative chances of achieving middle-class entry and avoiding lower working-class entry.

Ability is only one part of the meritocracy thesis. The other key element is 'effort' which involves both the desire to succeed and a commitment to behaviour (e.g. hard work) which is thought likely to bring success. In a

Table 9.4 Social mobility disparity ratios above and below threshold ability score for class I/II entry (whole sample in brackets)

(a) Those scoring high enough for class I/II entry:

| | Relative chances of being in: | |
	Class I/II	Class IV/V
Father class I/II	1.67(2.21)	set at 1
Father class III	1.23(1.29)	1.71(2.18)
Father class IV/V	set at 1	3.50(3.47)

(b) Those scoring below threshold entry for class I/II

| | Relative chances of being in: | |
	Class I/II	Class IV/V
Father class I/II	2.13(2.21)	set at 1
Father class III	1.15(1.29)	1.72(2.81)
Father class IV/V	set at 1	2.31(3.47)

meritocratic society, bright individuals will only succeed if they are motivated to do so, and people of lesser ability may still achieve relatively high positions if they are committed, motivated and hard-working. A rigorous test of the meritocracy thesis thus requires adequate measures of effort as well as ability.

In the NCDS survey, there are various possible indicators of 'effort'. From among these we shall examine (a) a 32-point motivation scale based on attitude questions answered by the children at age 16 (*motivation*); (b) an 'absenteeism' factor based on school truancy records and reports of trivial absences (*absenteeism*); and (c) a 'job commitment' factor based on answers to three attitude questions at age 33 (*work attitudes*). Taken together with the ability scores (between 0 and 80) at age 11 (*ability test score*), these represent the major indicators for testing the meritocracy thesis.

What, then, are the comparable indicators for evaluating the SAD thesis? One, clearly, is parental class (*parental class*) which is measured on a 3-point scale and which refers to the social class of father or mother when the child was aged 16, whichever is the higher. Linked to this is the educational level of the parents, for not only will this affect what Bourdieu calls the 'cultural capital' available in the home, but it may also influence the values which parents have and the decisions they make regarding the importance of a good education for their children. For fathers (*father's education*) and mothers (*mother's education*), educational level is a dichotomous variable based on whether or not they completed their schooling at the minimum leaving age. Other variables and factors measuring possible class advantages/disadvantages associated with social background include the higher class of either grandfather (*grandparents' class*), a measure of overcrowding in the home based on persons per room while the children were growing up (*overcrowding*), and a measure of lack of basic amenities in the home (*home amenities*).

Also related to the SAD thesis are a number of variables and factors associated with the education of the child and the support it received from the parents. *Pre-school education* indicates whether or not children attended any pre-school or nursery education facility before the age of 5, and *type of school* distinguishes those receiving a private education at 16 from those attending state schools. *Father read* and *mother read* indicate the degree to which father and mother respectively read to the child at age 7 (weekly, occasionally or hardly ever), and *parental interest* is a measure of parental interest in the schooling of the child at age 11 based upon the school's assessment of the interest demonstrated by the father and mother plus evidence on whether they had made contact with the school during the previous twelve months. There is also a factor, *parental aspirations*, expressing the degree to which parents had high aspirations for their child at age 11 (this is based on their wish that the child should remain at school beyond the minimum leaving age, together with their hope that it should go on to some form of further education). Finally, the sex of the child is measured by *gender*.

Taken together, these thirteen measures cover a large number of the material and cultural advantages/disadvantages which sociologists down the years have identified in an attempt to explain why class origins should be expected to influence educational and occupational success later in life. Not everything, of course, has been included – there are no measures of peer group pressure, nor of the quality of personal interaction with teachers, nor of the capacity to mobilize contacts and social networks. Nevertheless, a range of measures encompassing class of parents and grandparents, education of parents, indicators of household deprivation such as overcrowding and lack of amenities, private schooling, pre-schooling, early exposure to books in the home, parental interest in and support for education, and parental aspirations for their children would seem to offer a fair basis for testing most of the fundamental claims on which the SAD thesis rests.

We can begin an empirical evaluation of the meritocracy and SAD theses by considering why some working-class children succeed when others do not, and why some middle-class children fail when others maintain or enhance the position achieved by their parents.

Table 9.5 gives the results of a logistic regression model, in which 4 meritocracy variables and 12 SAD variables are used to predict whether individuals born to class IV/V parents will remain where they are or move all the way up to class I/II. It demonstrates clearly that it is meritocratic variables – ability, motivation and attitudes to employment – which are the key factors distinguishing successful lower working-class children from those they leave behind them.

With 183 of these individuals ending up in class IV/V as compared with 258 ending up in class I/II, the best initial prediction that we can make of any individual's class destination is that he or she makes it to class I/II. Such a prediction will be accurate in 59 per cent of cases (see the first line in the 'per cent *correct*' column of Table 9.5). What we now try to do is to improve this predictive accuracy by taking account of additional information. The model tells us that the single most important piece of information which we need

Table 9.5 A logistic regression model predicting class IV/V children entering class I/II against those remaining in class IV/V

Step	Variable	% correct	Final R	Final exp (B)
0		58.5		
1	Ability test score	69.6	0.26	1.06
2	Motivation	73.0	0.16	0.90
3	Work attitudes	74.1	0.15	1.59
4	Gender (female)	75.7	0.10	2.05
5	Grandparent's class	76.0	0.09	0.63

Variables not in the equation: *Mother read, father read, mother education, father education, pre-school education, type of school, home amenities, overcrowding, parental aspirations, parental interest, absenteeism.*
N = 441

to take into account is the ability test score achieved by these individuals when they were 11 years old. When these test scores are entered into our model ('step 1'), the accuracy of the predictions we can make rises sharply from 59 per cent correct to 70 per cent correct. We can improve this still further ('step 2') by taking account of the level of motivation at school when aged 16, for we see that this information improves our predictive powers by a further 3 per cent. One of the two remaining meritocracy indicators (work attitudes in adult life) plus just two of the SAD indicators (gender – women perform rather better than men; and grandfathers' class – those with grandfathers above class IV/V perform better) also have effects significant enough for them to be included in the final model, but together they only raise the level of predictive accuracy by a further 3 percentage points.

In addition to telling us about how powerfully we can predict any individual's final class position, the model in Table 9.5 also tells us the relative contribution made by each factor in influencing this outcome. This is expressed by the final 'partial correlation coefficients' ('*Final R*') which indicate the relative effect of each variable in the model when the effects of all other variables are taken into account. From Table 9.5 it is clear that ability ($R = 0.26$) is by far the strongest influence on working-class success, with motivation ($R = 0.16$) and attitudes to work ($R = 0.15$) as contributory factors.

The final column in the table ('*Final exp B*') tells us, for each of the variables in the model, the factor by which the odds of entering class I/II change for each unit increase in the variable in question. For example, the odds of a class IV/V child entering class I/II relative to the odds of remaining in class IV/V are 258/183=1:1.4. These odds are improved by (1.4×1.06) for each point scored on the ability test, by (1.4×0.9) for each point on the motivation scale,[2] by (1.4×2.05) if the individual is female, and so on.

Perhaps the most striking feature of Table 9.5 concerns the list of variables which fail to enter the model. Some, like private schooling, are hardly surprising, for very few of these children attended fee-paying schools. Others, however, are surprising from the perspective of the SAD hypothesis. Material deprivation in the home (measured by overcrowding and by lack of basic amenities) has no significant effect. Nor do parental levels of education, exposure to books at an early age, pre-school play group or nursery attendance, parental interest in the child's schooling, or parental aspirations for the child's future. To the extent that we can predict success for children from classes IV and V, the key factors have to do with their ability and their attitudes to work (at school and in later employment) and have very little or nothing to do with material conditions or 'cultural capital' in the home.

We saw earlier that ability tests such as the one utilized in the NCDS are often criticized as in some way class-biased. In Table 9.5 (and in Table 9.6), however, all children come from the same class background, so this sort of criticism cannot apply in these cases. The test which all these children took at age 11 is a good predictor of eventual occupational destination even when the children being compared come from comparable backgrounds. Clearly, the test results do indicate differences in individual aptitudes which cannot be explained away as merely the effects of social class background.

Table 9.6 outlines a similar logistic regression model, this time predicting failure (i.e. downward mobility out of class I/II) of middle-class children. Again, the basic message is the same – ability is the key factor with an *R* (0.19) twice as strong as that of any other variable in the model, and motivation is entered second. Private schooling appears as the most important of the SAD indicators, suggesting that the private schools may (as is often argued) offer middle-class parents some means of insuring their less able offspring against downward mobility. Parental education levels, absenteeism at school, attitudes to work and gender (where this time males prove rather more successful than females) all achieve statistical significance but make only tiny contributions to the final model.

Clearly, the meritocratic thesis proves much stronger than the SAD thesis in explaining why some individuals succeed while others from comparable social backgrounds do not. The meritocracy thesis has, however, to be subjected to a much stronger test. Supporters of the SAD thesis may well be willing to accept that individual qualities can make *some* difference to where people end up in life – that dull and lazy middle-class children are more likely to fail than bright and hard-working ones, or that intelligent and motivated working-class children are more likely to succeed than their less intelligent and less committed peers. The key question, however, is whether such individual qualities outweigh the initial advantages or disadvantages experienced by children growing up in *different* social environments. For example, are dull middle-class children still likely to do better than bright children from class IV/V backgrounds?

The short answer to this is that they are not. Class I/II children who

Table 9.6 A logistic regression model predicting class I/II children entering class I/II against those who are downwardly mobile

Step	Variable	% correct	Final R	Final exp (B)
0		60.0		
1	Ability test score	66.1	0.19	1.04
2	Motivation	66.6	0.10	0.94
3	Type of school	67.5	0.07	1.92
4	Mother's education	67.7	0.05	1.36
5	Absenteeism	68.1	0.04	0.79
6	Father's education	68.1	0.04	1.34
7	Work attitudes	68.9	0.04	1.15
8	Gender (male)	68.7	0.04	0.76

Variables not in the equation: *mother read, father read, pre-school education, grandparents' class, home amenities, overcrowding, parental aspirations, parental interest.*
N = 1830

retained their middle-class position had achieved an average score of 54. 2 on the general ability test as compared with 46.2 for those who fell to class III and 41.5 for those falling to class IV/V. Class IV/V children who achieved entry to class I/II had an average score of 47.2 as compared with 39.0 for those entering class III and just 33.0 for those who stayed in class IV/V. These are statistically highly significant differences (F = 131.0 with 5 df). Not only do ability scores within each class of origin sharply distinguish those who later succeed from those who do not, but class IV/V children entering the middle-class have significantly higher average ability scores than class I/II children leaving it.

Given that the IQ test sat by these children may well have favoured those from middle-class homes, this is a particularly striking result. Despite the cultural advantages which might have been expected to inflate their test scores, the middle-class failures scored lower on average than the successful children from the least advantaged semi-skilled and unskilled manual worker backgrounds. The 'real' difference in average levels of intelligence between them was almost certainly greater than the difference recorded in their test scores, given the likelihood that the middle-class children over-achieved on this test while the lower working-class children under-achieved. Clearly, the occupational system has sorted them out by intelligence to a much greater extent than it has selected them according to their class origins.

In order to evaluate the relative importance of ability and effort on the one hand, and social advantages and disadvantages on the other, we can develop what is called a 'multiple regression model' which includes all the meritocracy and SAD variables and factors and sorts them out in terms of the relative contribution which each of them makes to individuals' final destinations. To do this, we take as the measure of occupational success at 33 the ratings of their jobs on a 70-point occupational prestige scale.[3] All of the variables entered into the model are the same as in Tables 9.5 and 9.6, and the results are summarized in Table 9.7.

In Table 9.7, the *'Change in R^2'* column tells us how well the model is predicting occupational status at each step in its construction. For example, at step 1, we include ability test scores as the single most powerful predictor of people's occupational status at age 33, and these scores immediately explain 14 per cent of the variance in occupational statuses. At step 2, the next most powerful predictor, motivation, is added, and this raises the proportion of variance explained by the model to 16 per cent. And so on. The standardized Beta coefficients in the last column of the table (headed *'Final Beta'*) express the relative strength of each item in the model, after allowing for associations between the items. For example, with a coefficient of 0.25, the ability test scores have an effect on occupational status which is twice as strong as motivation (0.13), three times as strong as class background (0.8), and so on.

All four of the meritocracy variables enter the model, but, as before, ability is entered first and has by far the strongest effect (Beta = 0.25) of any of the

Table 9.7 A multiple regression model with Hope–Goldthorpe rank scores as dependent variable[4]

Step	Variable	Change in R^2	Final Beta
1	Ability test score	0.14	0.25
2	Motivation	0.16	0.13
3	Parental class	0.18	0.08
4	Absenteeism	0.19	0.07
5	Mother's education	0.20	0.06
6	Work attitudes	0.20	0.07
7	Gender (male)	0.21	0.07
8	Father's education	0.21	0.05
9	Parental interest	0.22	0.05
10	Type of school	0.22	0.05
11	Overcrowding	0.22	0.03

Variables not in the equation: *father read, mother read, pre-school education, grandparents' class, home amenities*.
Tests for multicollinearity: no variables correlated at higher than 0.5. Lowest tolerance (0.68) and highest Variance Inflation Factor (1.46) on *ability test score*. Inspection of variance proportions on eigenvalues shows some dependency between *mother's education* (59%) and *father's education* (63%), and between *ability test score* (60%) and *motivation* (35%).

variables and factors in the model, while motivation at school enters second (Beta = 0.13) and absenteeism at school and work attitudes enter fourth and sixth respectively, each with Beta = 0.07. The strongest SAD variable in the model is parental class (Beta = 0.08). Parental education levels, gender, parental interest in the child's schooling, private schooling and overcrowding in the home all achieve statistically significant effects, but they make only a tiny contribution to the overall model-fit. Grandparents' social class, pre-school education, early exposure to books and the level of basic amenities in the home all fail to achieve statistical significance. Basically, the model improves hardly at all after step 4 – occupational status at age 33 is explained (to the extent that it is explained by any of these factors) mainly by ability, motivation, parental class and absenteeism, and, of these four, ability appears roughly twice as important as motivation and three times more important than parental class and absenteeism.

It has also to be recognized, however, that the final model R-square (the total proportion of variance explained by the model) of 0.22 is fairly weak. The meritocracy thesis appears much stronger than the SAD thesis, but even when the two are combined, over three-quarters of the variance in occupational prestige scores remains unexplained. In part, this is because the model does not include direct measures of achievement which are obvious stepping stones to later occupational success. Three important measures are examination success at school, the occupational status of the first job taken after completing full-time education, and the achievement of further qualifications after leaving school. These three variables have been excluded until now because they are common to both the meritocracy and SAD theses. Both theories of social mobility accept that formal qualifications are important in influencing inter-generational mobility chances, and both accept that initial entry into the labour market is an important pointer to final class of destination. Where they differ is in the explanations they offer for why some people gain more qualifications than others, and why some enter the occupational system at a higher point than others.

Table 9.8 presents the results of a second multiple regression model entering the same variables and factors as before while adding school examination results summarized on a 9-point scale (*Exam passes at 16*), the occupational prestige of the first job after leaving school (*Class first job*) and additional qualifications achieved after leaving school summarized on a 5-point scale (*Further quals*). The model-fit is improved substantially (*R*-square = 0.32) and all three variables are entered into the model before any of the meritocracy or SAD variables. With Beta values of 0.19 and 0.22 respectively, the model clearly demonstrates the importance for final occupational status of formal qualifications achieved through school examinations and through further study after leaving school. The status of first job plays an important but less powerful role in the model (the NCDS panel members have undergone substantial intra-generational as well as inter-generational mobility), and the only other variable which continues to have a relatively strong effect on class of destination is ability (Beta = 0.13). This suggests that bright people tend to end up in higher status jobs, partly because they accumulate more qualifications, but also because their ability comes to be recognized and rewarded independently of their paper qualifications.[5] All three motivational factors are also included in this final model, as are parental class and overcrowding (which is probably an indicator of childhood

Table 9.8 A multiple regression model including qualifications and status of first job as independent variables

Step	Variable	Change in R^2	Final Beta
1	Exam passes at 16	0.23	0.19
2	Further quals	0.28	0.22
3	Class first job	0.30	0.13
4	Ability test score	0.31	0.13
5	Parental class	0.31	0.06
6	Absenteeism	0.32	0.04
7	Gender (male)	0.32	0.05
8	Motivation	0.32	0.05
9	Work attitudes	0.32	0.04
10	Overcrowding	0.32	0.03

Variables not in the equation: *mother's education, father's education, mother read, father read, pre-school education, type of school, grandparents' class, home amenities, parental interest.*

Tests for multicollinearity: no variables correlated at higher than 0.5 except *exam passes at 16* with *ability test score* (0.54) and *exam passes at 16* with *further quals* (0.54).

poverty), but all make only tiny contributions with standardized coefficients of 0.06 or below.

How are we to summarize the evidence presented in this chapter? The evidence has been presented in three parts. First, we have seen that ability correlates more strongly with class of destination than with class of origin. Middle-class children tend to score higher than working-class children on ability tests (and on more specific tests of literacy and numeracy), but this is consistent with both the meritocracy and SAD hypotheses and in itself does not therefore tell us a great deal. What is more interesting is the relatively higher correlation between ability test scores and the class of destination achieved over twenty years after the test was taken, for this shows that the occupational class system is to some extent selecting by ability irrespective of social class origins. This finding is consistent with the meritocracy thesis but is inconsistent with the SAD thesis.

Second, we have also seen that ability and motivation are the key predictors of lower working-class success and of middle-class failure. Low ability does not necessarily prevent entry into the middle-class (not even for children from lower-class backgrounds), and this suggests that other personal characteristics – a willingness to take risks, perhaps, or an engaging personality – may provide other routes to occupational success. High ability does, however, tend to safeguard individuals against failure, for very few high ability people ended up in classes IV and V irrespective of where they started out from. Bright and committed children tend to end up in the middle-class irrespective of whether they began life there or started out with class IV/V parents, although the former still enjoy a higher chance of success than the latter. Social mobility disparity ratios comparing class I/II origins with class IV/V origins are roughly halved once ability differentials between the classes are taken into account.

Third, we have seen that class destinations reflect individual merit (ability and motivation) much more than class background. Many of the factors which have attracted so much academic attention from sociologists down the years – private schooling, parental contact with schools, material conditions in the home, the 'cultural capital' passed on by middle-class parents to their children, and even gender bias in the school or the workplace – turn out, even when statistically significant, to exert only relatively minor effects on people's class destinies. By contrast, the factors which sociologists have so often ignored, or even dismissed as self-evidently absurd or unimportant – factors having to do with the intellectual capacities of individuals and the tenacity they display in working towards a given objective – turn out to be much more important.

None of this is sufficient to justify the claim that occupational class recruitment in Britain is entirely based on meritocratic principles. The high degree of variance left unexplained by the various models indicates that there are other factors at work which have little to do with either social advantage/disadvantage or meritocracy, and the models also suggest that both of the theses we have considered have something to offer to an overall explanation of class destinations. Nevertheless, the evidence does conclusively demonstrate that the occupational class system in Britain is more meritocratic than has commonly been assumed, and that initial patterns of social advantage or disadvantage are much less significant than has generally been claimed. In a straight evaluation of the meritocratic and SAD theses as explanations of social mobility and class recruitment, the former receives much more empirical support than the latter.

NOTES

1 Looking first at class of origin, the social class of fathers of panel members was last collected in 1974 (sweep 3) when the children were aged 16 and when 14,761 of them remained in the panel. The percentage of these fathers occupying each class position can be compared with the class distribution of all males at the 1971 census (although it has to be remembered that most of the fathers will have been in middle age at this time while the census reflects the occupations of all males including those much younger, who may still be on an upwards trajectory):

R-G class:	Panel Fathers (1974)	All Males (1971 census)	% over/under represented
I	5.4	4.7	+15
II	20.0	17.1	+17
IIIN	9.6	11.3	−15
IIIM	44.4	37.0	+20
IV	14.8	17.2	−14
V	5.8	8.2	−29

As regards the social class achieved by panel members themselves by age 33, comparison can be made (for males) with the social class distribution of men at the 1991 census (again remembering that we should not expect the occupations of a cohort of 33-year-olds to match those of the whole male population between 16 and 65):

R-G Class:	Panel Males (1991)	Census Males (1991)	% over/under represented
I	7.4	4.7	+15
II	32.3	17.1	+17
IIIN	10.7	11.3	−15
IIIM	33.3	37.0	+20
IV	12.9	17.2	−14
V	3.4	8.2	−29

Both tables indicate that the most significant bias created by panel wastage has occurred as a result of the under-representation of those born into and/or entering class V (unskilled manual work).

2 In the original NCDS data, low scores on the motivation scale indicate high motivation. Because this is counter-intuitive, and hence potentially confusing, the scale has been reversed here.

3 See Goldthorpe and Hope (1974). This scale is used because it provides a dependent variable measured at interval level. This enables multivariate analysis based on least squares regression and (in chapter 8) the development of a path model derived from structural equation models. Goldthorpe himself abandoned this scale (in favour of a categorical class schema) when he applied log-linear modelling techniques to the analysis of social mobility tables, but regression-based models remain more appropriate if the concern is to understand how different individuals end up in different positions, as opposed to Goldthorpe's major concern with analysing the effects of relative mobility rates on class structuration. For a discussion of these issues, see the papers by Kelley and Marshall, together with Goldthorpe's reply, in Clark, J., Modgil, C. and Modgil, S (eds.), *John H. Goldthorpe: Consensus and Controversy*, London: Falmer Press, 1990.

4 Variables are entered/deleted stepwise with $p < 0.05$ as criterion for entry and $p > 0.10$ as criterion for deletion. Missing data are replaced by group means based on gender.

5 The fact that ability has a clear effect over and above its association with educational qualifications is further evidence that we cannot rely (as Marshall does) on paper qualifications as substitute indicators for IQ when attempting to explain patterns of social mobility.

Chapter 10

Educational reform, gender equality and school cultures

M. Arnot, M. David and G. Weiner

In 1994 the Equal Opportunities Commission (EOC) funded a one-year study to consider educational reforms and gender equality in schools in England and Wales in the period 1984–94, in particular, assessing whether the various educational changes of the late 1980s and early 1990s had strengthened or interrupted trends towards greater gender equality.

The research had a threefold aim: to map student examination performance in terms of gender over a ten-year period; to evaluate the impact of government reforms on gender equality in schools; and to ascertain any noticeable changes in student and/or school cultures, and in equal opportunities policy-making.

The historical point at which the research was carried out (1984–94) followed, first, a period of equal opportunities activity in education which reached its height in the mid-1980s, in which local education authorities (LEAs) took a major role; and second, a period of considerable educational change. Such reforms were instigated by central government reforms which encouraged greater central control over schools, as well as choice, competition and the introduction of educational markets, through self-managing schools and new school provision.

Two recent clusters of reforms were identified in the project. The first focused on the establishment of a National Curriculum, assessment, testing and examinations, monitoring of school performance, and publication of school examination results. The second cluster focused on changes to the administration and organization of schools, namely, shifts from LEA responsibility for the organization of schools to greater school autonomy and diversity with local management of schools (LMS), open enrolment, increased power of school governing bodies, grant-maintained status (GMS) and city technology colleges (CTCs).

Few of these reforms were framed or developed with increased gender equality primarily in mind and hence there is relatively little explicit reference to gender equality in the policy documentation. The research found that in order to incorporate equality issues more explicitly teachers and LEAs developed broader concepts of equal opportunities to fuse more readily with government priorities and demands. This led to a wider focus within the research, on shifts in perception and interpretation of equal opportunities and/or gender policies and issues.

Three different approaches to data collection and analysis were used in the study in order to describe and explain the various patterns and trends in gender equality in schools since 1984. These were:

1 An analysis of statistics on examination entry and performance data for the period 1984–94.
2 Questionnaire surveys of

- a national sample of primary and secondary maintained and grant-maintained schools (including all CTCs) in England and Wales
- all LEAs in England and Wales.

3 Case studies of equal opportunities policy and practice in seven selected LEAs in England and Wales, named Shires LEA, North West LEA, Home Counties LEA, Midlands LEA, North East LEA, London LEA and Welsh LEA.[1]

The examination mapping exercise and the school and LEA questionnaire surveys provided trend analyses of patterns of subject choice and qualifications, and of levels of equal opportunities awareness, policies and practices. The value of the case studies was that they offered a more detailed and up-to-date picture of how equality issues were being experienced within schools and at LEA level. What they also showed was the variability in awareness, commitment and experience of equal opportunities policy-making and implementation within and between LEA areas.

In this summary, three themes have been taken from the report: context and effects of educational reforms, changing gender cultures of schools, and new practices, projects and initiatives.

CONTEXT AND EFFECTS OF EDUCATIONAL REFORMS

A range of factors have affected the ways in which recent education policies impacted upon equal opportunities practice in schools. These include economic and geographic conditions, the history of individual school policy-making on equal opportunities, the levels of support previously experienced by schools, and the patterns of achievement already in place prior to the reforms.

Taking budget cuts as an example of an outcome of the reforms which appears to have had a profound effect on equal opportunities, it is clear that tighter financial constraints have severely limited such work. For example, at North West LEA secondary schools with falling numbers, staff have found it increasingly difficult to fill all the posts required under the Education

Reform Act 1988 with the school having lost ten staff members (out of over fifty) since April 1994, and due to lose more in 1995. According to a long-serving member of staff:

> Staff have suffered from the drop in numbers. All are having to do more duties, they have difficult classes to deal with, with larger class sizes. When the school was larger, it was easier to 'swop' disruptive students around – now this is not possible.

The leakage of staff has meant that the member of staff responsible for gender recently had her responsibility extended to include all areas of equal opportunities.

> Until the previous year there had been a B allowance, race relations co-ordinator in the school. Now, as no one else is 'doing race', she has been given the responsibility by default.

(Case-study notes)

There are differences in how the reforms have been experienced in the schools in relation to past histories of equal opportunities activism or lack of interest. Thus in inner city and/or traditional working-class areas with a history of support for equality issues, the impact of the reforms is likely to have been rather different, and more negative, to that experienced in schools coming to such issues for the first time.

In the former case, the demise of the power of the LEA, and with it the ability to pursue and fund coherent policy development on equal opportunities, will be seen as a blow to widening gender equality. In the second instance (through LMS), newly semi-independent budget-controlling head-teachers and school staffs perceive new equal opportunities possibilities as they break away from low-spending local authority restrictions, for instance, by developing confidence-building strategies for female students or a more balanced curriculum for male students.

The outcomes of the reforms and their impact on equality issues are thus likely to be patchy. In North West LEA, for example, officers regarded gender equality as currently less of a priority than previously, and more likely to be treated as but one aspect of equal opportunities generally. As schools were being let off the equal opportunities 'hook' by the withdrawal of LEA influence, officers were seeing very little evidence in secondary schools of genuine interest in equality issues and at the primary level even less.

In contrast, for Shires LEA, equal opportunities has rarely been a policy issue and, at school level, has been an equally forgotten or ignored area. Schools are now able, if they wish, to 'buy-in' to equal opportunities support services; however, 'uptake is very low indeed and courses barely take off. Equality is not seen as a priority in schools' (case-study notes). In fact, the thrust of the authority's stance to equal opportunities is reflected in one primary head's view: 'if it is not an issue, don't make an issue out of it – let sleeping dogs lie'.

The survey data reveal a complex picture of the perceived impact to specific policies and practices. The LEA questionnaire focused on a range of social and educational reforms, covering issues that might not be seen as strictly education but may have had an effect upon gender equality in schools or on equal opportunities policies. Here, the aim was to explore the effects of attendant policy developments such as the financing of local authorities through the community charge and/or council tax.

The primary and secondary school surveys focused on specific educational reforms which were separated into two sets, those which affect pupil performance, achievement and standards – such as the National Curriculum, standard assessment tasks (SATs) and league tables – and those generating wider organizational changes, such as LMS. The aim here was to compare the contrast between such reforms through questions relevant to the specific school context. Thus fewer questions were asked of primary school respondents than secondary school respondents, the latter of whom were additionally required to report on sector-specific reforms such as General Certificate of Secondary Education (GCSE), Technical and Vocational Educational Initiative (TVEI), Certificate of Pre-Vocational Education (CPVE), General National Vocational Qualification (GNVQ) and work experience.

Tables 10.1, 10.2 and 10.3 illustrate the perceptions that LEAs and primary and secondary schools have of the impact of specific educational and social reforms.

What is noticeable from such data are the different perceptions of the curriculum, assessment and monitoring reforms to those relating to administration and organization of schools. A number of trends are identified below:

Curriculum assessment and monitoring reforms

1 The changes to the curriculum, monitoring and examinations, whether academic (such as the National Curriculum) or vocational (such as TVEI), and the monitoring of pupil performance and standards through the Office for Standards in Education (OFSTED) and data collection, were seen to have had largely positive effects on the promotion of equal opportunities.
2 TVEI was seen as positive by nearly all the secondary schools in the survey.
3 GCSE was seen as positive by 75 per cent of LEAs and 70 per cent of secondary schools in England and Wales.
4 The National Curriculum was seen as a positive reform in terms of gender equality by 85 per cent of LEAs and more positively by secondary schools (60 per cent) than by primary schools (40 per cent).
5 SATs were perceived as potentially having positive outcomes for equal opportunities by 60 per cent of LEAs, though 84 per cent of primary and 72 per cent of secondary school respondents gave more muted responses.

Table 10.1 Perceptions on the part of of LEA of the impact of educational and related social reforms (per cent)

	Very negative			Negative			Positive			Very positive		
	E	W	E&W	E	W	E&W	E	W	E&W	E	W	E&W
TVEI	—	—	—	2	—	2	38	67	40	60	33	58
GCSE	—	—	—	17	67	20	76	33	76	6	—	6
National Curriculum	6	—	5	13	33	15	82	67	81	4	—	4
SATs	12	—	11	37	33	37	57	67	58	—	—	—
Publication of exam results	—	—	—	34	67	38	51	33	50	2	—	2
OFSTED inspections	—	—	—	7	—	6	78	67	77	16	33	17
Increased power of parents	—	—	—	41	67	43	59	33	57	—	—	—
Parent governors	10	—	9	32	67	34	63	33	61	5	—	5
Governing body	16	—	15	48	67	49	43	—	40	—	33	2
Parent's charter	18	—	16	36	33	35	48	67	50	—	—	—
Teacher unions	6	—	6	6	—	6	72	67	72	21	33	22
LMS	13	—	12	60	67	61	23	33	23	—	—	—
Open enrolment	41	—	39	65	33	62	23	67	27	—	—	—
Opted out schools	13	—	12	59	100	61	—	—	—	—	—	—
Community charge	9	—	8	78	100	80	9	—	8	8	—	—
Council tax	—	—	—	86	100	88	5	—	4	—	—	—
GNVQ	—	—	—	26	33	27	66	67	66	—	—	7
N	49	3	52	49	3	52	49	3	52	49	3	52

E = England
W = Wales
E&W = England and Wales

Table 10.2 The perceived impact of curricular and educational reforms in primary schools (per cent)

	Very negative	Negative	Neutral	Positive	Very positive
SATs	1	3	84	11	—
National Curriculum	1	1	60	38	2
Equal opportunities as a cross-curricular theme	—	1	44	48	7
Levels of attainment	1	5	78	17	—
England and Wales *N*	390	390	390	390	390

Table 10.3 The perceived impact of curricular and educational reforms in secondary schools (per cent)

	Very negative	Negative	Neutral	Positive	Very positive
SATs	4	9	72	11	5
National Curriculum	1	4	36	54	6
Equal opportunities as a cross-curricular theme	1	1	35	56	7
Levels of attainment	2	9	68	19	2
GCSE	—	1	27	52	20
TVEI	—	—	14	56	31
CPVE	1	3	57	34	5
Work experience	—	1	21	43	35
Other (e.g. GNVQ)	7	7	7	43	37
England and Wales *N*	235	235	235	235	235

6 GNVQs had a mixed reception with only 27 per cent of LEAs seeing the new qualifications as having positive effects for equal opportunities.

7 LEAs also gave a mixed reception to examination tables, with 52 per cent claiming them to be positive and 47 per cent negative. OFSTED, in contrast, attracted mainly positive responses, although the case studies indicated a rather cooler response from schools.

Behind such largely positive responses to our surveys were complex scenarios. Here two headteachers of very different secondary schools commented:

The reforms have undoubtedly helped to put equality issues higher up the educational agenda, though certainly this has not been prioritized or anticipated by government measures. The inclusion of equal opportunities in OFSTED inspections and in TVEI has been bound to have an effect. Also schools have had more independence to explore chosen priorities and there has been much more media coverage of equal opportunities issues. These have created an atmosphere where equal entitlement to all aspects of the curriculum is expected, particularly girls' access to the sciences. Publication of exam results has focused on emergent patterns of achievement.

(North West community school)

Similarly the head of a mixed comprehensive in a traditional working-class area experiencing relatively high levels of unemployment and relatively low GCSE results who confirmed his deep political commitment to give all pupils a chance, commented:

> The educational reforms? ... It's an interesting conundrum ... but generally the reforms the Conservatives brought in terms of the ideas, I think we would support nearly all of them. However the implementation of them has been appalling ... the raw league tables say nothing about the value that has been added ... in terms of parents knowing our exam results, it is absolutely rubbish. . .
>
> (Shires secondary school)

Administration and organization of schools

The range of views on administration and organization of schools depended to a large extent on the context in which such reforms work and whether they are to be supported. The data revealed that:

1 The LEAs considered most of the administrative reforms of schooling to have largely negative consequences for equal opportunities and gender equality.
2 Open enrolment was seen as positive by only 27 per cent of LEAs (most were negative – 62 per cent); and all LEAs considered the effect of grant-maintained status to be negative for gender equality.
3 LMS was perceived by 77 per cent of LEAs as having predominantly negative effects on equal opportunities.
4 The role of trade unions in equal opportunities was seen as positive or very positive by a large majority of LEAs.
5 The effects of the imposition of community charges and the council tax on strategies to promote equal opportunities through LEAs were overwhelmingly considered to be negative or very negative, though this was not an issue of particular importance in the case studies.

CHANGING GENDER CULTURES OF SCHOOLS

Despite such negative connotations of organizational and administrative reforms, and perhaps in spite of the lack of support facilities – e.g. equal opportunities advisers, networks, finance, in-service training (INSET) equal opportunities courses – interviews with local authority officers, advisers and inspectors, and teachers and student in schools yield insights into the extent to which school cultures have changed.

Two themes in this section highlight current school priorities: management and school cultures, and matters of concern in relation to achievement.

Management and school cultures

One of the most worrying features to emerge from the research has been the evident continuing dominance of white male cultures in school and LEA hierarchies. A quote from a male headteacher usefully illustrates the perceptions of LEA management held by some as 'grey-suited men running the authority in a paternalistic rather than partnership sort of way' with 'blunt autocratic reputations' and with 'uncomfortable, defensive, dismissive, sceptical [and] hostile' responses to gender issues.

In fact, in the secondary school survey more than three-quarters of the secondary heads (and two-thirds of CTC principals) were male. In the primary school survey, slightly over half the primary school headteachers were male. The Welsh surveys had a higher proportion of male headteachers in both primary and secondary schools. While these findings may be viewed as skewed in favour of males, they constitute a movement away from a starker gender imbalance of headteachers in the early 1980s, in particular in the case of primary schools – although data for this period was frequently incomplete.

Significantly, it was also found that the gender balance of the current chairs of governing bodies also favours males. In 1993–4 in the case of both primary and secondary schools (and CTCs separately) the chairs of governing bodies are male in about three-quarters of the cases. (These data were not available for 1983–4.)

Similar patterns of high (white) male representation were also apparent at virtually every level of organization within the case-study LEAs and schools. In only one of the seven LEAs visited was there any satisfaction expressed about staff issues (in London LEA where there had been a long history of equal opportunities awareness and policy initiatives) with explanations commonly offered for the low level of interest in gender equality issues within LEAs, drawing attention to the lack of movement and over-representation of male staff in the senior management of schools and LEAs.

Apart from schools in the two LEAs with a strong and continuing tradition of equal opportunities policy-making and development which both had a presence of women at senior management level (although still a minority), the prevailing management culture across the other case-study areas appeared to be almost exclusively male and white. A typical mixed-sex secondary school might have, to quote an example from the case-study notes:

A senior Management Team [which] is largely male and white: head, two deputies (one male, one female), four senior teachers (male). Heads of Department are mainly men and pastoral posts have mainly gone to women (three out of five).

In a number of cases reported to the project, the white, male management culture has led to an ethos antithetical to women staff. For example, in a Shires primary school:

In a culture where staff are called 'Brains', 'Sergeants' and 'Ladies', women teachers felt uncomfortable and out of place. Many I [the researcher] spoke to were aware in a quiet way of gender issues but had failed to find opportunities to develop strategies in the school. They had come across issues in training or on INSET courses.... Few of the teachers had ... a chance to discuss this work in staff meetings. They did not feel 'listened' to generally and were aware therefore that gender issues were unlikely to be discussed either.

(Case-study notes)

It seemed that within such male management cultures, approaches to gender issues could be dealt with in a number of ways. They could be ignored, or, as one adviser described it in respect of a number of primary schools, equal opportunities became a 'twilight zone'. Or gender issues might be deemed irrelevant – for one largely male management team, the position taken was 'why make an issue of something that is not an issue?'. Yet in the same school, female staff had identified parental concern about boys becoming too effeminate; they were concerned themselves about girls not gaining sufficient access to the computer, girls' and boys' under-achievement in maths and English respectively and significantly, the lack of respect (and promotion prospects) accorded to female staff.

In other male school cultures, gender equality had become absorbed into the language and rhetoric of the school but had not made an impact on policy or ethos. Thus, for example, when required to provide an equal opportunities policy statement prior to an OFSTED visit, one headteacher asked the LEA for help in the form of 'drafted paragraphs'. In this case, he had little sense of how equal opportunities might be integrated into overall school policy or into the school's development plan.

Matters of concern in relation to achievement

There appears to be a clear trend of increasingly positive attitudes towards girls' schooling. In terms of gender differences in performance, 64 per cent of respondents from the secondary schools survey claimed to have noted that girls are increasingly out-performing boys at various assessment levels, a claim that also proved a major feature of the case studies. However, primary school respondents were not nearly so unequivocal with 49 per cent denying evidence of any gender difference and only 17 per cent reporting girls' higher achievement levels.

Evidence from the case studies suggests that parents also have changed perceptions of girls' educational opportunities. As a deputy head in a shire county put it:

You get very few parents who say it's not worth girls doing that [staying on] or girls going on in education, but the recession has helped that because lots of families are resting on the female income now.

(Case-study notes)

Such awareness of changing labour market patterns was reflected in comments from students. A personal and social education (PSE) female teacher noted the changing values in working-class communities as follows:

There is great awareness in the classroom of the breaking down of barriers, about what is a traditional girl's job or boy's job. Actually, if you ask the question, they will see no problem with girls wanting to be bricklayers or whatever. Whether that actually affects what happens in reality...

(Case-study notes)

Consequently, girls (from all social backgrounds) appear to see achievement at schools as of benefit to them in the labour market and in their future lives. Even in areas of high unemployment where stereotypical perceptions of male and female roles continue (as in areas of North East LEA) 'women are increasingly taking on both the childcare and working roles'. Thus, girls see a twin future of childcare and occupational opportunity, though eventual jobs are often in low-paid and low-status areas and they are well aware of the obstacles preventing them escaping from stereotypes. As a female student from a working-class background put it 'the boys have got stereotypes of women and women have got stereotypes of women. Men prefer women to wait on them hand and foot' (case-study notes).

The role of men within the family seems to be particularly problematic for some girls. For example, while the career aspirations of a group of 10-year-old girls in a Catholic junior school in an area of high unemployment, viz gymnast, lawyer, lifeguard, detective, lawyer, footballer and nurse, might be thought of as fantasy rather than to do with labour market reality, several challenged existing stereotypes and their view of the role of men in their future lives was instructive, to say the least. They suggested for instance that:

Men could be on drugs – [you] can't trust men to be there all the time. [You] can't trust men full-stop ... [They] don't see future lives as staying at home to look after children ... [They had] all sorts of ideas ... about how to look after children when working.

(Case-study notes)

Significantly, as the researcher noted, the girls seemed very practical and focused: 'very independent and unromantic/unsentimental'.

At secondary school age, girls seemed to be more motivated than many of the boys. As a headteacher put it: 'girls now have ambition and employers are beginning to see them as reliable and employable. Girls don't see any forbidden areas as in the past.'

There are also indications of an emerging generation of 'new' boys and girls, conscious and supportive of equality issues. Interviews with students suggest that while attitudes of many male (and to a lesser extent female) adolescents remain traditionally narrow and stereotyped, the new generation has a larger share of more confident girls and 'softer' boys. An illuminating instance of a new 'caring' male generation was a 17 year old (from London LEA), who in reflecting on the CTC's longer school day and its ethos, argued that the longer day might be dangerous for young students in the darker months of the year. He also expressed concern about the apparent down-grading of the 'softer' humanities in the CTC's avowedly commercial environment, suggesting that it would be detrimental to the curriculum balance offered by the school (although he, himself, was currently occupied with technological subjects).

This trend was confirmed by a secondary member of staff (in the same London LEA) who reported noticing that a group of 'softer boys' seemed to be emerging from the primary schools 'no doubt influenced by much of the equal opportunities that has gone on in the local borough'. And, in an LEA in a different part of England, the promotion of a 'caring, creative masculinity' was the concern of one head of a selective GM boys' school who was at pains to break through traditional sport-centred competitive masculine codes in his school.

Interviews with, and observations of, male and female students also emphasized their acceptance of the idea of the importance of women in the labour market, especially with endemic male unemployment in some parts of England and the formation of dual career families in other, more prosperous areas. As the researcher of Shires LEA noted: 'In secondary schools pupils seemed to be aware of the need for women to earn a living, especially in the context of economic recession'. However, she also noted that it was 'only a few girls though [who] were actively considering a range of non-traditional occupations (noticeably not often in engineering or industry) and seemed confident of success'.

Boys appeared to accept the need (or perhaps the inevitability of) 'working wives' although for most the issue of childcare remained vague and un-resolved. For girls, childcare appears to be becoming incorporated into a wider sense of possibilities and opportunities for them in the future, at least for the higher achievers.

Boys' achievement

A number of new areas of concern relating to equality issues emerged during the project. One of the most common has pointed to an apparent loss of motivation among working-class and black boys. It was claimed time and time again that as traditional areas of male employment have collapsed or altered, working-class (and/or black) male students now tend not to see themselves as benefiting academically or vocationally from schooling. They appear to be less motivated than girls, therefore, and more alienated from the classroom. Further, while working-class boys seem increasingly to stay on into the sixth form, they tend to study for vocational qualifications such as GNVQs (rather than A Levels).

In North East LEA, special schools placed particular emphasis on boys with language difficulties (boys are consistently over-represented in such schools) and secondary schools have attempted to tackle the fact that boys seem less able to cope with more informal systems of schooling – 'They [boys] can get on if someone stands over them but otherwise they are not as mature as girls and discipline problems arise ... Boys find it less easy to sustain a level of effort' (case-study notes).

In Midlands LEA, concern about boys' under-achievement, particularly in reading and language, has led to the requirement for a shift in practice from some teachers.

> The teachers ... who had a long involvement with equal opportunities issues were reluctant to devote too much to boys, because it will weigh against the still unresolved issues around girls' education. However, their action plan resulting from OFSTED inspection has highlighted the achieve-ment of boys as an area of concern. This appears to be less driven by equal opportunities issues as by the need to raise the overall performance of the school.
>
> (Case-study notes)

The under-achievement of white boys, in particular, was identified in the OFSTED inspection of a Midlands LEA comprehensive. In its response the school accepted that external factors led to under-achievement, such as local unemployment, though it also identified behavioural, disciplinary and aca-demic reasons. After some discussion the recommendation was:

> That we move away from looking at the under-achievement of boys, to looking at the disruptive behaviour of a small minority of mainly white boys which affects the achievement of the majority.
>
> (School discussion paper)

For middle-class areas and, in particular, for selective boys' schools, English (particularly literature) was perceived as the weak point in boys' curriculum profile. For example, in a Shires LEA boys' school, 70 per cent of whose pupils gained A–C grades at GCSE, only 30 per cent of the boys achieved such grades in English.

> The head put this pattern down to the failure of the examination boards to reward the particular forms of male creativity and literary styles. Course work too seemed to cause difficulties even to these boys. [However] by changing to a different examination syllabus with less course work, he

was able to bring the English Literature results in line with the pattern in other subjects.

(Case study notes)

A concern related to boys' general under-achievement has been the apparent over-representation of boys in disciplinary procedures and in exclusions. In Midlands LEA it was noted that disruptive behaviour primarily stemmed from a minority (though a significant number) of boys and that 'the concentration of the failure of poor white boys was potentially dangerous'. Similarly, from the records of a London LEA primary school over two years, the head noted that the proportion of boys relative to girls kept in at play-time for disciplinary reasons, was 90 per cent and 97 per cent respectively. He also expressed the view that girls tended to be punished more severely by teachers than boys for misdemeanours – 'it happens that a well-behaved girl is severely punished when she is a little less well-behaved'. Yet again, in a high school in Welsh LEA, exclusion numbers, particularly for boys, seemed to be on the increase – from seventeen boys and three girls for September 1993 to July 1994, to twenty-five boys and two girls for September 1994 to February 1995.

However, there also remain what have been termed 'unresolved problems' for girls: for example, the hidden curriculum still appears to produce girls with low self-esteem and confidence – 'girls creating themselves as boys want to see them'. And schoolgirl pregnancy and the general destabilization of families and communities, rarely mentioned in equal opportunities terms, were also identified as 'unresolved' issues.

NEW PRACTICES, PROJECTS AND INITIATIVES

Case-study visits revealed a range of initiatives and positive practices showing how issues are being taken forward into the new circumstances and conditions created by the reforms: at the level of the school and the LEA and with involvement of other bodies. In some cases, the values/social justice dimension of the first wave of equal opportunities (in the 1980s) and the 'standards' dimension of the second wave (post-1988) appear to have fused together to produce new forms of policy-making and innovation. For instance in the case of a CTC, past history and present structures have come together both to re-create policy and to aid recruitment:

The head of PSE carries responsibility for equal opportunities across the college. There was a long-standing equal opportunities group in the girls' school which continued its work after CTC status, then involving staff from the boys' school which had no such group. The 'mixed' group together with students updated the earlier policy and created the colourful equal opportunities poster which is very visible around the school and leaflet for the school brochure.

(Case-study notes)

Most of the initiatives being developed in schools and LEAs were not widely disseminated even within any one authority. Thus documentation on, and descriptions of, these initiatives were available only from the school or authority directly involved. In this section we describe some of the best examples of school creativity and action.

Personal and social education: gender module (Shires LEA)

One of the few places in the school curriculum where equality issues can legitimately be discussed is in the cross-curriculum area of personal and social education; a number of schools had developed supporting materials for this. Here, the school had developed a module which aimed to address equal opportunities and to 'offer differentiated tasks within Careers work in PSE'. The contents of the module included discussion of stereotyping, prejudice, sex-roles and 'acceptable gender occupations', and was principally designed to 'encourage students to think about their skills and interests when making career choices and to consider areas of work traditionally associated with the other sex'.

A variety of teaching and learning strategies were employed for the module including group work, brain-storming, debates and whole class discussion. 'Differentiation' or recognition of differences between pupils was acknowledged in

- inclusion of a wide range of teaching and learning styles
- degree of autonomy and choice for pupils
- supported self-study
- choice of presentations by pupils
- use of study guide.

To develop the materials, the school had allocated two teachers (part-time) who extensively research the range of resources on the topic before designing the module for the PSE curriculum.

Mixed comprehensive: strategies to address boys' under-achievement (Shires LEA)

This school, in a traditional working-class area and fairly low down the league tables (20 per cent gaining five or more GCSE A–C grades), perceived two main areas of under-achievement: working-class male students with little interest in academic subjects, and girls' lack of interest or achievement in science. There has clearly been a deep commitment from the whole school to equal opportunities, and among other strategies, 'all sorts of mechanisms' had been instituted to tackle boys' lower academic performance, particularly in English. These include:

1 Careful supervision of homework with teachers making thorough checks.
2 Senior management involvement in cases where homework has not been completed, with 'family work' reviews and the setting of attainable targets.
3 Review of students' test scores on entry to the school (at 11+) with the aim of raising teacher and parental expectation.
4 Development of language and reading skills through small group teaching and highly structured activities.
5 Experimentation with a variety of more effective teaching styles, for example, devoting more attention to differentiated work in the classroom.
6 Widening language activities for boys, for example, by encouraging them to join a travelling drama group or dance group, or to engage in public speaking.
7 Making the improvement of boys' performance levels in English a target for all staff involved including the English department, senior management or student-teachers.
8 Placing the emphasis in careers advice on students continuing their education post-16 and considering the possibility of non-stereotyped occupations.
9 Careful evaluation of students' progress at the English departmental annual review, and in the broader monitoring of staff patterns and students' achievement levels, and in the appraisal of teachers' performance in the classroom.

Governor training on equal opportunities (Welsh LEA)

The authority had been one of the first to develop a governor training module on equal opportunities. Through developing a 'pool' of school governors willing and able to deliver training, the authority was able to provide support for governors, not only on equal opportunities, but on other topics such as discipline and bullying, the National Curriculum, how to run meetings and salaries.

> Coming from a variety of backgrounds, each of them [the trainers] has in common a commitment to the education of our children and a belief in the value of governor training.
>
> (Extract from LEA brochure)

Praised by researchers from the local university for good practice and for the positive evaluation of participants, take-up for the module by governors nevertheless appeared to be quite low.

As the county equal opportunities adviser observed:

> The trouble with governor training is you can't impose it on them. Governors will ask you to lay on some training for them to do the INSET they need . . . but take-up varies.

Football for girls (Welsh Sports Council/Welsh LEA)

The equal opportunities dimension of sport has emerged as a feature of the project. In this initiative, ten primary schools in the county were involved with the Welsh Sports Council in extending football to girls. A primary school involved in this initiative employed a trainee teacher (female) to take twenty Year 5 girls for weekly football sessions.

> The ideas is to get girls using the playground space and joining the County's under-13 girls' league.
>
> (Student teacher)
>
> The boys get jealous 'cos we've got our own coach and she teaches us skills. They say 'can we be a girl today?' [giggles] . . . they won't let us play at dinner time though.
>
> (Year 5 girl in track suit)

CONCLUSIONS

Cultural, demographic and labour market changes have influenced the way students and teachers think about the schooling of girls and boys, such that most now consider girls' education to be equally important. High-scoring female students are proving attractive to schools in the competitive climate of the 1990s, and it is poorly behaved and low-achieving boys up to 16 who appear to be the subjects of greatest concern.

The research revealed a mixed picture of beneficial procedures and policies arising from some of the reforms, and pockets of thoughtful and knowledge-able practice from committed individuals and groups, but overall, no infra-structure for the delivery of equal opportunities on a wider and more systematic basis.

There remain wide areas of concern about the impact of social class and minority ethnic origins on male and female student achievement and the extent and depth of understanding and perception of gender issues in schools. If the shifts towards greater gender equality identified by the project are to continue, efforts need to be made to explore those issues which were not addressed by the project, to create a sound infrastructure for the delivery of equal educational opportunities and to build upon the commitment of the many involved in education to provide genuinely better opportunities for future generations of female and male citizens.

ACKNOWLEDGEMENTS

We are grateful to the Equal Opportunities Commission for funding the research. The report, *Educational Reforms and Gender Equality in Schools*, Research Discussion Series no. 17, is available from the EOC, Manchester. The views expressed in this article and in the original report are those of the authors and do not necessarily represent the views of the Commission. We would like to acknowledge the help of Ed Puttick, Liz Speed and Anne Madden on the report, and the support of the research team who conducted the case studies, Jackie Davies, Sally Mitchell and Jane Salisbury, and Jonathan Trotter who worked on the LEA and school surveys.

NOTE

1 The case studies were as follows: Shires LEA – large rural authority, pre-dominantly white, low level (*laissez-faire*) approach to EO involvement; North West LEA – urban, high minority ethnic population, declining population and high level of inner city disadvantage; Home Counties LEA – wealthy commuter belt, high achievement in school examinations, and history of entrepreneurial EO activities; Midlands LEA – mainly urban, concentrations of minority ethnic groups and strong record of EO involvement; North East LEA – mix of rural and urban, mainly white, past history of EO policy-making; London LEA – spanning inner and outer city, past history (when ILEA) of EO initiatives; Welsh LEA – urban and rural mix, some EO involvement.

Chapter 11

Feminist theories

L. Measor and P. J. Sikes

Feminism is not one theory but has many different perspectives within it. Feminism is usually divided into three main categories – liberal feminism, radical feminism and socialist feminism. However, in recent years psycho-analytic theories of feminism have become important and post-modernism is also beginning to develop an influence.

There are some similarities between all of the theories. What unites them is the emphasis they place on how central gender divisions are to the way a society works. Feminism starts from the position that the ways that women are treated are unfair and is based on a commitment to a political project – to developing strategies of change in order to create full rights and opportunities for women. It is important to note that the different perspectives not only are significant at a theoretical level, but also affect views of what should be done.

The issues which distinguish the different approaches from each other can be organized into three areas:

1 The causes of women's oppression, and the importance they give to 'patriarchy'.
2 The programme for change.
3 The ultimate goal for society.

PATRIARCHY

Partriarchy is a significant concept, with a central role in the disagreements between different feminist theories. There are differences between men and women in society, and it is important to look at the way these differences are ranked and to recognize that these differences make for powerful forms of inequality. This involves an examination of power and politics. In all the societies which have been reliably studied, males have more power and authority than females, and specifically they have power over females. The degree and the character of their power vary considerably and there is no universal pattern. Men and women are not just different, but are in a power relationship with each other. Some men can exercise more power than others, but partriarchy emphasizes the benefits that come to all men from the domestic labour and sexual subordination of women.

There is a great deal of controversy over what the term patriarchy means, but it is important to note that it implies a hierarchy of social relations and institutions through which men are able to dominate women, and also men who are younger or who have less power.

We need to try to establish the main points of each of the feminist theories, to clarify the ways in which they relate to established traditions of political thought, and to indicate the effect they have each had upon the study of education. We shall not deal with post-modernist feminism, for it has yet to have much influence on the feminist analysis of education, although post-modernism is beginning to have an effect more generally in the field of sociology of education (Ball 1990; Walkerdine 1984, for work on discourse in child-centred education theory; B. Davies 1989 and Calder, forthcoming, for a post-structuralist account of early years' education).

LIBERAL FEMINISM

Liberal feminism is based upon the political philosophy of liberalism. Liberalism starts from a belief in the rights of the individual as based essentially on the fact of the individual's humanity, but also on the individual's capacity for rationality. All individuals have rights to freedom and autonomy and to a voice in how they are governed. Liberal feminism appeals to the central principles of liberty, equality and fairness for all to justify women's rights.

Liberalism first emerged as a political force in the seventeenth century in Britain. The first feminist statements based on the philosophy were made a little later. In the *Vindication of the Rights of Women*, written in 1792, Mary Wollstonecraft argued that women have as much potential as men, but are stunted by being reared to fit an image of weakness and femininity, and degraded by having always to please men. Women need to be offered the same civil liberties and the same economic opportunities as men in order to develop their true potential.

John Stuart Mill in the nineteenth century developed these ideas further, arguing that equal rights for women are necessary to remedy the injustice done to them. Moreover, these rights are also essential to promote the whole moral and intellectual progress of humanity. Women's inequality is unfair, and must be remedied if the goals of liberalism are to be realized for the society as a whole.

What is to be done: the liberal feminist programme for change

Today liberal feminists emphasize the fact that all men and women should have equal rights and that any legal or social constraints that block the achievements and development of talented individuals from whatever gender, class or race should be abolished. Their programmes for change are set by their belief that individuals should have occupations and positions that are based on their ability and nothing else. Liberal feminists place reliance on legal remedies, and have taken up the cause of legal reform to ensure that women have equal opportunities with men. Women are urged to take up opportunities offered to them and to realize their full potential at work and in public as well as private life.

Criticisms of liberal feminism

Liberal feminists are criticized on much the same basis as liberalism itself, namely that they over-emphasized individual freedom at the expense of the needs of the community. There is a limit to what the individual can achieve and her/his rights must be reconciled with those of others in the community. Other feminists suggest that the view of the self as a rational autonomous individual which is at the heart of liberalism is in itself a very male view of the way people and society work.

Socialist feminists are critical of liberal feminism for its emphasis on formal legal rights and the provision of equal opportunities. They allege that this programme fails to tackle the problems of poverty and economic oppression which prevent women and other deprived groups from taking advantage of opportunities.

Other feminists, particularly black feminists, have suggested that liberal feminism is a middle-class white movement. They have claimed that it is little more than a self-improvement programme which encourages women to compete for top jobs and live by the same values as men. Instead of the sexy chick or the perfect homemaker we now have a new image to live up to: the liberated woman (E. Willis 1975: 170). The problem is that this is only relevant to an elite and ignores the difficulties of many women from disadvantaged groups in society.

Radical feminists argue that liberal feminism which views men as fellow victims of sex role conditioning fails to recognize the power men have over women in a patriarchal society. They also allege that liberal feminists want women to become more like men and that their goal for society is a system in which women can compete with men and behave like them.

Education and liberal feminism

Education has always been important for liberals, who are committed to the view that it replaces ignorance and prejudice by knowledge and enlightenment. They started from a belief that education allows the individual to attain self-fulfilment and develop their potential to the full. Wollstonecraft and Mill both emphasized the importance of education for the emancipation of women. Early liberals worked to establish provision of education for girls and their rights of access to educational institutions. Later the issue of developing a legal framework to ensure equality of access and equal opportunity in educational settings became important too.

Assessment and conclusions

It is important to note that much contemporary feminist thought defines itself in reaction to liberal feminism. More radical thinkers have been critical of its reform orientation, denying that any important change can be achieved under the existing political and social system. However, liberal ideas and values have been the basis for all central political and legal reforms achieved in the last hundred years, so their achievements should not be trivialized. Educational and legal reforms to increase women's professional and occupational rights are still not complete, there are still areas of discrimination, and not all the gains are yet secure. Liberal principles still have scope and power in the public mind to uphold feminist claims.

SOCIALIST FEMINISM

Socialist feminism is an umbrella term, and a number of different approaches are included in this category. The most important differences between them are the extent to which each accepts the principles of Marxism.

Marxism

The political philosophy of Marxism developed in the nineteenth century and grew from Marx's own experience and view of industrialization. The Marxist perspective argues that inequality is the result of the economic, social and political structures in which people live. Marx started from a 'materialist' idea of society, and from the concept of the 'mode of production'. The mode of production refers to two things: forces of production and the 'relations of production' – that is, the way in which production is organized by people. In western industrialized nations the system is capitalism, which is responsible for exploitation and inequality. Other economic systems produce different patterns of inequality.

This material 'base' of a society generates a 'superstructure'. The superstructure is the layer of legal, social and political agencies and institutions that have power in that society, and the social, political and legal ideas that dominate in the society. Education can be seen as an important agent in the superstructure.

Marxism and women

Marx has little to say that is specific to women; women's oppression is simply part of the inequality produced by the capitalist system. Other Marxists have looked at the role of the family in generating women's inequality in capitalist society. Engels (1884) suggested that as private property grew in importance the family changed its character, and women became more oppressed. The growth of capitalism meant an enormous growth in the significance of private property and succeeded in obliterating any equality that had existed in the human community.

What is to be done: the Marxist programme for change

In the Marxist view the working class, which is oppressed by capitalism, must make a revolution to liberate themselves. There is no possibility of reforming the system peacefully or gradually. Capitalism must be replaced with a socialist system in which the means of production belong to one and all. The oppression of women will disappear simultaneously, as it is part of class inequality.

Criticisms of Marxism

The Marxist analysis of society and history is highly controversial; in this chapter we consider only the feminist view of Marxism. A number of feminist groups have criticized Marxism for being 'gender blind', and for its 'silences' about the position of women and their subordination.

Socialist feminism and Marxism

Socialist feminists have tried to take account of this criticism while holding on to the basic insights that Marxism offers. They acknowledge the importance of material factors in the oppression of women, but do not see that living in a class society is the only source or even the primary source of women's oppression. Socialist feminism suggests that both patriarchy and capitalism have to be taken account of, and that both must be defeated.

What is to done: the socialist feminist programme for change

Socialist and Marxist feminists share a belief that only limited change can be achieved within the capitalist system. This is the main point of difference with liberal feminists. However, socialist feminists have pressed for change within the present system, concentrating on the issue of women's participation in the workforce, and on the state welfare support system which discriminates systematically against women.

Women's participation in the labour force is determined by the division of labour. Since the development of capitalism, they are not considered as being primarily engaged in productive, waged work outside the home. They do unpaid domestic labour, look after children, men and the old in our society, and hence reproduce the next generation of workers. The domestic work that women do is not seen as being as important as the work that men do outside the home, and this contributes to their subordinate status. One programme for action has been to suggest that the status of domestic labour could be improved if women were paid wages for housework (Dalla Costa and James 1972).

When women do enter waged work they tend to be poorly qualified and skilled because it is not seen as their main 'job'. This also contributes to their lack of status in society. Socialist feminists argue that women's position could be greatly enhanced by their achieving a greater degree of equality with men in the public sphere. They share this objective with the liberal feminists but not their optimism that change can be easily achieved by the passing of equal opportunities legislation and greater knowledge and awareness on the part of employers. Socialist feminists assume that the process of women gaining equality in the workplace will create conflict and will require a struggle.

The socialist feminist programme has tried to take account of the needs of disadvantaged groups in society. It recognizes that many women currently work in the lowest paid, unskilled jobs and that it is therefore essential to strengthen their unionization and press for better pay and conditions. Socialist feminism has also underlined the inadequacies and injustices of social welfare services. It is the most disadvantaged women who are dependent on these services and socialist feminists have campaigned for changes in the way they work.

Criticisms of socialist feminism

Liberal feminists have criticized socialist feminists for going too far in challenging a system which they believe does not need to be changed in any fundamental way but merely fine-tuned to redress a balance for women. Radical feminists have criticized socialist feminism for not going far enough. In their view socialist feminists continue to emphasize the significance of social structure and capitalism in the oppression of women and fail to give enough space to patriarchy. Radical feminists argue that if Marxism or socialism is to ensure the liberation of women it must further incorporate some understanding of patriarchy as an incredibly powerful and tenacious system which intersects with capitalism but is separate from it.

Radical feminists have also criticized socialist feminists for making the economic well-being and independence of women their main concern. Non-Marxist feminists believe that this is simplistic and that it misses out on a large area of women's oppression. They question whether a change in women's work and economic status is enough to change women's position in society.

Education and socialist feminism

Marxist and socialist feminists have looked critically at the role that education systems play in creating and justifying social inequalities. We will outline the arguments.

Reproduction of inequality through education

We have already discussed the fact that most sociologists recognize that schools are a sophisticated mechanism for selection. Marxist sociologists take the view that the main role of schooling is to transmit inequality between the generations. The selection procedures ensure that the class structure is reproduced from one generation to the next. In addition they ensure that the values that are necessary for the capitalist system to function are transmitted to children. Education in the Marxist view is an important agent in reproducing the capitalist system (Althusser 1971; Bowles and Gintis 1976).

Socialist feminists have drawn attention to the role that gender plays, arguing that schools reproduce both gender inequality and class inequality. They suggest that class and gender are connected to each other and so interwoven that it is theoretically difficult to draw them apart. Working-class girls are in a doubly disadvantaged position in schools; they undergo the same experience of class inequality as their male counterparts but they also receive messages about their subordination to men. The division of labour is a crucial factor in socialist feminists' thinking. They suggest that schools direct a range of messages about appropriate roles and activities to girls and thereby occupy a central place in reproducing the division of labour across the generations.

Winning consent

In recent years Marxist scholarship has moved away from a purely determinist position. Marxist sociologists have argued that schools do not simply force or coerce people into a subordinate role but rather manage to win consent for the allocation process (P. Willis 1977). In school everyone is seen to have had a fair chance and talented children do well and leave the others behind. In this way education convinces people that it is fair that they occupy the place to which they have been assigned.

Gender is involved here too. Socialist feminists suggest that schools play a part in gaining the consent of girls to their subordinate status and to their place in the domestic sphere. Schools are also involved in winning the consent of boys to a definition of masculinity which makes them primarily responsible for the economic support of the family.

Resistance

However, 'winning consent' is not a simple task, and it is not accomplished without struggle. One of the issues that is important for Marxists and socialist feminists is that children, and working-class children in particular, do not passively accept the socialization process that is happening to them in schools. They try to resist what is going on, which leads Marxists to a particular interest in the forms of rebellion and deviance that occur in schools. Socialist feminist research has shown that girls have different forms of rebellion and resistance from boys. Resistance seems to have different meanings for them, and a different significance for the process of reproduction of gender differentiation and class inequalities.

Marxist sociology has described the processes involved in producing and reinforcing social class inequality. The argument is therefore at first sight very different from the liberal feminist one, which sees education as a liberating agent and a force for good. However, socialist and Marxist feminism share this view of the potential that education has to benefit society and the individual; but they emphasize that the way it operates in our society prevents working-class children from receiving those benefits.

Assessment and conclusions

Socialist feminism and Marxist feminism have drawn our attention to the importance of social structure and class in the patterns of inequality in our society. While acknowledging that we need to know about gender discrimination in school, socialist feminists insist that we cannot fully understand the problem without taking account of the whole social context and the class system. They argue that the strategies of both liberal and radical feminists cannot in themselves achieve really significant change. This is because they cannot have any significant effect on the division of labour at the workplace or in the home. Only a wholesale change in the way capitalism operates can do that.

RADICAL FEMINISM

Radical feminism is a perspective which is still evolving and changing. Much of the writing of the 1970s and 1980s which originated from this section of the women's movement cannot be classified in terms of existing political theories. It is new and original and, as its name suggests, radical. There are two key ideas in radical feminism: first that patriarchy is of overarching importance, and second that the personal is political.

Radical feminism asserts that it is patriarchy that oppresses women and that their subordination stems from the social, economic and political dominance of men in society. It is men who have forced women into oppressed situations and functions. Women's domination is therefore the deepest and strongest form of inequality and the most difficult to eradicate.

In contrast to the socialist writers, radical feminists argue that patriarchy must override all other forms of inequality. Radical feminists point to the fact that women are oppressed by men and in a worse position than men whatever the economic and political system of society. They are critical of socialist feminists for the stress they place on class oppression. Radical feminists attack liberal feminism, on the other hand, for its failure to recognize the power of men, and for its assumption that those who have power will voluntarily give it up.

For radical feminists relationships between men and women are governed by patriarchy. Personal and sexual relationships reflect those power relationships, are tainted by the deep power imbalance, and therefore need to be changed. Sexuality has become a crucial issue for radical feminists, and they have emphasized that men aim to control women's sexuality. They have focused on different varieties of male sexual domination – pornography, prostitution, sexual harassment and violence against women – and have been prepared to fight politically against these issues and problems in our society.

Radical feminism has also been critical of the family, since it too is permeated by patriarchy. Greer (1981), for example, saw the nuclear family living isolated in its own individual home as a prison. There have been demands for the abolition of the nuclear family, and attempts made to create alternative communal structures.

Initially radical feminists were preoccupied with the enslaving aspects of women's biology and psychology, and were concerned to minimize differences between men and women: androgyny was the ideal. They accepted implicitly that traditional masculine pursuits were superior to traditional female ones like child-rearing and domestic work and consequently they rejected the traditional female role. This approach has been changing in recent years, with the development of the idea that a feminist revolution must mean more than women simply imitating men. This led to a re-evaluation of the traditional values of femininity and the talents of women. Radical feminists have come to view women's biology, especially their reproductive capacities and the nurturant personality that they believe derives from it, as a potential source of liberation for women. If men can adopt some of the characteristics that are now seen as female there is hope for change throughout society.

What is to be done: the radical feminist programme for change

In the radical feminist view, existing legal and political structures must be abolished to achieve women's emancipation. The programme is a radical one; social and cultural institutions need fundamental revision and the family is an especially important agency for the reform of personal lives.

However, individuals too must be prepared to make sweeping changes, as significant areas of personal life need to be restructured. Women will always be subordinate to men unless sexuality and the forms of sexual relations between the sexes are changed. Radical feminists therefore call for an end to patriarchal structures, but also insist that women must take more control over their own lives, and refuse to bow to the power of men. The most extreme radical feminists advocate a complete separation of the sexes. They believe that a complete commitment to feminism means becoming lesbian, and perhaps separatist. They engage in total non-co-operation with men, believing that only with their own institutions can women really find freedom.

This is a very different approach from liberal feminism where men are seen as fellow victims and each sex can be liberated by education, legal change and good will. It also stands in great contrast to socialist feminists, who wish men and women to fight together to bring change from a system that oppresses them both.

Some radical feminist writers feel that inequality between men and women is rooted basically in the nature of human reproductive biology. For most feminists this has meant demanding access to contraception and abortion as a basic right for women. Firestone (1979) went further. She argued that until there is some new technological way of reproducing the human species which frees women from pregnancy and childbirth, then women will not be able to be fully liberated.

Radical feminists do not see that it is possible to change social and political institutions by legislation and piecemeal reform, since men will not give up the power they have willingly or easily. Legislation cannot eradicate sexual inequality anyway. A transfer of power to the working class will not necessarily liberate women either. What is needed is a transfer of power from men to women. Radical feminists emphasize that this means that struggle is necessary to change the way society works. Patriarchy can never be reformed in the radical feminist view; instead it must be ripped out root and branch.

Criticisms of radical feminism

Radical feminist accounts emphasize the role of male power as universally important; radical feminists therefore fail to distinguish between various forms of male power, or between different classes and types of men, who have varying amounts of power. They ignore issues of 'race' and class, and the fact that not all men have equal ability to oppress all women. Moreover, radical feminists can tend towards an assumption that the female nature is all 'good' and that male nature is essentially bad. This means they see all men as victimizers who are by nature incapable of being anything other than exploitative.

Education and radical feminism

The radical feminists' account of education is concerned to analyse the way patriarchy spreads its web in schools, and has concentrated on the power relationships between boys and girls there. They suggest that boys dominate schools and classrooms and that this has a very negative effect on girls' chances of success at school. Boys are seen as a major source, although not the sole one, of the problems that girls have in school. The general argument is that boys dominate classrooms and take the lion's share of the teacher's attention. Their interests dominate the curriculum and leave girls out. Teachers have to concentrate on boys, and the way teachers treat girls in comparison with the boys works to lower the self-esteem of girls.

The other issues for radical feminists is that of sexual harassment. They argue that there is a good deal of sexual harassment of girls in school by both fellow pupils and male teachers. Mahony considers that 'Boys spend an enormous amount of time and energy in the social control of girls. A great deal of what is said by boys to girls constitutes verbal abuse and all girls suffer some form of harassment in school' (Mahony 1985: 53).

In this analysis, boys have the power to reduce girls' chances of success at school. Girls do not 'retire gracefully from academic competition', but rather are pushed out by being treated negatively by the boys. Boys behave as if girls as a category are laughable and may become even more so as they mature. This may go some way towards explaining the polarization and voluntary segregation of girls from boys which characterizes the late phase of schooling (Shaw 1980: 73). The suggestion is that girls withdraw from the danger zones in schools, where their presence simply invites abuse. The boys' sexism therefore shapes the image the girls have of their future lives.

Assessment and conclusions

Liberal and socialist feminists argue that if we look in detail at the daily working of the school classroom, then there are problems in substantiating the radical feminist analysis. There is great variety in the way that boys behave, and not all are confident enough to oppress girls (Connell 1989). Wolpe comments that we have very little research on the ordinary boy who goes through schooling doing minimal work but not domineering or sexually abusing or harassing girls (Wolpe 1989: 92). Research by Troyna and Hatcher (1992) documents the fact that there is also more resistance on the part of at least some girls to the boys' oppressive behaviour than is suggested in some of the feminist accounts (L. Davies 1984 gives many examples).

The radical feminist analysis has brought issues of reproduction, sexuality and children's socialization into the debate about women's rights. It has therefore enlarged the debate and moved it away from issues of work, status and public life, which both liberal and socialist feminists had dwelt upon. It has allowed a re-evaluation of femininity and the characteristics of empathy, caring and nurturing which are usually defined as feminine, and it has stressed the importance of the support and warmth that women can and do offer to each other.

PSYCHOANALYTIC FEMINISM

One of the important issues for psychoanalytic feminist is sexuality and particularly female sexuality. They start from an assertion that we live in a society which has many taboos on sexuality in general, but women's sexuality in particular. Through the process of gender socialization girls learn guilt and confusion about their sexual feelings, and this means their sexuality does not develop fully. In a sense girls' sexuality is taken away from them, they are dispossessed of it.

Psychoanalytic feminism asserts that the oppression of women affects their emotional life and sexuality as well as their place in the workforce and institutions of society. In this way psychoanalytic feminism is like radical feminism in that it draws our attention to private as opposed to public areas of life.

What is to be done: the psychoanalytic feminist programme for change

Psychoanalytic feminists find the roots of women's oppression embedded deep in the emotional psyche. Mitchell (1974), for example, emphasizes that in order for women to free themselves, an 'interior' revolution is necessary. This is not to deny the reality of social, economic and legal disadvantages which every woman faces, but it is to insist that 'she must do more than fight for her rights as a citizen, she must also probe the depths of her psyche' (Mitchell 1974). In a sense Mitchell sees women as colluding with men; they allow men to be dominant, therefore women need to challenge their own oppression. She acknowledges that this will be a difficult and painful process.

The other change that can affect future generations lies in child-rearing practices. Psychoanalytic feminists suggest that a number of changes in the child-rearing practices of modern society are advisable. Chodorow, in particular, is convinced that mothers dominate child-rearing and that this is the source of a great many problems in the emotional make-up of the individual, and has argued for more fathers to become deeply involved in childcare (Chodorow 1978).

Criticisms of psychoanalytic feminism

Other feminists criticize psychoanalytic feminism for underplaying the significance that economic, social and legal factors have for women's position in the family and society. This material oppression makes it very difficult for women to reflect critically on their individual and social position. Nevertheless, psychoanalytic feminism has the advantage of drawing our attention to the way that oppression is experienced by each individual, and to how it feels.

Education and psychoanalytic feminism

At first sight it may not seem that these theories have a great deal to do with what goes on inside the schools of the western industrial world, but they have been used to explain some of the processes at work there. The first issue is that of sexuality. Schools are involved in gender socialization, and therefore communicate messages about the nature of sexuality. If they do not do this 'officially', then at least the hidden curriculum has a role.

The second set of ideas that has direct relevance is of those that deal with gender identity. Psychoanalytic theories suggest that males and females use a set of symbols to signal gender identity. When boys come into contact with girls in mixed schools, it is likely that there will be a division between them according to interests, activities and aspirations. Boys and girls in schools will choose to do and be very different things from each other as a way of signalling that they are male or female. This may help us understand what happens in relation to curriculum choice, when boys choose the sciences and girls choose the arts and domestic sciences. Adolescence is the time when sex role differentiation is at its most intense, 'when pupils are consumed with a concern to establish themselves as feminine or masculine' (Measor 1984: 173). As Kelly puts it, 'Each sex when educated with the other is at puberty almost driven by developmental changes to use subject preference and where possible subject choice as a means of ascribing its sex role' (Kelly 1981: 102). The constant presence of the other sex creates pressure to maintain boundaries, distinctiveness and identity, in Shaw's view (1980). Subject choice and different activities in schools may be a very useful resource for adolescents at this stage in their lives.

Assessment and conclusions

Psychoanalytic feminism can therefore be seen as complementary to liberal and socialist feminist ideas and concerns. Where the latter emphasize the importance of social factors or the struggle for legal rights and equal access to public life, the psychoanalytic approach emphasizes internal and emotional issues, and indicates the sense in which women do have some power to bring about change.

MASCULINITIES

Since the mid-1980s, a new area of study of gender has been developing. A number of men, mostly starting from a Marxist perspective, have become interested in the study of 'masculinities'. They begin from a concern about the inequalities of power between men and women, and the injustices of patriarchy. Hearn (1987), for example, writes that men exact a human 'tithe' from women, which they take directly and without any recompense. He suggests that the main principle governing the lives of women is their pervasive powerlessness in relation to men, and he recognizes that this is expressed most clearly in the area of sexuality and sexual relationships.

Those researching masculinity are aware that social and economic change has created pressure for alterations in the way masculinity is defined. Factors like widespread unemployment and the decline of traditional industrial settings have had an effect, as has the growth of the welfare state, which has eroded the amount of power that men enjoyed within the family.

Writers on masculinity concentrate on the price that men have had to pay for the power they have. They lament the fact that 'The nurturing and gentler side of men has been obscured through the socialisation process' (Hearn 1987: 11). They consider that there is now an opportunity to change the power differential between men and women, and in the process for men to rediscover the 'shadow' side of their natures. However, this will not be an easy matter. Hearn draws up the balance sheet:

> The pessimism lies in men's remorseless and potential domination at almost all times and in almost all spheres. The optimism jumps out from the fact that men can be different, can be loving, sharing, caring and intimate.
>
> (Hearn 1987: xi)

Assessment and conclusions

The study of masculinities is an interesting new development, which has the advantage of presenting the meaning of masculinity from the 'inside'. At the moment the work is confined to a small audience, and has little chance to create widespread change. It is also the case that much of the fabric of the study of masculinities does seem to be built upon the work and the insights of feminism, and in a sense therefore is parasitic upon feminism.

CONCLUSIONS

There are major differences between the different feminist groups in their approach, understanding and goals for the future. However, there is much that is shared as well. In terms of education it is clear that, despite the differences and the difficulties, the feminist movement has succeeded in making girls 'visible' in the research on schools, for previously a great number of studies had researched only boys. The work that feminists have done has got the issue of discrimination against girls on to an official agenda and into the minds of teachers and education policy-makers.

It is possible to argue that the attempt to create distinct boundaries between the different categories of feminist thought and the different groups is artificial. It is difficult to place particular writers in categories and to put a label on them. McFadden (1984) has argued that dividing feminism up in this way is unhelpful. What we need is new categories which will allow for more open-endedness and fluidity, and which recognize the overlaps and the connections that exist between different groups and individuals. Tong concludes: 'All of these perspectives cannot be equally correct, but each have made a rich and lasting contribution to feminist thought, and feminist thought is still growing and changing' (Tong 1988: 237).

REFERENCES

Althusser, L. (1971) *Lenin and Philosophy*, London: New Left Books.

Ball, S. (1990) *Foucault in Schools*, London: Routledge.

Bowles, S. and Gintis, H. (1976) *Schooling in Capitalist America*, London: Routledge & Kegan Paul.

Calder, P. (forthcoming) 'Different discourses? Psychology and feminism at the interface: women, childcare and the training of childcare workers', *Gender and Education*

Chodorow, N. (1978) *The Reproduction of Mothering*, Los Angeles: University of California Press.

Connell, R. W. (1989) 'Cool guys, swots and wimps: the interplay of masculinity and education', *Oxford Review of Education* 15(3): 291–303.

Dalla Costa, M. and James, S. (1972) *The Power of Women and the Subversion of the Community*, Bristol: Falling Wall Press.

Davies, B. (1989) *Frogs and Snails and Feminist Tales: Pre-school Children and Gender*, Sydney: Allen & Unwin.

Davies, L. (1984) *Pupil Power, Deviance and Gender in School*, Lewes: Falmer.

Engels, F. (1884) *The Origin of the Family, Private Property and the State*, Moscow: Foreign Languages Publishing House.

Firestone, S. (1979) *The Dialectic of Sex*, London: Cape.

Greer, G. (1981) *The Female Eunuch*, London: Granada.

Hearn, G. (1987) *The Gender of Oppression*, Brighton: Harvester.

Kelly, A. (ed.) (1981) *The Missing Half*, Manchester: Manchester University Press.

McFadden, M. (1984) 'Anatomy of difference: towards a classification of feminist theory', *Women's Studies International Forum* 7(8): 495–504.

Mahony, P. (1985) *Schools for the Boys*, London: Hutchinson.

Measor, L. (1984) 'Gender and the sciences: pupils' gender-based conceptions of school subjects', in M. Hammersley and A. Hargreaves (eds) *Curriculum Practice*, Lewes: Falmer.

Mitchell, J. (1974) *Psychoanalysis and Feminism*, Harmondsworth: Penguin.

Shaw, J. (1980) 'Education and the individual: schooling for girls, or mixed schooling – a mixed blessing', in R. Deem (ed.) *Schooling for Women's Work*, London: Routledge & Kegan Paul.

Tong, R. (1988) *Feminist Thought: A Comprehensive Introduction*, London: Unwin Hyman.

Troyna, B. and Hatcher, R. (1992) *Racism in Children's Lives*, London: Routledge.

Walkerdine, V. (1984) 'Developmental psychology and the child-centred pedagogy: the insertion of Piaget into early education', in J. Henriques, W. Holloway, C. Urwin, C. Venn and V. Walkerdine, *Changing the Subject*, London: Macmillan.

Willis, E. (1975) 'The conservatism of *Ms.*', in Redstockings (eds) *Feminist Revolution*, New York: Random House.

Willis, P. (1977) *Learning to Labour*, Farnborough: Saxon House.

Wolpe, A. (1989) *Within School Walls*, London: Routledge.

Chapter 12

Boys will be boys?

Racism, sexuality and the construction of masculine identities among infant boys

P. Connolly

I think it is very important to describe the values of masculinity in the working class. It's a social fact like any other, but one that's badly understood by intellectuals. . . . It goes without saying that I don't present the lifestyle of the working class and its system of values as a model, an ideal . . . I try to explain the attachment to the values of masculinity, physical strength, by pointing out for example that it's characteristic of people who have little to fall back on except their labour power, and sometimes their fighting strength . . . the idea of masculinity is one of the last refuges of the identity of the dominated classes.

(Bourdieu 1993: 4)

There is no uniformity in the particular aspects of masculinity and physicality that are valued among working-class boys (Dollimore 1986; Brod 1987; Hearn and Morgan 1990; Segal 1990). Specific values will differ not just for White, Irish and Black boys,[1] but also in terms of how the discourses on 'race' gender, class and sexuality articulate for these boys in specific contexts. This chapter is concerned with the construction of masculine identities among a friendship group of 4-, 5- and 6-year-old boys, collectively named the 'Bad Boys'[2] (one African/Caribbean, two mixed-parentage[3] and one White). It aims primarily to address the way in which, as Bourdieu commented, masculinity is 'badly understood' by intellectuals. It is an attempt to shift the focus away from innate cultural and familial-based explanations of masculinity towards an explanation of masculinity as a response to broader social processes – a shift from 'blaming the victim' to problematizing 'society'. The chapter draws upon data from a much broader ethnographic study of a multi-ethnic inner-city primary school – a study concerned with examining the ways in which racialized and gendered cultural identities are formed among infant children.[4]

The African/Caribbean[5] boys considered in this chapter see themselves not just as working-class but also as Black. So these boys have more than their labour power to fall back on. Their masculine identities are also formed within the context of, and in resistance to, racism. However, racism and class relations are neither expressed nor experienced uniformly (P. Cohen 1987;

Donald and Rattansi 1992). In general, the African/Caribbean children in the school studied have very diverse biographies: they bring differing experiences to the school and respond to situations with differing knowledge bases and, accordingly, in differing ways (Fuller 1980; Gillborn 1990; Mac an Ghaill 1988; Mirza 1992). Moreover, the nature of relations within the school will largely depend on how various discourses articulate and manifest themselves in specific contexts. Nothing is predetermined. The boys discussed here are in no way representative of other African/Caribbean boys in the school. The aspects of masculinity that they valued, especially in relation to sexuality, differ markedly from the other Black boys. The main concern of this chapter is to examine the specific nature of their masculine identities and identify the way in which particular social processes have contributed to their construction. Rather than making any claims to be representative, the chapter therefore starts from the premise of diversity. It attempts to understand how discourses on racism, gender, sexuality and class articulate within specific contexts to inform the formation of masculine identities among the Bad Boys. Their focus on physical competence (at sports and fighting) and sexuality is not because they are Black[6] *per se* but because of the specific contexts and set of social relations in which they are located.

In focusing upon the complex nature of masculine identities and the variety of social processes that articulate in their construction for the Bad Boys, this chapter will also illustrate the active role that infant children themselves play in negotiating and forming social relationships. It will show the cognitive ability of children as young as 5 and 6 to make sense of and actively construct their own identities around a number of discourses on childhood, masculinity, racism and sexuality (James and Prout 1990; Chisholm *et al.* 1990; Wagg 1988).

In doing this, the chapter will draw out the contradictory nature of children's experiences of schooling and their responses to it. It will be shown how gendered and racialized identities are relatively fluid and contingent and, as a consequence, how the constructions of identities are only ever contradictory in their outcomes. In this sense, not only are the Bad Boys *Black* but also they are *boys*. Their construction of specific masculine identities in response to schooling and racism are, especially in their reliance upon particular discourses on gender and heterosexuality, never simply 'progressive' in their own right. As Walkerdine has argued:

The contradictions, the struggles for power, the shifting relations of power, all testify the necessity for an understanding of subjectivities not a unique subjectivity. These contradictions also point to the necessity to re-think our strategies for action within education. It shows too how resistance on the part of children is not necessarily progressive in and of itself, and that the consequences of resistance are, to say the least, contradictory.

(Walkerdine 1981: 24)

MANOR PARK ESTATE AND ANNE DEVLIN
COUNTY PRIMARY SCHOOL

The 'Bad Boys' all live on the Manor Park estate which provides the main catchment area for Anne Devlin County Primary School.[7] It is a distinctly working-class inner-city council estate located in the heart of an English city with high levels of unemployment and a high population of young children and single-parent families. Manor Park is composed of maisonettes and high-rise tower blocks separated from its immediate surroundings by four main dual-carriageways and with its own shopping precinct, neighbourhood and health centres and tenants' association. While there are high proportions of Black (mainly South Asian) people to be found in the immediate neighbourhoods, the estate itself is predominantly White with only 14 per cent South Asian and 8 per cent African/Caribbean.

Within this overall context Manor Park has gained a notoriety with the police and other professional agencies serving the area for being 'rough'. While such a reputation has, as with many others, been the product of various moral panics (S. Cohen 1972; Hall *et al.* 1978) and is not one particularly shared by the residents themselves, the estate does experience higher rates of crime (particularly burglary, theft and robbery) and higher levels of domestic violence compared with the county as a whole. The incidence of racist attacks is also relatively high and many of the (particularly Asian) parents are unable to use the local playgrounds and other facilities without fear of verbal abuse or attack – often by children from Anne Devlin Primary School. Such attacks could partly be related to contestations over territory amongst the White working-class youth on the estate (see P. Cohen 1987) and their perceptions of being one of the 'last posts' of White areas within a city 'dominated' by Black communities. This was certainly one of the underlying themes that emerged in discussions with the children and parents on the estate.

Five years old at the start of the school year, the Bad Boys had come to construct and negotiate their identities largely in the domestic environment of parent(s), older peers and friends living on the estate. The emphasis on Manor Park was one of survival and this provided the context for the creation of specific forms of working-class masculinity which emphasized its 'street-wise' nature and drew heavily upon various expressions of popular culture. Such cultural forms and identity played a large role in the Bad Boys' attempts to re-construct and re-negotiate their masculine identities within the more public arena of the school. It is here that the Boys, in being confronted with social relations on a much larger scale and more ethnically diverse than before, while also being the object of various discourses on racism and childhood, drew upon and introduced these wider working-class cultural forms in their responses.

The Anne Devlin is a relatively large school with 407 children on roll at the start of the 1992/93 academic year. It is more ethnically diverse than its catchment area with roughly half its children being White, one-quarter South

Asian and the other quarter African/Caribbean and mixed-parentage children in equal numbers. Each child on the estate is entitled to spend at least one term full-time in one of the school's three nursery classes before moving up to the Reception/Year 1 classes. There are four Reception/Year 1 classes (three of which formed the basis of my study). Children move up to these classes at the start of the term following their fifth birthday. At the start of the 1992/93 academic year each of the Reception/Year 1 classes began with a total of eighteen and nineteen children rising, by the summer term, to between twenty-four and twenty-seven.

RACISM, SCHOOLING AND BAD BOYS

The Bad Boys – Stephen (African/Caribbean), Jordan (mixed-parentage), Paul (mixed-parentage) and Daniel (White) – who provide the focus of this chapter were all in the same Reception/Year 1 class – Mrs Scott's class. They had all been there for two terms prior to the start of the academic year 1992/93 and were all 5 years old at the start of that academic year. For much of the time these four (or at least a combination of three of them) could he seen together, either sitting at the same table in the classroom (unless purposively split up by Mrs Scott) or outside in the playground playing football or other group games such as tick or wrestling.

The Bad Boys' experiences of schooling need to be located within the broader schooling experiences of African/Caribbean boys. In essence, it was one of greater surveillance, chastisement and disciplining from teaching and non-teaching staff compared to any other group within the school (Wright 1986; 1992a; 1992b; Mac an Ghaill 1988; Gillborn 1990). Such control was heavily dependent upon the specific contexts. Teachers were more likely to make important distinctions between African/Caribbean boys in terms of beliefs and actions in more relaxed, less stressful situations. This was also true in more one-to-one, private contexts (Connolly 1993). It was, in the more public, and often highly stressed context of classroom management, however, that these boys were more likely to share a relatively common experience of surveillance and control.

It was common practice in the school for staff in public situations such as in assemblies, the playground, dinner hall or classroom to 'single out' certain children quite publicly when order was being challenged. By directing their wrath at one or two individuals rather than the group as a whole and quite publicly chastising them, order was soon regained. It was in this context that the Bad Boys' more adverse experiences of schooling need to be located. For it was their 'visibility' as *African/Caribbean* children which meant that they were by far the most likely to be called to the front of assembly, excluded from the classroom and made to stand in the corridor, or ordered to stand by the wall in the playground.

The Bad Boys' increased 'visibility' to school staff, at times when staff are struggling to maintain order, is in part underwritten by the broader racializcd view of African/Caribbean boys being stubborn, aggressive and moody. The fact that they had formed a friendship group and were therefore more 'visible' as a *group* of African/Caribbean boys, increased their likelihood of being singled out by school staff relative to other African/Caribbean boys. This was certainly the case for Mrs Scott whose end of year school report[8] for Jordan commented on how:

> He persists in kicking and thumping other children despite the fact that he has been kept in at playtime frequently. He takes no notice at all ... colouring seems to have a calming effect on him. ... I must add that Jordan's stubbornness prevents him from doing as well as he could; today he refused to look at the alphabet on the wall when trying to write about his new baby. He can be *extremely* difficult to deal with [original emphasis].

Similarly, during a brief talk I had with Mrs Scott in the playground one morning she also had this to say about Paul's father, who was in prison:

> I shall imagine Paul's father is a big West Indian man, because Paul is quite big and the mother's blonde, and I can imagine, you know, perhaps have to be in maximum security if he's got a temper or some other thing.

These broader views of the Bad Boys were often reinforced in public situations. A typical example of this was in the following incident in the classroom where Mrs Scott, sitting at a table with Stephen, Daniel and two other children, was asking Stephen about his planned visit that evening to his father in prison. Interesting here is not only the public vilification of Jordan but also Stephen's contradictory identity as created by Mrs Scott; 'good' at one level but always within the shadow of being Black (with the potential this creates for a 'deviant' way of life):

Mrs Scott: So you might be visiting him tonight?
Stephen: [*nods*]
Mrs Scott: You're good. I don't think you'll be going to prison [*louder, some children in the class look up*]. You'll have to remember when you're a man not to fight, steal, throw bricks. [*pause*] In fact even when you're 10.
Daniel: Can you go to prison when you're 10?
Mrs Scott: Well not prison but you can certainly be taken away.
Daniel: Go to a naughty children's home eh?
Mrs Scott: Something like that – a young offenders' centre they call it, that's right; a young offenders' centre. [*She then looks over to Jordan on another table on the far side of the room who is busy with his head down, colouring in his picture and shouts over*] You'll have to remember that over there! [*Most of children in class stop what they are doing and look*

over to Jordan's table] If you kick and fight when you are over 10 you'll have to go to a special school – a young offenders' centre.

(For an explanation of typographical conventions used in transcribed dialogue see p. 186.)

PEER GROUP RELATIONS

It is this frequent public reinforcement of African/Caribbean boys as 'bad' that provides the specific context for the playground interaction with their peers and thus the basis within which their masculine identities are then constructed. These continuous public vilifications of African/Caribbean boys generally helped to create and reinforce a distinct reputation they had for being 'troublesome' within the school. For the Bad Boys, being seen as a *group* of African/Caribbean boys, this was a reputation much more marked. It was a reputation that created, for some of the White boys in the school, a number of responses. On the one hand, while the Bad Boys have obviously been set-apart and racialized by such processes, the White boys, in comparison to their almost universally derogatory views of the Asian boys, held a kind of grudging 'respect' for the Bad Boys. They were in their eyes, after all, obviously strong and defiant – why else were they attracting the wrath of the teachers so much? Moreover, they were also regarded as 'good at sport' and especially football – something that the school encouraged the boys to be involved in (Connolly 1994; see also Carrington 1983). The centre-stage, both visually and spatially, that the older African/Caribbean boys took in the playground at dinner time with their highly organized games of football, provided both distinct role-models for the younger boys and consolidating evidence, for the White boys, in their views.

On the other hand, such competent displays of masculinity were also the main source of feelings of insecurity and of threat for the White boys (Hewitt 1986; Back 1991). It was a 'threat' experienced more acutely in public situations and when African/Caribbean boys played together and were thus more 'visible'. The consequent need, among the White boys, to 'prove themselves' and re-assert their own 'macho' credentials provided the context for regular public contestations. Such contestations were at times particularly violent and would be set off for no particular reason. Not surprisingly, the Bad Boys were more likely than other African/Caribbean boys to be singled out and challenged by the White boys. These resultant contestations were witnessed periodically throughout the year, arising at certain conjunctures and within specific contexts and occurring often enough to become a significant experience in the lives of the Bad Boys (Daniel, by association, being implicated in this as much as the others).

On most occasions, however, these attacks and confrontations were sparked off by a complex mixture of factors. One main factor was group loyalty. Groups were constantly formed and re-formed in various contexts and, for the boys, most commonly around the factors of age, which classes they were in, and 'race'. Membership of a group demanded loyalty to other members and the ability to help and/or defend them at times of either verbal or physical conflict (Hewitt 1986). This construction of the group or 'gang' had important implications for a second main factor which influenced confrontations between boys and that was gender. Girls were treated as property that boys could lay claim over either by defining them as girlfriends or, more generally, by virtue of the girls being in their class. The fact that the Bad Boys could be seen playing kiss-chase and other games with girls from another class was interpreted by one particular gang of White boys, who were a year older and predominantly from that class, as a challenge to their status. Moreover, the fact that the Bad Boys were Black and the girls were all White appeared to exacerbate the situation and render conflict inevitable. This is illustrated in the following interview with Jason and Craig, two of the leading members of the White gang, who were telling me why they had attacked Daniel and Paul:

PC: [. . .] but tell me about before, you know Daniel and Paul
Jason: Ah yeah!
PC: From Mrs Scott's – what was all that about?
Jason: Erm, er, were you [*to Craig*] playing with us? [*Craig nods*] That means Mark, Nicky, me, Craig started it [. . .] we started it but/
Craig: /and, and, and we made a plan didn't we
[. . .]
PC: You started it – you started it with Daniel and Paul? Why?
Craig: It, it started when/
Jason: /Ah-a-a, I'm saying it, because erm, you know John, John was catching Christine
PC: Yeah
Jason: That's why we just done it
PC: John from Mrs Scott's class?
Jason: Yeah – they got Christine in *our* class
PC: Right, and you didn't like that?
Jason: No!
Craig: No!
PC: Why not?
Jason: [*to Craig*] You saying it not me now – I've said something
Craig: No, you, I didn't even do anything/
Jason: /Yes you did you said your gang had a plan did they?
Craig: The plan was to, erm, get John out of the way [. . .] with er just me right who made the plan up
[. . .]
PC: I don't understand if you were trying to get John then why were you fighting with Paul and Daniel?

Jason: But Paul and Daniel are on their side!
PC: Oh, right! So what were Paul and Daniel doing then?
Jason: Er, erm/
Craig: /Chasing after Jason's girlfriend!
Jason: Oye! Shush!
PC: Jason's girlfriend? Who's that?
Craig: Emma!
[. . .]
PC: Do you not like them chasing after Emma then?
Jason &
Craig: No!
[. . .]
PC: So do you think Emma likes to be chased by the boys?
[. . .]
Jason: I don't know!
PC: You don't know? So why did you try and stop John then if you don't know whether she liked/
Craig: /I, I was trying to stop him!

The sense of ownership of girls provided one key context for conflict between boys and for affirming classroom loyalties. But the fluid nature of such groupings became apparent as the confrontations which developed over the following few weeks became less class-based and distinctly racialized, drawing in other boys from different classes and differing ages into the conflict. At its peak there were between ten and fifteen boys involved split quite visually into two groups – one all-White and one predominantly African/ Caribbean. The highly physical and vicious nature of the fights ensured that a certain level of tension and resentment between the two groups remained and would flare up, on occasion, throughout the year.

Such attacks, both physical and verbal, against the Bad Boys were found to emanate not only from these specific groups of White boys but also from other infant children – both boys and girls – in their and the other Reception/Year 1 classes. John, for instance, was heard later on that year telling some of the girls in his class not to play with Stephen and Jordan because they're 'Bad Boys'.[9] Indeed this label of 'Bad Boys' that having been created by a combination of the teachers' tendency publicly to chastise the Bad Boys and other African/Caribbean boys more generally together with the presence, moreover, of racist discourses within and beyond the school, was now being taken up by significant numbers of the infant children to varying degrees in the classroom and playground. It created the classic self-fulfilling prophecy where the Bad Boys were forced into more fights and were then identified and publicly vilified by the teacher for being more aggressive (note Jordan's school report above). The boys were then set up with an even stronger 'masculine' identity which other boys within the school felt it necessary to challenge.

A similar process was also observed to be the case in the classroom where children would jump, without hesitation, to blame misdemeanours on the Bad Boys when they had not been involved. During story time one afternoon at the end of the day, for instance, when all the children were sitting on the carpet, one of the children near the back belched; Mrs Scott stopped reading, closed her book and asked in a stern voice who it was. Without hesitation, two girls sitting at the front offered Jordan's name as the culprit even though he was not at school that day.

RACISM, MASCULINITY AND RESISTANCE

It is within this overarching context of racism, manifest both in pupil–teacher and pupil–pupil interaction, that the construction and negotiation of the Bad Boys' masculine identities takes place. From the foregoing discussion it is not surprising to find that the first, and central, tenet of such an identity is associated with the ability to defend yourself and to fight back. This was particularly true for the Bad Boys who, more than other African/Caribbean boys in the school, were more frequently singled out and attacked. This tenet of their identity can be seen in the following discussion between Paul and Daniel following the first physical encounters with Jason and his gang over Christine and Emma. While there was obviously some exaggeration and bravado in the account, it does reflect quite accurately the physical nature of the confrontations described earlier and the way in which physical strength and the ability to 'look after yourself' are negotiated, constructed and re-constructed in the act of story-telling and recounting of incidents:

PC: You said when they came up to you to start with you were playing with some girls?
Paul: Yeah, I had some fighting but he [*Daniel*] didn't!
Daniel: Yes I did!
Paul: No you didn't!
Daniel: Jason pushed me in a puddle!
Paul: Yeah, what did you do? – nothing!
Daniel: No
Paul: So you didn't fight did you? – I did! Cos I got, erm, one of them over
Daniel: Yes I did fight! When I was running, I was going to kick them
Paul: But missed them didn't you?
Daniel: What?
Paul: Missed them!
Daniel: No I never!
Paul: Well I got, I got, I had two people over from me
PC: You had two what Paul? What did you say – you had two people what?
Paul: Down!

PC: Down?

Paul: Three! – Sean, Craig and Jason

Daniel: Yeah, I, I, you got Sean down by kicking him didn't ya?

Paul: No! He ran and I got my foot out so he tripped over

Daniel: Yeah and then he was going to kick you weren't he?

Paul: Yeah but he couldn't – he was running and trying to get me but [*gets up to rehearse the actions – Daniel also gets up*]/

Daniel: /But he missed didn't he?/

Paul: /I put my foot out and he went over!

[. . .]

Paul: Then I tripped Karl over, and I punched Jason down so he was, so he was down

Much obviously depends upon how such episodes are remembered and recounted. The contestation between Daniel and Paul both over the nature of the events and the status that rides with it was as much for my benefit as their own. Indeed, my role, as an adult providing an audience for such arguments, is a significant one. It is in these interviews, through the introduction of 'adult' ways of knowing, talking and acting that the Bad Boys could subvert their position as objects within specific discourses on childhood and gain a certain level of power. As will be seen, it is through the introduction of certain 'adult' themes that the boys know are 'taboo' for children of their age, such as those associated with violence, sexuality and 'cusses' (curses or swear words and/or phrases) that my authority, as an adult within the school, was challenged (Walkerdine 1981).

Interviews were therefore very popular with the children as an arena where past events could be re-constructed and re-told and 'adult' knowledge could be paraded and exchanged. The central role played by the acquisition of 'adult' knowledge for the construction of masculine identities generally is illustrated in the following transcript where, with myself temporarily absent from the room, a whole range of violent and sexualized cusses are exchanged and learnt. There was no animosity between the children but rather the context was one of a contest or verbal sparring match. Note the active role played by the peer group itself where such cusses are not simply handed down from older peers but are taken up, customized and re-used in an almost rhythmic manner, by the boys themselves in interaction with each other.

Stephen: Come on then you fuck-in bitch!

Jordan: Come on then!

Stephen: Come on sit down!

Jordan: Eh! Miss Williams! [*pointing to photo on wall*]

Stephen: You fucking Sappa!

Paul: Zappa!

Stephen: Sit in your seat! Quick!

Jordan: Oye! There he is!

Paul: Who?
Stephen: You're a fucking bastard!
Jordan: You fuckin' dick-head!
Stephen: You fuckin' dick! Bitch!
Jordan: Bitch! Ass-hole!
Paul: Arse-hole!
Jordan: Ass-hole! Bitch! Dick-head! Fuck off dick-head! Fuck off fucker!
Paul: Fucker! Fuckin' bastard bum-bum!
Stephen: Come on then you fucking bastard! Calling me fucking names!
Jordan: Yeah like/
Paul: /you bastard!
Jordan: Fucker! Dick-head!
Stephen: Lickin' your arse off, pussy-sucker! You White pussy-sucker!
Jordan: You Black/
Paul: /You're blind you Black/
Jordan: /You Black bastard!
Stephen: You White/
Jordan: Pussy! You smell pussy!
[*inaudible – Creole accent. Boys seem to be standing and playfighting*]
Jordan: Booofff! [*play-hits Stephen*]
Stephen: No don't – don't fight me! Paul sit down quick! Quick Paul!
Stephen: [*banging out beat on table making bass noise through lips*]

The general use and appropriation of cusses – especially the more complex ones – was heavily guarded. In this, Stephen appeared to be the expert. In one interview he recounted the following rhyme at a speed which was intentionally hardly audible to the other boys: 'Hey Pakistani, Let me see your fanny, Let me smell [*sniff sniff*] fuckin' Hell!' The distinctly gendered and racialized nature of this is a theme that will be covered shortly; for now, the significance lies in the way that Stephen spent much of the session listening to the other infant boys trying to guess the rhyme and telling them that they were wrong while refusing to repeat it.

More generally, this drawing upon, experimentation with and adaptation of various discourses on adulthood emphasizes the importance of popular culture. It is the representations of women and sex in the tradition of American films such as *Police Academy*, and its language which has permeated through to popular youth cultures more generally (i.e. 'pussy', 'bitch', 'ass-hole', 'pussy-sucker'), that provide specific cultural building blocks from which identities, through interaction, can be constructed. The Bad Boys however, are also able to draw upon, and interweave within this, a whole host of Black cultural themes such as the use of creole and particular styles of dress and music. They are themes that often draw upon African and Caribbean heritage, focus on racism and, as such, are heavily guarded more generally among African/Caribbean youth. The appropriation of these Black cultural forms is therefore more problematic for White and South Asian boys who, as a consequence, find such themes less accessible (see Hewitt 1986; Jones 1988).[10]

The use of these Black cultural themes was noticeable with Stephen for instance who, at the end of the above transcription, was beating out the rhythm to 'Jump! Jump!' on the table – a rap-song by Kriss Kross, a popular teenage duo of American Black boys. In other interviews, where just Stephen and Jordan were present, they sang this song right through together with the dance actions. Stephen also tried to teach Jordan a song from the movie *Boyz 'n' the Hood*. These cultural forms, in drawing from Black cultural themes to varying degrees, do offer the potential for resistance; one which is treated with a grudging respect by many of the other (White) peers (Hewitt 1986; Back 1991). The increased victimization of the Bad Boys relative to other African/Caribbean boys, and the particular subcultural responses generated between them, provided a fertile context within which such cultural forms were appropriated.

The ability to take up and use such Black cultural forms was, however, often contradictory and conditional. Daniel, the only White boy of the four, faced the most difficulty. While being keen to learn and use various cusses he rarely entered into verbal competition with the other boys. His almost passive acceptance of their 'prior claim' to use such Black cultural capital was quite observable through interaction (Hewitt 1986). For Jordan and Paul, being mixed-parentage meant that their access to and use of these Black cultural forms were no less precarious; their identity had to be worked on. In the context of (often racial) verbal sparring and insult-trading their light skin colour led to their identity as African/Caribbean being questioned and contested, as the following transcript illustrates:

PC: What about the girls in your classroom do you play with any of them?
All: No-oo! No.!
Daniel: Some are Indians!
PC: Are they? What, do you play with Indian girls then?
Stephen: NO-WAY!
Daniel: Jordan kisses um!
Jordan: No!! I'm West Indian!
Daniel: Eh??
Jordan: I'm West Indian – I'm English and I'm half-White ain't I?
Paul: Yeah but then if you say that – d'you know what? – you're an *Indian*!
Jordan: No! . . . Are you still my friend then?
Paul: Not if you talk like India! No – talking like an Indian!
Jordan: I bet I am!
Paul: If you do I'm not, we're not playin' with ya!
PC: Why's that Paul?? Don't you like/
Paul: /We don't like Indians!

PC: Why?
Paul: We don't like Indian talkers!
PC: Why?
Jordan: [*indignantly*] Well I ain't a Indian!

What the above transcript illustrates is the way in which such racist taunts are often highly gendered and also the contradictory and fluid nature of racial identities (P. Cohen 1987; 1992). This 'carving out' of a distinct identity by the 5- and 6-year-old boys, partly in terms of what they are not provides a significant context for the reproduction of various racist discourses. These are aimed almost exclusively at South Asian children in the school and are overwhelmingly clustered around notions of inferiority and disdain unlike the discourse within which African/Caribbean children are located. Such discourses are most likely to be found within distinctly public spaces within the school where identity and status are much more keenly displayed and guarded. Football, because of its high status amongst boys and its inevitably public nature, provided one of the key sites at Anne Devlin where racist discourses flourished and Asian children were systematically excluded (see Connolly 1994). For this chapter, however, we will focus on the discourse on sexuality and how it came to inform the Bad Boys' views of girls whilst also mediating relations between the sexes. What will be shown is not only the largely symbolic and public nature of boyfriend–girlfriend relationships but also the ways in which they form a central component of these 5- and 6-year-old boys' masculine identities and are, as a consequence, highly racialized.

KISS-CHASE, GIRLFRIENDS AND SEXUALIZED IDENTITIES

Certain derogatory and sexualized images of girls and women central to masculine discourses have already emerged above. The main arena through which sexuality most overtly manifests itself, however, is through the rituals of kiss-chase and the identification of boyfriends and girlfriends. Kiss-chase was a game consistently present in the playground throughout the year of the study. It involved both girls and boys encouraging and initiating the chases. A range of actions were observed to take place when a child had been caught. They might be let go, kissed, or, on occasions, a group of boys would hold girls down on the floor, or pin them against the school gates and sexually abuse them. This might involve groping them or simulating sex on top, or against them. These games were played equally by Black and White children. South Asian children were never observed being encouraged to play kiss-chase by other children – either boys or girls – in the playground during the whole year of observations.

Discourses on Black, particularly African/Caribbean, male sexuality have a long history in popular culture. They are discourses which are equally likely to articulate among infant children and inform peer group relations. The Bad Boys' reputation for being 'hard', and the way in which they were constituted as highly 'visible' subjects within such discourses, provided the context within which these discourses on Black male sexuality were more likely to become prominent. They were discourses manifest, most directly, in the greater attention that some of the infant girls paid to the Bad Boys compared to other boys. It was interesting to note that the (mainly White) girls in Mrs Scott's class, together with Emma and Nicky (the two girls at the heart of the fighting during the Autumn term), were more frequently observed encouraging and initiating kiss-chase games with the Bad Boys than with any others. Of course, the more the Boys were encouraged to play kiss-chase, the more they gained a reputation in this area. This was a process quite specific to the Bad Boys compared to other African/Caribbean boys, who were only ever tangentially involved, if at all, in such games.

These processes can be seen as providing one key aspect of a complex self-fulfilling prophecy within which the Bad Boys, specifically, constructed identities around notions of heterosexuality. The more they responded to the girls and engaged in games of kiss-chase and boyfriend–girlfriend relationships, the more they developed a reputation in this area. Moreover, notions of sexuality and the construction of sexualized identities among infant children was regarded as one of the most 'taboo' subjects for children as young as these. The appropriation of such discourses can be seen as constituting a powerful means to resist such dominant discourses on childhood on the one hand, and reinforcing a distinctly male and adult identity on the other. Thus the more the Bad Boys were encouraged into games of kiss-chase, the more cultural building blocks they had with which to construct a specific identity along these lines.

It was within this context that the Bad Boys constructed masculine identities which drew upon a range of discourses on heterosexuality as in 'kiss-chase' and the identification of 'girlfriends'. While boys and girls would often be seen playing together in the more personal and private spaces of the playground (by the walls, in the bushes, behind the benches), kiss-chase involved the use of large areas of playground space and was therefore, by definition, an essentially public activity. In this sense kiss-chase was another public parading and exhibition of status but it was also the only 'legitimate' arena within which the Bad Boys could play with girls so openly. As the following extract illustrates, a distinction was made between girlfriends and girls-as-friends for, while girls provided one crucial way in which masculinities can be forged, the girls themselves, outside of their roles as girlfriends, were treated with distaste and belittled. To have a girl as a friend would bring the Boys' masculine identities – so heavily guarded and carefully constructed – crumbling down. The following argument, between Stephen and Daniel concerning the ownership and control of girlfriends, illustrates the way in which, within such arguments, Daniel's attempts to associate Stephen with girls-as-friends can be seen as an insult:

PC: So Stephen, before, remember before break time when Nazia [*South Asian girl in his class*] wanted to look at your work and you wouldn't let her? Why didn't you let her have a look?

Stephen: I hate girls!

PC: You hate girls?

Stephen: Yeah!

[. . .]

Daniel: Why, well why do you chase girls then like ours?

Stephen: No I don't chase you lots of girlfriends!

Daniel: Yes you did!

Stephen: No I didn't!

Daniel: Yes you did!

Stephen: No I don't, no I never this morning!

Paul: No, last morning didn't you?

Stephen: Last morning? What last morning? What last morning? Yesterday – that was yesterday though – that was yesterday!

Paul: After dinner that thingy! Yes you do get a lot of girls!

Stephen: No I not, no I don't Paul!

Daniel: You do!

Paul: Why do you get Nicky and Emma then?

Stephen: No I don't – I only got 'em yesterday!

Paul: So why did, so why sometimes you chase your girlfriends so why, so you must like girls!

Stephen: [*angry*] So what if I've got a girlfriend! It doesn't mean I like girls does it?

Daniel: Yes it does!

Stephen: [*to PC*] Does it?

PC: Doesn't it?

Stephen: [*more subdued*] No it don't!

Within the context of these interviews where the arena is set for the re-interpreting, verbal jousting and construction of fantasy, discussions of girlfriends, sex and sexuality take on a specific form; especially with myself as a spectator to such contestations and an adult in a position of power over the children (Wolpe 1988; Walkerdine 1981). Sexuality, especially its emphasis on violence and power, manifested itself most frequently in the boys' conversations in terms of verbal abuse and insults (see also Willis 1977). Such themes of power and violence are also significantly evident in specific conversations about girlfriends. The following transcription illustrates both the knowledge that these 5- and 6-year-old boys have about sex as well as the symbolic power that kiss-chase has come to hold for them:

PC: I was just wondering what you've been playing in the playground recently?

Jordan: We're playing races, kiss-chase

PC: Kiss-chase? Who with?

Stephen: Kissy-cat!

PC: Kissy-cat?

Jordan: Yeah, when you catch somebody then you kiss them on the lips!

PC: Who've you played that with?

Stephen: Our girlfriends!

PC: Your girlfriends Stephen? Who's that?

Stephen: [*laughs*] I said it last time!

Jordan: Marcia!

Stephen: And Samantha!

[. . .]

PC: So what do you play with them?

Stephen: Kiss

PC: Kiss?

Stephen: Chase!

PC: Do you?

Stephen: And you have to kiss 'em and sex 'em!

Jordan: Ahh! No!

PC: And sex them? What does that mean?

Stephen: Arhh – I'm not saying that!

PC: You can tell me if you want to

Stephen: No way!

Jordan: Do you want me to tell him?

PC: Yeah you tell me what it means Jordan!

Stephen: I know – up and down!

Jordan: No! No! It means shagging and things!

PC: It means shagging? What do you mean by 'up and down' Stephen?

Jordan &

Stephen: [*loud laughter*]

Jordan: Stick in your fanny!

Stephen: Snogging!

PC: Stick in your fanny you said?

Stephen: Yeah he just said!

Jordan: He's well dirty!

Stephen: Not like you are!

The specific issue of power and the objectification of girls can be seen in the following conversation where the context provided by the interview setting of competitive and verbal sparring adds significantly to this process. Girls are situated within such a discourse as being emotionally dependent and possessive upon one boyfriend while the boys come to treat girls as little more than inanimate objects to 'sex' in a kind of production-line fashion:

PC: Which girls do you like to play with the best?
Paul: Nicky and Emma!
Daniel: And Emma!
Stephen: I like Natasha [*mixed-parentage*] and Marcia and Samantha. I like, I've got fourteen girlfriends!
Paul: Woo-woo!
Stephen: I've got a hundred girlfriends!
Daniel: If you've got one you can't have no more!
Stephen: Yeah!
Daniel: Your girlfriend will tell you off!
Stephen: No!
Daniel: Yeah!
Stephen: No!
Paul: How you going to sex 'em then?
Stephen: I'll put all of them on top of each other and when I've done one – put her over there, then when done another one put her over there, then another one put her over there, then over there, and over there and over there
Paul: I've got, I've got a million!
Stephen: I've got four hundred and eighty-two!
[. . .]
PC: Stephen, when you say you've done one what do you mean when you say you've done one?
Paul: Sexy baby!
Daniel: He throws it over and then he puts, then he has another one then he picks her up throws her over and has another one

Contradictions emerged later in this conversation where all the boys accept that girls can also have a hundred boyfriends. While wider discourses on power are deeply engrained, it would seem that, in the realms of fantasy and the telling of stories, there is a certain inherent logic which opens up a significant array of contradictions and spaces for the introduction of altern-ative stories and understandings (Billig *et al.* 1988). The overwhelming message from these discussions, however, is one of power, violence and domination (see also Mahoney 1989). This can be seen in the following extract where I asked the other three boys where Jordan was that day:

PC: Where's Jordan today?
Stephen: He's at home boiling his head off!
Paul: No! Kissing his girlfriend!
PC: Kissing his girlfriend? Who's his girlfriend?
Stephen: He's waiting at his girlfriend's house
PC: Is he? Who's?
Paul: Yeah, waiting for her
Stephen: And when she comes in, he's hiding right, and when she comes in

he's going to grab her and take her upstairs and then she's going to start
screaming and he's going to kiss her . . . and sex her!

PC: And sex her? And why's she going to be screaming?

Stephen: Because she hates it!

PC: Because she hates it?

Stephen: Yeah!

PC: So if she hates it why does he do it?

Stephen: I don't know!

Paul: Because he loves her!

Stephen: He'll sing 'I want to sex you up!'

This creation of a distinctly uneven and disturbing power-relationship with
girlfriends seems, to a certain extent, to be symbolic of the actual relationships
that the boys had with their 'girlfriends'. Paul and Daniel, especially, could
be observed fairly frequently in the playground physically abusing Emma
and Nicky; pushing them over, swinging them round and kicking them.

GIRLFRIENDS, RACISM AND SEXUALITY

Discourses on girls, girlfriends and sexuality are highly racialized, as
illustrated in some of the transcripts reproduced earlier. Having a girlfriend is a particularly public affair and thus to be associated with an Asian
girlfriend is definitely a term of abuse. This is illustrated in the extract
below where the conversation is preceded by a general argument about
whose girlfriend is whose. Annette (mixed-parentage) occupies a contradictory position; on the one hand, she is the only girl in the class who is
treated by the Bad Boys as a member of their group and whose physical
and sporting prowess is acknowledged. On the other, this distinctly
masculine identity renders her less attractive and desirable as a girlfriend:

Paul: Annette does love you! Annette does go out with you!

Stephen: I bet! Is that why . . . Alright then, if Annette goes out with me
then Nazia goes out with Daniel!

Paul: You have two girlfriends – Nazia, Kelly [*mixed-parentage*] and her,
Annette.

Stephen: And I know, and I know you go out with Rupal, Rakhee and [*saying
last name slowly and pulling face*] Neelam!

[. . .]

Daniel: You've got a Paki girlfriend!

Stephen: Who?

Daniel: That one there with that dot! [*on another poster*]

Paul: [*laughs*]

[. . .]

Stephen: You go out with Neelam!

Daniel: And so do you!

Stephen: You go out with all the girls in our class!

Daniel: You go out with all the Pakis! [*laughs*]

Stephen: I said you go out with everyone in the whole world mate!

Daniel: So do you [*laughs*]!

Stephen: How can you say I do when I've already said you do?

Daniel: You do!

Stephen: You do!

Daniel: You go out with all of the Pakis, I go out with all the Whites [*laughs*]

Stephen: You go out with all of the Pakis! Because I, do I look like a Paki
   though – you do! You go the Mosque mate where all the Pakis go!

[*general laughs*]

When pressed to justify their derogatory views of Asian girls, the boys not
only illustrate their cognitive ability to reason at a relatively sophisticated
level but also, as a consequence, raise a whole host of contradictions:

Daniel: [*laughs*] And do you know what? He's [*Paul*] got a girlfriend in that
   class! [. . .] – Nadia! [*laughs*]

Paul: No I haven't – he's lying! I ain't got a girlfriend anyway!

PC: Who's Nadia?

Daniel: A PAKI!

[. . .]

PC: Do you, do you like/

Paul: /Indians!

PC: Indians?

Daniel: No!

PC: Why?

Paul: [*to Daniel*] Why you say it then?

Daniel: Because they're brown!

PC: They're brown? You don't like them because they're brown?

Daniel: Yes

[. . .]

PC: What are you Paul?

Paul: Brown

PC: So you like Paul don't you Daniel?

Daniel: Yeah 'cause he's in our class!

PC: He's brown!

Daniel: Only people in our class!

PC: So Prajay is in your class – do you like Prajay?

Daniel: Yeah!

Stephen: He's an Indian! And you like him?

PC: And you like Neelam and Rakhee?

Daniel: Yeah

The contradictions inherent within the above as lines of friendship are drawn
and re-drawn around differing boundaries – gender, 'race', their own class-

loyalty – can be seen as can the spaces created for work to be done in challenging and offering alternative perspectives with which the children can make sense of their world. This contradiction is apparent within the Bad Boys' racial discourses on Asian girls where, in opposition to the distinctly non-sexual and derisive view of Asian girls outlined above, there exists a parallel discourse which raises the supposed exotic, unknown and threatening sexuality of Asian girls. The following extract, from an interview with three White boys, illustrates both of these themes:

Dean: He don't know what I mean, he don't know what I mean, he talks English
Jason: English, I'm talking English now!
Dean: Yeah like Paki [*laughs*]
Jason: You talk French!
Dean: You talk like Paki language [*laughs*] you talk . . .
PC: What's that language?
Jason: You talk French
Dean: When you got a girlfriend, no way you want to play with them [*Asian*] girls, right, they might, you might, you might, you might [*in soft voice*] 'come on baby want to suck you off'
PC: You want to what?
Dean: Nnaaahhh not . . .
PC: What girls are those? What do you mean by them girls?
Jason: Downstairs
Dean: In our class/
Jason: Like Reema
[*laughs*]
PC: You don't want to play with those then?
Dean: No
PC: Why?
Dean: She's a Paki!

This is a contradiction, to a more coded, and less frequent extent, reproduced by the Bad Boys in this study. In the following extract, Asian girls are characterized as tigers who are unpredictable and dangerous as girlfriends:
Daniel: I don't like 'um [*Asian girls*]
PC: Why don't you like 'em?
Daniel: Because they're Tigers! [*laughs*]
PC: They're Tigers?
Daniel: Yeah! They've got a mask on their face like a Tiger!
Paul: Daniel, if there, if you go with one of them – you know what will happen, you know what, what they'll do?
Daniel: What?
Paul: Bite ya!

Stephen: Eat you!
Daniel: Bite your bum off!

African/Caribbean girls are also subjects of such discourses on sexuality and desirability but in a more 'positive' and sexual manner:

Stephen: I'd just go to my Black girlfriends!
PC: Your Black girlfriends?
Stephen: Yeah [. . .] And do you know why I like 'em?
PC: Why?
Stephen: Because they're sexy!
PC: Because they're sexy?
Jordan: No dirty words today!
PC: Well you can if you want! Who's, who's sexy then?
Stephen: My girlfriend
PC: Your girlfriend?
Jordan: Yeah and my girlfriend!
PC: Why are they sexy?
Jordan: 'Cos, erm, 'cos they're shiny!
[. . .]
PC: So who's, who's shiny then? Jordan?
Jordan: Erm Marcia
Stephen: My girlfriend – especially my girlfriend!
PC: Why especially your girlfriend?
Stephen: 'Cos my girlfriend puts too much cream on her
Jordan: Mine, er, mine just puts some cocoa-butter on and she puts some cocoa-butter on
PC: What Samantha [*who's White*] put some cocoa-butter on?
Jordan: Yeah
Stephen: Yeah but she don't even know what cocoa-butter is – she asks her mum what cocoa-butter is
PC: What Samantha does?
Stephen: Yeah she goes: 'mum, what's cocoa butter?'
PC: What else makes them sexy then?
Jordan: [*inaudible first two words*] skirts
Stephen: Skirts – we have to pull down their knickers!
PC: You pull down their knickers?
Stephen: Yeah to see them sexy! Init Jordan?
Jordan: [*giggles*] No! I don't!
[. . .]
Stephen: [*singing/chanting*] And I wanna kiss my girlfriend, and I wanna love my girlfriend, and I wanna sex my girlfriend, and I wanna snog my girlfriend!
Jordan: Don't Stephen!

IDENTITIES OF RESISTANCE: SOME
CONCLUDING REMARKS

This chapter makes no claims to be representative. Indeed, the Bad Boys were unique among other African/Caribbean infant boys in the school in relation to their appropriation and combination of physical and sexual themes in the construction of their identities. The main concern of this chapter has been to examine how and why various discourses on 'race', sexuality, childhood and gender articulated in the specific ways that they did for the Bad Boys. It was their presence in the school as a *group* of African/Caribbean boys that was central in increasing their 'visibility' and subjecting them to a number of racist discourses. These discourses operated in a complex manner and, through their articulation with other discourses, helped to create a complex set of social processes whereby the Bad Boys were constituted as aggressive, hard and sexual.

The Bad Boys were far from passive subjects within such discourses, however. This chapter has highlighted, more generally, the active role that children as young as 5 play in the construction and negotiation of their identities. It has illustrated the relative sophistication of the children's understandings of issues of racism, gender and sexuality at that age and, moreover, the cognitive ability they have in terms of being able to draw upon and reframe such discourses in the course of trying to make sense of their own experiences. However, as also highlighted, such views are given with contradictions and are inherently fluid. In this sense the chapter not only has highlighted the need to do anti-racist and anti-sexist work with young children but also has pointed towards some of the spaces – within the contradictions of the children's own perceptions and narratives – where such work could be done (see also Carrington and Short 1989; 1992; Troyna and Hatcher 1992; Thorne 1993).

Furthermore, the chapter has, within this, drawn attention to the complex nature of masculine identities and the variety of processes that articulate in their construction and negotiation. Above all it has argued for the need to locate the forging of Black masculinities within the specific contexts provided by racism (see also Westwood 1990). It is here where the ongoing debates surrounding African/Carribean boys and their 'under-achievement' [*sic*] should be located. What the chapter has shown is not only the central role of the school and its teaching staff in the labelling of African/Caribbean boys as 'bad' and the consequent self-fulfilling prophecy that results (see, for instance, Wright 1986; 1992a; 1992b; Mac an Ghaill 1988; Gillborn 1990) but also the importance, within this, of peer-relations and their role in the creation of specific masculine identities among some African/Caribbean boys as young as 5. Significantly one of the teachers in this study had complained despairingly to me that she had read all the research regarding African/Caribbean boys and the self-fulfilling prophecy and was ever-mindful of that in her own work and yet, unfortunately, found that all the African/Caribbean boys in her (Reception/Year 1) class were already 'aggressive' and/or exhibiting 'behavioural problems'. This, more than anything, emphasizes the need to develop a more comprehensive understanding of the schooling experiences of Black children, one which incorporates the active role of peer group relations with that of student–teacher interaction (see Connolly 1993).[11]

Finally this chapter has drawn out the contradictory nature of children's responses to schooling. In this sense the Bad Boys' forging of masculine identities of resistance, while needing to be located quite specifically within the context of racism and the school, also needs to be understood in terms of its highly gendered and sexualized nature. The Bad Boys are not only *Black* but also are *boys* and *children*. They therefore occupy a number of subject positions. Their use and adaptation of Black cultural forms and a 'hard', street-wise image in response to racism forms only one facet of their identity. It is also their use of and experimentation with adult ways of knowing, in response to the discourses on childhood manifest within the school, that plays a significant part in the formation of their masculine identities. Whilst the adoption of Black cultural forms and a street-wise image represents attempts at being an 'adult', it is apparent from the above that it is not so much that the Bad Boys are experimenting with being 'adults' generally but with being 'men' more specifically. Their introduction of adult themes are therefore highly gendered and draw upon an array of representations and meanings that tend to provide the backdrop to boy–girl relationships.

The status of the data reproduced above obviously needs to be borne in mind. The transcripts are not simply a clear representation of 'reality' but of boys, in a specific context, taking up, experimenting with, and adapting a variety of discourses on adulthood. The use and adoption of such identities varied from one context to the next. Consequently, their masculine identities emphasized above were specific to the interview context. They structured interaction in the classroom and playground only ever partially and complexly and represented more of an ideal-typical fantasy picture of masculinity for the boys rather than what was conveyed day-to-day through interaction with others. Nevertheless, such discourses are powerful and emphasize the contradictory nature of children's responses to schooling and the need to be more critical in understanding resistance on the part of children rather than simply assigning it as 'progressive' and celebrating it in its own right (Walkerdine 1981).

KEY TO TRANSCRIPTIONS

/ indicates interruption in speech
[. . .] indicates extracts edited out of transcript
[*text*] indicates descriptive text added by myself to clarify/highlight the nature of the discussion
. . . indicates a pause

ACKNOWLEDGEMENTS

The above data are drawn from my broader doctoral research funded by an ESRC Postgraduate Training Award. I should like to thank my supervisor, Sallie Westwood, and Janet Holland, Maud Blair, Karen Winter, Cecile Wright and Steve Wagg for their insightful comments and guidance on earlier drafts of this chapter.

NOTES

1 'Black' here is used as a political term to denote those of African/Caribbean and South Asian heritage. While I am mindful of the fact that such a term is essentially socially constructed and is inclusive of a range of people whose identities appear to be becoming increasingly fractured and diverse (see Rattansi 1992; P. Cohen 1987; 1992) there is a space where a qualified use of the term 'Black' is still appropriate in relation to the general marginalization, alienation and conditional citizenship that South Asian and African/Caribbean people experience.

2 This was a name used by the boys themselves during one interview where, in complaining about the way in which the teachers and their peers label them as poorly behaved and 'bad' (see also note 8), they significantly reverse the meaning of the term ('bad' now meaning 'good') as in broader Black cultural forms (Hewitt 1986), and reclaim it for themselves.

3 Unless stated otherwise, mixed-parentage refers to those children who have a White mother and African/Caribbean father.

4 The data reproduced below form part of a much broader ethnographic study of a multi-ethnic, inner-city primary school where I spent a full academic year focusing on the school's three parallel, vertically grouped Reception/Year 1 classes (Connolly 199). Methods included participant observation, semi-structured interviews with all teaching and non-teaching staff and a series of group interviews with the children. The data drawn on for this study derive from ten interviews held with two or more of the 'Bad Boys' – in various combinations – over the whole of the academic year. Three other interviews with differing groups of White boys from two Year 2 infant classes are also drawn upon. These interviews varied from ten to fifty minutes in duration and were held in a separate room within the school away from other children and teachers and were distinctly non-directive, with the children being given the space and opportunity to discuss whatever they felt to be relevant and/or significant with the assurance of total confidentiality.

5 In this chapter 'African/Caribbean' includes those children of mixed parentage (see note 3 above) unless stated differently. While their specific racial identity is significant in certain contexts, in many respects mixed-parentage children do occupy similar subject positions to African/Caribbeans within the school with regards to the prevalent racist discourses which emphasize the aggressive, sporting and sexual nature [sic] of such boys.

6 See Willis (1977), for instance, and the way in which the 'Lads' in his study – a group of White, working-class adolescents – greatly valued notions of aggression and sexuality.

7 All names of places and people in this study have been altered to maintain confidentiality.

8 I have drawn upon not only reports written for, and sent home to, the parents for each child, but also their 'internal' reports, which are kept in the child's individual

file at the school and are mainly for internal consumption. As such, many of the teachers admitted that they felt they could be more truthful in these than in the ones written for parents.

9 Indeed it was when this was discussed with the Bad Boys during one interview that they adopted and inverted the term 'bad' to describe themselves.

10 Again it needs to be stressed that these boys have agency and that nothing is predetermined. Indeed the appearance of Apache Indian, a South Asian male rap artist, is a case in point. The issue is, however, that for such a man the ability and effort it takes to construct and maintain such an identity will be much greater than for an African/Caribbean.

11 Maybe this is where Foster's (1990) work could have been more fruitfully focused. His research claimed that there were no instances of racism in the sample school he studied, whilst also explaining away the differing social and educational experiences of African/Caribbean boys in his study in terms of their possibly higher levels of aggressiveness and/or lower educational ability within that year (see also Connolly 1992). His measure of 'racism' was, not surprisingly, focused almost entirely upon the role of teachers and their detrimental treatment of Black students.

REFERENCES

Back, L. (1991) 'Social context and racist name calling: an ethnographic perspective on racist talk within a south London adolescent community', *European Journal of Intercultural Studies* 1 (3): 19–38.

Billig, M., Condor, S., Edwards, D., Gane, M., Middleton, D. and Radley, A. (1988) *Ideological Dilemmas: A Social Psychology of Everyday Thinking*, London: Sage.

Bourdieu, P. (1993) *Sociology in Question*, London: Sage.

Brod, H. (ed.) (1987) *The Making of Masculinities: The New Men's Studies*, London: Allen & Unwin.

Carrington, B. (1983) 'Sport as a side-track: an analysis of West Indian involvement in extra-curricular sport', in L. Barton and S. Walker (eds) *Race, Class and Education*, London: Croom Helm.

Carrington, B. and Short, G. (1989) *'Race' and the Primary School: Theory into Practice*, Windsor: NFER-Nelson.

—— (1992) 'Researching "race" in the "all-White" primary school: the ethics of curriculum development', in M. Leicester and M. Taylor (eds) *Ethics, Ethnicity and Education*, London: Kogan Page.

Chisholm, L., Buchner, P., Kruger, H. and Brown, P. (eds) (1990) *Childhood, Youth and Social Change: A Comparative Perspective*, London: Falmer.

Cohen, P. (1987) 'The perversions of inheritance: studies in the making of multi-racist Britain', in P. Cohen and H. S. Bains (eds) *Multi Racist Britain*, London: Macmillan Education.

—— (1992) '"It's racism what dunnit": hidden narratives in theories of racism', in J. Donald and A. Rattansi (eds) *'Race', Culture and Difference*, London: Sage.

Cohen, S. (1972) *Folk Devils and Moral Panics: The Creation of the Mods and Rockers*, Oxford: Martin Robertson.

Connolly, P. (1992) '"Playing it by the rules": the politics of research in "race" and education', *British Educational Research Journal* 18 (2): 133–48.

—— (1993) 'Racism, schooling and resistance: the construction of masculine identities amongst African/Caribbean boys'. Paper presented to postgraduate conference 'Representation, Identity and Agency', University of Manchester, December.

—— (1994) 'Racism, anti-racism and masculinity: contextualising racist incidents in the primary school', Paper presented to International Sociology of Education Conference, University of Sheffield, January.

—— (199X) 'The formation of racialised and gendered cultural identities amongst working class infant children: an ethnographic study of a multi-ethnic, inner-city primary school', Unpublished PhD thesis, University of Leicester (in process).

Dollimore, J. (1986) 'Homophobia and sexual difference', Oxford Literary Review 8: 5–12.

Donald, J. and Rattansi, A. (eds) (1992) 'Race', Culture and Difference, London: Sage.

Foster, M. (1990) Policy and Practice in Multicultural and Anti-Racist Education: A Case Study of a Multi-Ethnic Comprehensive School, London: Routledge.

Fuller, M. (1990) 'Black girls in a London comprehensive school', in R. Deem (ed.) Schooling for Women's Work, London: Routledge & Kegan Paul.

Gillborn, D. (1990) 'Race', Ethnicity and Education, London: Unwin Hyman.

Hall, S., Critcher, C., Jefferson, T., Clarke, J. and Roberts, B. (1978) Policing the Crisis: Mugging the State and Law and Order, London: Macmillan.

Hearn, J. and Morgan, D. (1990) Men, Masculinities and Social Theory, London: Unwin Hyman.

Hewitt, R. (1986) White Talk, Black Talk: Inter-Racial Friendship and Communication amongst Adolescents, Cambridge: Cambridge University Press.

James, A. and Prout, A. (eds) (1990) Constructing and Reconstructing Childhood: Contemporary Issues in the Sociological Study of Childhood, London: Falmer.

Jones, S. (1988) Black Culture, White Youth: The Reggae Tradition from JA to UK, London: Macmillan.

Mac an Ghaill, M. (1988) Young, Gifted and Black: Student–Teacher Relations in the Schooling of Black Youth, Milton Keynes: Open University Press.

Mahoney, P. (1989) 'Sexual violence and mixed schools', in C. Jones and P. Mahoney (eds) Learning Our Lines: Sexuality and Social Control in Education, London: Women's Press.

Mirza, H. S. (1992) Young, Female and Black, London: Routledge.

Rattansi, A. (1992) 'Changing the subject? Racism, culture and education', in J. Donald and A. Rattansi (eds) 'Race', Culture and Difference, London: Sage.

Segal, L. (1990) Slow Motion: Changing Masculinities, Changing Men, London: Virago.

Thorne, B. (1993) Gender Play: Girls and Boys in School, Buckingham: Open University Press.

Troyna, B. and Hatcher, R. (1992) Racism in Children's Lives: A Study of Mainly White Primary Schools, London: Routledge.

Wagg, S. (1988) 'Perishing kids? The sociology of childhood', Social Studies Review 3 (4): 126–31.

Walkerdine, V. (1981) 'Sex, power and pedagogy', Screen Education 38: 14–24.

Westwood, S. (1990) 'Racism, black masculinity and the politics of space', in J. Hearn and D. Morgan (eds) Men, Masculinities and Social Theory, London: Unwin Hyman.

Willis, P. (1977) Learning to Labour: How Working Class Kids Get Working Class Jobs, Hants: Saxon House.

Wolpe, A. M. (1988) Within School Walls: The Role of Discipline, Sexuality and the Curriculum, London: Routledge.

Wright, C. (1986) 'School processes: an ethnographic study', in J. Eggleston, J. Dunn and A. Madju (eds) Education for Some, London: Trentham.

—— (1992a) 'Early education: multiracial primary school classrooms', in D. Gill, B. Mayor and M. Blair (eds) Racism and Education: Structures and Strategies, London: Sage.

—— (1992b) Race Relations in the Primary School, London: David Fulton.

Chapter 13

Swimming against the tide

Liberal parents and cultural plurality

J. Grimes

This is an extract from an ethnographic study that examined the concept of cultural capital in relation to the educational aspirations and experiences of pupils in an urban first school where 40 per cent of the pupils were Asian (the majority of these being British-born of Pakistani Muslim parents), and the remainder of the children were White British children. One aspect of the study focused on the treatment of cultural diversity by the school staff, and in particular, the ways in which they perceived, and responded to, the relationship between the children's various home cultures and the culture of the school. This extract describes the teachers' and parents' perceptions of controversy that arose when the White parents were required to relinquish some of their power and influence in the school in order to accommodate the wishes of the Asian parents.

The school had its own swimming pool and each class had one swimming lesson a week that was led by the class teacher. The practical arrangements for these lessons were commonly agreed to be unsatisfactory because there was only one group changing room, which the girls used while the boys changed behind a screen next to the pool, but no suitable alternative had been found for many years. However, during the study new guidelines were introduced for the teaching of swimming, requiring all children to be taught by an adult with a lifesaving qualification. None of the staff had such a qualification and the school was obliged to employ a swimming instructor, which led to unavoidable changes to the swimming timetable.

The governors took this opportunity to address the changing room problem, and make the swimming arrangements more sympathetic to the wishes of the Muslim community, whose representatives had stated that they wanted their children to swim in single-sex groups. This was because the Muslim parents felt that the combination of the children having their bodies uncovered while mixing with children of the opposite sex who were not members of their families presented an intolerable conflict with Islamic requirements concerning appropriate behaviour between the sexes. As a consequence four or five Asian children had been explicitly withdrawn from swimming lessons and another five or six regularly failed to bring their swimming kits to school. The governors believed that the difficulties which the existing swimming arrangements raised for the Muslim community were undermining a significant number of children's entitlement to swim; and so when the swimming instructor was employed a new swimming timetable was introduced to allow all the children to swim in single-sex sessions.

This decision produced an overwhelmingly hostile response from the majority of White parents, who saw the segregation by sex in these lessons as a violation of their interpretation of equal opportunities. They were also angry that the decision had been made without consulting them; they demanded that the governors held a public emergency meeting to justify their decision, and a working party was set up to devise alternative swimming arrangements which were acceptable to both the Asian and White communities. After a short period of consultation it was agreed that the majority of swimming lessons would remain single-sex, although there would be a few supplementary lessons for those children whose parents wished them to attend mixed lessons.

This decision had significant repercussions for community relations within the school. Many of the White parents felt that their understanding of the school's ideals and policies had been undermined and consequently they no longer exhibited the same degree of support for the school. Although they managed to sustain their good relationships with the class teachers they were extremely critical of the headteacher and the governors for failing to take their wishes into account. It appeared that this was the first time that many of the teachers and White parents had been required to acknowledge the complexities of living in a multicultural community which aspires to grant all members equal rights. Moreover, although they had multicultural aspirations, the swimming episode appeared to be the first occasion when the White parents were obliged to relinquish some of their power and influence in the school in order to accommodate the wishes of the Asian parents.

This raised a number of issues about the role of parents as consumers of education and the extent to which the school was willing to allow all parents to influence school policy and practice. It revealed the White parents' assumption that the school should reinforce their particular beliefs and values (even if they are not shared by the rest of the school community) and the Asian parents reported that it confirmed their perception that stating their concerns and requests to the staff would be problematic, and possibly destructive to community relations within the school. The problem of differential confidence and power experienced by the two ethnic groups is evident in the following comment made by the Year 1 teacher:

Teacher: The problem with this school is that we have a few very powerful
        [White] parents who have got a lot of influence and a lot of intellect,
        and they have a voice; and we have another group of [Asian] parents who
        are now gaining a voice in the community and it's good that they can

say how they feel about issues that are important, and I think that they are getting a voice, the Muslim community. Don't you think so?

Researcher: Yes I do. It's a very big obstacle to overcome isn't it, to be able to have equal influence.

Teacher: They are saying, and I think the swimming was a thing about . . . they wanted to be listened to, and I think in a way they have never . . . it's never really been . . . well it is addressed here but it's . . . their [the White parents'] power and influence . . . it's a good thing, they {the Asian parents] can now say how they feel.

The episode appeared to provoke such strong feelings in the White parents because it revealed the tensions between anti-sexist and anti-racist education, and many of the White parents had either been unaware of, or had ignored, the potential difficulties involved in attempting to address the two in a multicultural school. This attitude also appeared to be held by most of the class teachers, who disagreed with the governors' decision because it conflicted with their interpretation of equal opportunities, which emphasized gender issues (and in particular treating girls and boys identically, and never segregating groups of children by gender) at the expense of multiculturalism. These issues all crystallized in the shared perception of the White parents and teachers that, in principle, the Muslim community should have equal rights to express their wishes in the school, but that the request to have their particular cultural values taken into consideration in this context was an unreasonable demand. It was apparent that many of the White parents had difficulty resolving the conflict between their commitment to the principle that all cultures should be accorded equal respect and their realization that there were aspects of Islam which they opposed, and which they were unwilling to have impinge upon their children's lives. The following comment by the mother of a White child in the Year 2 class exemplifies the reactions of many who found themselves experiencing difficulties resolving this dilemma:

Parent: I feel very cross about the swimming for various reasons. I don't actually think there should have been a decision to have separate swimming. I think that if the Muslim families were upset about it, I don't know how many of them were, I really think that then there should have been a special swimming time for them rather than affect all our children. [. . .] I'm cross about it, he's cross about it. I think it's to do with the demands of the Muslim community. As a general issue I don't think the Muslim community should make those kind of demands.

Researcher: Do you think they had a justifiable demand for their own community?

Parent: Yes, but I think one has to look at how one reorganizes things for them or whether they should find the time and helpers to . . . because it has disrupted the whole swimming and increased teacher time. It's really made me feel antagonistic towards them.

Many of the White parents felt and expressed similar hostility towards the Asians at the school, despite claiming to remain committed to the principle of multiculturalism. Their comments on the issue suggested that the majority of White parents perceived the function of multiculturalism to be the promotion of similarities between various ethnic groups and expected the school to overlook any potential points of conflict between the different cultures. This is exemplified in the following comment by one of the White mothers:

There are a lot of similarities. Wherever you are there's good and bad in everything. But if you pick out the similarities and see how they harmonize, which is what I think this school does, and celebrate each other's feasts and talk about each other's religions and how similar they are, because I mean, Muslims follow the Old Testament in everything, so the base is there, it's all very similar. I think that's where this school has its strength.

However, it appeared that the White parents and teachers expected the Asian community to suppress those aspects of their culture which conflicted with the western notion of a liberal society. When this did not happen (as in the case of the swimming episode) the White parents were required to respond in a way that did not undermine their declared commitment to multi-culturalism. Consequently many of the White parents rationalized the antagonism they were feeling towards the Muslim parents by suggesting that the Muslim community was being misrepresented by a few fundamentalist fanatics. One of the White mothers stated:

It brought about an awful lot of feeling about the subjugation of women, big things like that, which other than the fundamentalists, I don't think the others are bothered about it in the slightest, but they felt that they had to.

The common justification for this perception was that the apparently sudden upsurge of debate was led by a few men from the Muslim community, when the majority of the Muslim parents had not complained officially about the former swimming arrangements. The White women in particular felt that the Asian women's views were not taken into account, and that a few Muslim men were using the episode as an opportunity to impose their wishes upon the Muslim community. However, this was a misperception based on their presumption that the lack of formal complaints by the Muslim parents indicated that they were happy with the existing swimming policy and their failure to understand that it is not usual for Muslim women to contribute to public debates.

The presumption by the White teachers and parents that there was relatively little support in the Muslim community for separate swimming was mistaken. All the Muslim parents interviewed for the study categorically stated their desire for their children to attend separate swimming sessions, although in two cases the parents said that they would temporarily be willing to compromise on this issue because their children were still very young. Some also expressed regret about the detrimental effect the episode had upon community relations within the school. For example, Bilal's uncle commented that in retrospect, it would have been wiser for the Muslim community to continue to compromise on the issue of swimming because they would have avoided the racist backlash that he believed they were now experiencing.

However, the belief that the request for separate swimming was mis-representative of the majority of Muslim parents' views persisted among teachers and White parents for a number of reasons. First, in contrast to the White parents, the Asian parents did not typically express their opinions about the issue to their children's class teachers nor write letters to the headteacher stating their understanding of the situation. Some spoke to the headteacher about the issue and others had informal conversations with the Asian Section 11 staff. However, the main channel of communication between the Asian community and the school was through the representation of two or three community leaders. The Pakistani Section 11 teacher reported that this reflected the lack of confidence many of the parents felt about their ability to express themselves adequately in English (the Punjabi and Urdu speaking staff, in an attempt to remain neutral, did not volunteer to provide translation during the public meetings) and the decision made between herself, the headteacher and some of the community leaders that the debate would be more manageable if a small number of representatives were responsible for presenting the Muslim case to the rest of the school community. Second, prior to the governors' intervention, the Muslim parents had either reluctantly accepted the swimming arrangements, or in some cases had quietly asserted their concerns by repeatedly sending their children to school without swimming kit. Therefore it appeared that most of the Muslim community had no problem with the swimming arrangements until the issue was raised by a small minority, and this assumption appeared to be confirmed when two or three men dominated the Muslim contribution to the debate during the open meeting between parents and governors.

The episode was significant because it revealed a fundamental resistance shared by the majority of White parents to the Asian community having the same degree of influence upon school policy as themselves. However, this was often obscured by the White parents' facility for using liberal arguments and jargon to justify their concerns. This produced the ironic circumstance where the White parents attempted to justify their opposition to the Asian community's wishes by declaring that their concerns arose out of their commitment to equal opportunities. The majority of White parents stated they that believed segregated swimming undermined the school's commit-ment to anti-sexist education, and were concerned that this would have an adverse affect upon the girls, because they would be made to feel self-conscious about their bodies, and less important than the boys. The White parents were very effective at expressing these opinions to the teachers and governors. The headteacher received over twenty letters of complaint from White parents and was inundated with White parents requesting to speak to him about the issue. The White parents also used the informal meeting times at the beginning and the end of the school day to express their concerns to the class teachers, who felt torn between supporting the policy of the school and agreeing with the sentiments of the parents. White parents were also responsible for contacting the local paper and television station, both of which produced reports on the issue.

In contrast the Asian community restricted their comments to the representations of a few community leaders and informal conversations with the headteacher and Section 11 staff. They also seemed less involved in the negotiations to produce alternative swimming arrangements. Not only was this for cultural and practical reasons, but also it reflected the Asian parents' concern not to fuel the controversy any further. However, this resulted in a relative lack of tangible evidence of Asian support for separate swimming, which was interpreted by many of the White teachers and parents as an indication that the issue had been blown out of proportion and was not supported by the majority of the Muslim community. The following comments by the headteacher indicate the problems that this presented to the governors when they tried to consider how they could devise alternative arrangements which would be acceptable to all the parties involved:

I think one of the real difficulties about judging the whole thing is that there is an articulate part of the community and a relatively inarticulate part. Particularly meaning by articulate, whether one expresses one's views publicly and forcefully. It's extremely difficult to judge response, basically because does one brief comment just to say 'Oh thanks for that, that's good' ... how does one match that against a five-page letter setting out a deep philosophical position being very hostile? I don't think one does really. Again, ultimately I think where the people who lead schools, be they headteachers or other staff or governors, have actually at times got to bite the bullet to say 'One doesn't simply go along a populist line or respond solely to those who speak the loudest or in the most articulate way. One tries to look at issues in terms of philosophical statements one believes about the school, in terms of justice, in terms of 'rightness', in terms of listening to the disadvantaged and those sort of things.

The episode reveals how misrepresentations resulting from White parents' and teachers' misinterpretations of the Asian parents' needs, interests and behaviours contributed to the unequal status of the two groups of parents in the school, and the differential values that the teachers placed upon the home cultures of the children in their classes. However, it also gives two important indicators of how such a situation could be improved. First, it suggests that such misunderstandings could be avoided if the teachers were more informed about the complex relationship between anti-racist and anti-sexist policy when considering equal opportunities, and in particular, re-evaluated their assumption that identical treatment for different groups is synonymous with equal opportunities. Second, it suggests that such difficulties could be resolved more satisfactorily if the teachers improved their understanding of the potential conflicts and misunderstandings between minority cultures and the dominant culture promoted by schools. However, it is important to assert that this understanding cannot be achieved by merely describing how minority cultures differ from the dominant culture, but should be based on a thorough understanding and critical analysis, both of minority cultures and the cultural values and practices that are currently taken for granted in the school.

Chapter 14

Educational experiences of ethnic minority students in Oxford

D. McIntyre, G. Bhatti and M. Fuller

This is a report upon on a six-month investigation of the educational qualifications gained in one year (1991) by school students from different ethnic groups in the city of Oxford; and of the accounts of their school experience given in interviews by some of these young people.

THE STATISTICAL STUDY

This study was designed to provide information about the performance in General Certificate of Secondary Education (GCSE) and Advanced (A) Level examinations in 1991 of all students belonging to different ethnic groups in the city of Oxford. In the event it proved impossible to gain access to the relevant data from Oxford College of Further Education, but full data was gathered from the six upper schools in the City. The heads of each of the upper schools were approached in the early summer of 1991 and asked to gather data on students entered for GCSE and A Level examination, categorizing the pupils in terms of their ethnic origins on the basis of the LEA's Pupil Ethnic Monitoring guidelines. In November 1991, this information was collected from the schools, together with information on the performance of the students in the relevant examinations. Examination performances were coded according to the Audit Commission's systems. For A Levels, grades are translated into numerical scores as follows:

A	B	C	D	E
10	8	6	4	2

For A/S level grades, reckoned to be be worth half of A Levels, the translation is as follows:

A	B	C	D	E
5	4	3	2	1

and a total score is obtained by simply adding the numerical scores for all the grades a person is awarded. For GCSE, grades are translated into numerical scores as follows:

A	B	C	D	E	F	G
7	6	5	4	3	2	1

and total scores obtained in the same way.

The population of students concerned categorized according to ethnic origin, gender and examination for which they were candidates is shown in Table 14.1.

Table 14.1 Numbers in each ethnic group of students

Ethnic category	Total	Girls	Boys	GCSE candidates in 1991	A Level candidates in 1991
Afro-Caribbean	18	8	10	12	6
Bangladeshi	19	10	9	19	0
Chinese	13	9	4	12	1
Indian	34	14	20	26	8
Pakistani	57	26	31	45	12
White British	1,203	600	603	964	239
Other	44	17	27	33	11
Total	1,388	684	704	1,111	277

Embedded in Table 14.1 is the important finding that, just as the candidates from the five largest ethnic minority groups make up 10 per cent of GCSE candidates (114 out of 1,111), so the candidates from these ethnic minority groups make up 10 per cent of A Level candidates (27 out of 277). On this evidence, ethnic minority students as a whole are just as likely as other students to pursue their academic education to A Level standard.

Of the 1,111 candidates registered for the GCSE examination, 151 were 'missing cases', i.e. candidates for whom no grades were awarded. There were no significant differences between ethnic groups in the 'missing cases' category.

GCSE results for different ethnic categories

Excluding missing cases, the remaining 960 total GCSE scores varied from I to 76. The median score, which divides the whole distribution of scores into two equal halves, is 27. A simple way of looking at the success of any sub-group is to ask what proportion of its members' scores are above or below the median. If the sub-group is performing as well as the total population, about 50 per cent of its members should have scores on or above the median. Table 14.2 shows the results in these terms for the different ethnic categories.

Inspection of Table 14.2 shows clearly that the overall performance of the small Chinese group is very impressive, while the Bangladeshi group has on average done less well than others. There is little variation, however, among

Table 14.2 GCSE results for different ethnic categories

Ethnic category	Number on or above median	Number below median	Per cent on or above median
Afro-Caribbean	6	6	50
Bangladeshi	3	13	19
Chinese	8	1	89
Indian	10	14	42
Pakistani	17	24	41
White British	429	401	52
Other	11	17	39
Total	484	476	50

Table 14.3 Ethnic categories, gender and GCSE results

	BOYS		GIRLS	
	No. above or on median	No. below median	No. above or on median	No. below median
Afro-Caribbean	4	3	2	3
Bangladeshi	1	7	2	6
Chinese	2	0	6	1
Indian	6	9	4	5
Pakistani	6	15	11	9
White British	191	231	238	170
Other	9	12	2	5
Total	219	277	265	199

the other groups. Table 14.3 shows the results analysed further in terms of gender categories.

Two contrasting patterns are apparent. For most of the ethnic categories, the same trends seem to occur irrespective of gender, although numbers are so small that it is difficult to assert this with confidence. For the total population, however, and for the two largest sub-groups, there are strongly contrasting trends according to gender. Thus 58 per cent of White girls, but only 45 per cent of White boys, have scores on or above the median; and 55 per cent of Pakistani girls, but only 39 per cent of Pakistani boys, have scores on or above the median.

Ethnic category and A Level results

For the total A Level population in Oxford upper schools in 1991, the median overall score was 10.

The number of ethnic minority students taking A Level courses is so small as to make statistical statements difficult. There were no Bangladeshi A Level students and only one Chinese A level student (score of 8). For the other three groups, the scores were as follows:

Afro-Caribbean	Girls	12,	6,	2				
	Boys	16,	4,	0				
Indian	Girls	14,	8,	4,	2			
	Boys	30,	14,	10,	0			
Pakistani	Girls	10,	16,	8,	2			
	Boys	26,	14,	14,	2,	2,	2,	0,	0

There is nothing in these results to suggest that the students from any ethnic group are performing less well on the whole than others. An interesting feature of these results is the much larger spread of scores for boys than for girls. One might wonder, too, whether the four boys who failed to achieve a single grade (and indeed the six boys and girls who gained a single E grade each) were taking a course for which they had the prerequisite knowledge and motivation; but that is a problem which is far from being restricted to ethnic minority students.

The further question which can be asked is about how well ethnic minority students performed at A Level in comparison to others, given their level of performance at GCSE. Records of GCSE performance were available for 18 of the 27 ethnic minority students and for 205 of the 277 total of A Level candidates. Their scores were plotted on a two-dimensional graph which is summarized in Figure 14.1. For each broad band of GCSE scores, the median A Level performance of candidates was calculated; and the gradually increasing median A Level performance as GCSE scores improve is indicated in Figure 14.1 by the line connecting the crosses which represent these median scores. The eighteen individual ethnic minority students are shown on the table according to their GCSE and A Level scores.

It may be seen that the ethnic minority students' performances follow the general trends quite closely on the whole. More precisely, eight of the individual scores are within two points of the median lines, four are clearly above it and six are clearly below it. The one really exceptional case is of the Pakistani student who, with an A Level score of 26 after a GCSE score of 30, was relatively the most successful student in the whole population.

Overall, these figures once again give no indication of ethnic minority students in general performing either better or worse than the majority in A Level examinations.

THE INTERVIEW STUDY

Against the background of statistical evidence of ethnic minority students' formal academic achievements in city schools, an interview study was planned to explore the experiences and concerns of ethnic minority students. The aims of this interview study were

1 to understand the aspirations and expectations of individual ethnic minority students in educational contexts and how these aspirations and expectations have developed

2 to understand the experiences which have encouraged and facilitated, and those which had discouraged or constrained, the realization of these individual students' aspirations.

Selection of students for interview

In order to gather evidence on as wide a range as possible of the concerns and experiences of students from the main ethnic groups in Oxford (but not in order to make systematic comparisons between groups), it was decided that the students to be invited to interview should be selected by stratified random sampling, taking three factors into account:

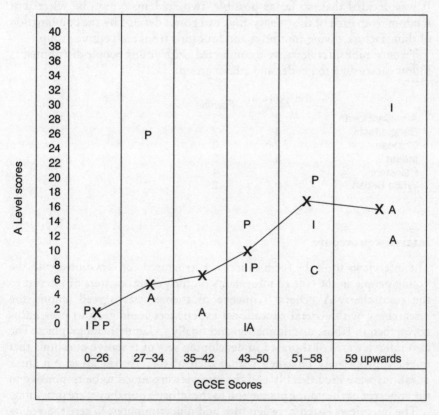

X = Median A Level score for given GSCE band of scores
P = Score of Pakistani individual student
I = Score of Indian individual student
A = Score of Afro-Caribbean individual student
C = Score of Chinese individual student

Figure 14.1 Relationships of A Level to GCSE results: general trends and ethnic minority individuals

1 the six largest ethnic groups in the student population:

Afro-Caribbean
Bangladeshi
Chinese
Indian
Pakistani
White British

2 boys and girls
3 those who fell above, and those who fell below, the median success rate in GCSE examinations in 1991.

It was decided that, so far as possible, two students would be selected at random from each of the twenty-four categories defined by the combination of these factors, giving four boys and four girls from each ethnic group.

Twenty-nine interviews were conducted, with young people distributed as follows according to gender and ethnic group.

	Male	Female
Afro-Caribbean	2	3
Bangladeshi	4	3
Chinese	2	0
Indian	3	2
Pakistani	4	4
White British	0	2

Interview procedure

The interviews took the form of loosely structured conversations, with the young people in the role of informants on the general matters of interest to the researchers. A general sequence of themes was agreed among the researchers, with general educational experiences leading on to peer influences, then to ethnic discrimination and finally to family demographics. The two interviewers collaborated in developing sets of tentative questions that might appropriately be asked within each of these broad areas; but these questions were used flexibly and the interviewers aimed to be responsive to the concerns of the young people and to the information they were providing.

The interviews lasted between fifty and ninety minutes. Where the young people seemed relaxed and uninhibited by the process, audio recordings were made of the conversations; but when in doubt, the interviewers took summary notes which they wrote out in full as soon as possible afterwards. Most of those interviewed had not consciously addressed all the questions which were being asked and seemed to be thinking aloud about some issues for the first time. Their answers were not therefore based on extended reflection.

Analysis of interview data

The two interviewers each wrote overall reports, identifying what had seemed to them major themes and concerns arising out of the interviews. They also prepared all their data in the form of detailed accounts of the substance of each interview, including a considerable amount of verbatim quotation. The data thus consisted of some seventy-five pages of closely typed reports.

Analysis of these data was conducted by first allocating each statement in it to one, or sometimes more, of ten very general categories including, for example, 'teachers', 'peers', 'school in general'. The data in each of these categories were then sifted at some length to establish recurring themes within them. Where the same themes were found in different general categories, they were treated as one. The data relevant to each theme thus identified were then summarized directly in a paragraph or more of the draft report. Finally this draft report was checked against the reports of the two interviewers to ensure that none of their insights had been overlooked.

The young people interviewed

The twenty-nine young people interviewed were all around 17 years old. All of them had attended one of the Oxford City upper schools for several years (or, in one case, for the one year since he had arrived in the UK). There were at least three from each of the six upper schools; and there was at least one young man and at least one young woman from each of the four mixed-sex upper schools.

Almost half of the twenty-nine had been born in Oxford. The remainder had arrived, in almost equal numbers, in infancy or in time to attend middle school or during the last preceding years. Those arriving in Oxford during middle or upper schools year came, in almost equal numbers, from elsewhere in Britain or from their country of origin.

The young people were from a variety of home backgrounds. No systematic information was sought about their homes or families, but from the information offered during interviews it was apparent that one or both of the parents of most interviewees were in manual occupations. However, a substantial minority of the parents were unemployed or were in fear of imminent redundancy. Parents' educational backgrounds varied widely: most were literate, not necessarily of course in English; a minority were well qualified, up to graduate level, although in several cases such qualifications were not reflected in their current occupations. A substantial proportion of the Asian parents, particularly the mothers, did not speak English; and the languages normally spoken in the homes of many, probably most, of those interviewed were languages other than English.

Of the twenty-nine interviewees, ten were currently retaking GCSE courses and eight were taking A Level courses at their schools, five were taking various Further Education (FE) courses, mostly at the Oxford FE College, five (all young women) were unemployed, and one was in employment.

The importance of individual teachers

The frequency with which individual teachers were mentioned in the interviews suggests that the young people's overall experience of school could be coloured to a remarkable degree, for good or ill, by one teacher.

Stories of teachers who helped

It is difficult to preserve anonymity while still giving the texture of these stories, but perhaps that is not something that need be worried about in this instance.

A had an Asian teacher of economics who was more strict than his White teachers. 'She frightened me that if I did not work I would fail. With the others it was up to me.' He felt he tried harder in her subject than in others. She used to borrow his Bhangra music tapes; and A found her both 'human and a teacher'.

B came to Britain in 1988. He was full of praise for the teacher who had taught him English, without whom he felt he would be 'nowhere'. Apart from the effort she had put into teaching him, she had also befriended him, giving him Eid cards and visiting him at home.

C was full of praise for most of her teachers, especially those who gave her extra help and attention when she was struggling to learn English. One of them, the ESOL (English for speakers of other languages) teacher, had given her, to keep, three dictionaries: Bengali–Bengali, Bengali–English and English–English. At the beginning, she remembered, everyone used to laugh because she opened a dictionary every two minutes. Two of her teachers had taken the trouble to visit her and her mother at home; and they continued to come at Eid time, even after she had left the school.

What stands out most for D about his school is his experience with the music teacher. Through her, he learned to play the bass guitar, the drums and the keyboard. She also got him to begin singing. Moreover, she put him together with three other students to form a band. He especially appreciates that she helped him to overcome self-consciousness in performing in front of other people. Through her, he has come to see that 'music can be an advantage to me', he realizes that he can use his knowledge of music to get a good and interesting job.

E's early career at her upper school was stormy. She became part of a group of girls who 'got blamed for everything' that went wrong in classes. She was sent out of classes rather frequently and was told she had an 'attitude problem'. E has survived all this and is now a hardworking and confident sixth-former, partly because of her mother's support and that of her own academically successful best friend. Her form tutor has also, however, been crucial. She has taught E about the politics of teacher–student relationships, advised her how to handle teachers, acted as her advocate when she got into trouble, and eventually persuaded her to accept that teachers have some authority over her.

More than half those interviewed told similar stories about one or more teachers whose help has been a critical beneficial influence upon them and their school careers.

Stories of teachers who did not help

The examples which follow are of stories which did not seem to relate obviously to the distinctive ethnic origins of the young people interviewed.

P had a teacher 'to whom I said I might go into medicine and the first thing she said was "That would be difficult. For a start you are a female. Then do you have relations in the medical profession?"'. From that time P learned not to share things with her teachers.

French at school for Q was an unpleasant experience. The teacher could not teach them properly and consequently lost control regularly. Some children including herself went to talk to the Head of Department. She told them that it was a foreign teacher and the children should try and put up with her, 'because she said we would get a new teacher next year, and we did'. But it was too late by then for Q.

R had had problems with GCSE English. 'Well in the first year I did not work. That was not just me. It was the whole class ... we had a terrible teacher ... the class was just ruling itself ... that is why we did not get our coursework done.' In the following year a much better teacher had ensured that all the students completed the necessary amount of work, 'But my bad teacher still messed me up ... we all lost didn't we?'

S had been persuaded to stay on at school for A Level courses, but had been disappointed by them and regretted the decision. For one course, the teacher's attendance had been uneven, he did not give much individual attention to the students, and he was not around for consultation after school. In S's other A Level course, the teacher was domineering and unsupportive of S's work, was not teaching what S feels he needs to learn, and S is finding it difficult to stay motivated.

T had one history teacher who 'couldn't cope ... she ran out of the class crying once' and who was replaced by another. 'All you were expected to do in his class was to copy from the board. We weren't learning anything so we complained and he went as well.'

U knew that Craft, Design and Technology was 'a boy's subject', but she chose it and found herself at the back of the class with another girl. The teacher 'was always angry, he picked on people. They were shy to ask him things ... anyway he would shout back ... He probably would not have shouted because we were girls but we didn't put our hands up anyway ... He gave us sheets. We didn't understand it. It was too complicated anyway.' U quickly lost confidence and motivation but when after six months she asked to change to another option she was persuaded to stay.

As with teachers who had been outstandingly helpful, more than half those interviewed had vivid memories of individual teachers who had made life at school significantly less rewarding and who in some cases were seen as having had a critical negative influence upon the student's school career.

School factors influencing academic success

The young people interviewed were generally very conscious that their academic success or failure had depended very largely on their own efforts. Those who had been relatively successful were naturally inclined to ascribe this more to themselves than were those who had been less successful; but even among the latter, the majority explicitly or implicitly recognized that harder work by themselves would have led to greater success. There was also a small, but rather sad, minority of interviewees who had concluded that they were not the kind of people who could benefit much from schooling, whatever efforts they made.

It was, however, about their experiences of schooling that the young people had been asked mainly to talk and they therefore had a good deal to say about what in their schooling had or had not been helpful to them in seeking academic success. Three main themes were apparent in their talk about such matters: facilities and resources; their needs for help and teachers' responses to these needs; and the ways in which teachers differentiated among pupils in terms of who was worth helping.

Facilities and resources

Only a minority of those interviewed raised questions of resources. Positive comments on school resources were restricted to appreciation of computer and (especially) sports facilities. However, various resource constraints upon learning opportunities were mentioned. Among these were the availability of books and other materials, library facilities and (once) class size. The resource constraints most frequently mentioned concerned teaching staff. Teacher turnover was one complaint, with three independent instances being given of classes having three successive teachers of the same subject in one year. Another recurrent complaint was of the disruptive effects of teacher absences, with supply teachers being seen as having a hopeless task and being quite useless to students. Also, grossly incompetent teachers were seen as a major constraint upon learning opportunities.

The need for teachers' help

'Help' is perhaps the word most commonly to be found in the interview data. Many of the students felt a need for help with their studies, and in preparation for their examinations. Some had received such help and were grateful for it, but others had not. At least three different kinds of help are repeatedly mentioned: extra classes, individual attention, and encouragement.

First, extra help in English after school, revision classes, practice examinations, workshops in different subjects at lunchtime or after school were all mentioned, sometimes by pupils who had benefited from them and rather more often by those who said they needed them but did not get them.

Second, many students felt a need for individual attention. As one explained, he had great difficulty in some subjects and often did not understand what was being taught. He did not always manage to ask the teacher to explain things; there were so many people that the teacher did not always get round to seeing everyone. This was the experience of several. Some reported with gratitude that, when they had been struggling with understanding English, teachers had spontaneously given them extra individual attention. Such spontaneous extra attention seemed however to be reserved for those in obviously greatest need. 'They think you can talk, you must be all right ... I get stuck with hard words ... and some teachers they just ignore you when you put your hand up ... so you feel sad ... and just write over words again.'

The strategies which teachers are seen to adopt in these circumstances tend in their students' judgements to be ineffective. These include relying on other students to help those in difficulty, setting the work to be done but not helping individual students to do it, and pointing out mistakes in students' work but not helping them to improve. Where teachers are not prepared, because of the numbers they have to deal with, to take the initiative 'to sit down and explain things' to individual students, then it is up to the student, as many recognized, to seek out the teachers and to ask for their help. This is not something which every student had the confidence and motivation to do, especially if experience has taught them that 'teachers at [this school] are not interested in your work'. None the less, as one interviewee made clear, if he made the effort to find the teacher, and if the teacher were free, he could go over things with the teacher. Those who had sought help in this way had met with varying reactions. While some teachers were not easily approachable, others made one feel comfortable about asking for extra help; and some were impressively willing to spend a lot of time helping one to understand.

The third kind of help mentioned was encouragement and being pushed. Some respondents recognized that, especially when they had been a year or two younger, they needed the help of external pressure. A few thought that a generally more disciplined school atmosphere was desirable, but others were concerned with a more focused academic pressure. One, who had experienced the benefits of this kind of help, recalled:

> You were definitely pushed by the teachers: 'You've got to hand this in.' And, I think some of the people maybe weren't pushed, like I've heard of from other schools, just didn't bother, where we felt we didn't have a choice in a way. So we did it. And I'm glad we did. And yet they were encouraging at the same time they pushed you. So you thought 'This is really hard', but it was encouraging once you got to the end and had a lot done. It was needed, the pushing was needed.

The absence of such pressure in the experience of other students was expressed in such disapproving comments as 'It's easier to not work here because the teachers don't do anything'.

One student who had had a difficult and frustrating school career made the following suggestions when asked what she wished had occurred in her upper school education:

1 Give me more attention.
2 Pressure me more to do my work.
3 If I don't learn, tell me what I've got to learn.
4 Tell me what I need to do to get a good grade.
5 If I'm holding back, push me forward.
6 Tell me how I feel, help me understand what I'm feeling.

Differentiation by teachers

A considerable number of the students talked, sometimes at length and with some passion, about how teachers in their view invested their energies in some students and not in others. This phenomenon was sometimes reported with approbation, sometimes in anger, and sometimes in resignation.

The earliest reported experience of this kind was from a student who, having enjoyed first and middle schools, had, shortly before coming to upper school, had a bad accident which interrupted the continuity of his schooling. Since then, he felt, teachers had not bothered with his problems and had generally 'given up' on him.

Other students used the same expression, 'being given up on', to describe what they thought had happened to them later, when they were on GCSE courses. Here the problem was twofold: on the one hand, they had found themselves in noisy classes, among 'dossers' who seemed content to be 'messing about' which in itself made serious work difficult; and on the other hand, teachers tended quickly to give up on not only the 'dossers' but on everyone in these classes. These students were angry, as were others. For example, an academically successful student had suddenly discovered that her 'mixed-ability' mathematics class was doing significantly less demanding work than her friends in another class, and concluded that the school was secretly denying her opportunities to which she was entitled. Another academically successful student suggested that teachers should tell children exactly where they stood in terms of sets, about how and when teachers decide which child to 'dump' and which one to 'choose'.

Several students, including successful ones, described their schools and teachers in terms such as:

'good only if you really can get down to your work'
'encouraging only successful students'
'keen to help, if you're already clever'
'if you're willing, you're given a chance'.

Although interviewees differed in their judgements of the merits of such states of affairs, there seemed to be a general acceptance that such differentiation was an important factor influencing students' academic success.

RACIAL DISCRIMINATION

There were only a few comments on schools' disciplinary practice in relation to racism. One student commended her school for being very strict about expressions of prejudice, it having responded very quickly to an isolated incident by making it very clear that no racist remarks would be tolerated. Students elsewhere seemed to have a more resigned attitude to racist remarks. Most of the racist incidents which occur are in the playground, one suggested, and children had to learn to deal with it themselves because teachers were not there. 'And even if they were there they wouldn't be interested.'

About one-third of the young people interviewed talked of having experience in their upper schools of 'racist' teachers. In most cases, they were talking of one or two very specific teachers and in all cases it was emphasized that only 'some' teachers could be described in this way. In at least one case, complaints to the headteacher had led to the departure of the teacher concerned.

While the term 'racist' probably meant different things to different people, about two-thirds of those interviewed reported ways in which they thought they had been disadvantaged in their dealings with schools directly as a result of their racial characteristics, or ethnic backgrounds. Some were clearly struggling to make sense of situations in which they felt powerless. One said: 'How can teachers be interested in Indian children? They are not Indian are they? Besides, we are living in their country and they make the rules.' Others tried to make light of it by trying to persuade us, and perhaps themselves, that it was all in fun. For example, one young man reported that teachers stereotyped Asians about arranged marriages, but that 'you learn to joke your way out of it'. Another young man of Chinese origin similarly reported that it did not bother him that his physical education teacher calls him 'Karate Man' since 'he means it as a joke'.

Some young people who felt they were treated sometimes not as individuals but merely as members of an ethnic group, were unhappy about this, but were for example willing to say 'There's no discrimination at [the school]. We are all treated the same', at the same time as 'if one [black] gets in trouble, then they all get in trouble. They [the teachers] don't see you as an individual. They see you as part of that group.' Students did, however, feel aggrieved when they thought that they or their friends had been recurrently 'picked on', neglected or denied opportunities because of their colour or ethnic background.

One young woman believed that teachers noticed her talking inappropriately in class more than they noticed her white friends behaving in exactly the same way. The major complaints, however, tended to be directed against specific individual teachers. One interviewee has been taught by a teacher with a well-established reputation of 'always picking on black kids', and his experience too had been that in a class of twenty-five students, in which there might be three or four blacks, they always got blamed by this teacher for any problems. Another student had found that a particular senior teacher at his school would always single him out from his white friends for punishment when they had all been seen doing the same thing, such as smoking.

Several of the young people interviewed claimed to have experienced consistent neglect in comparison to others. In three cases this claimed neglect was in classrooms, where it was claimed that white children were given priority by racist teachers over those from ethnic minority groups; one young man claimed to have stopped going to such a class because of the futility of his attempts to gain attention or to learn there. Another student claimed more generally that ethnic minority children had to try very hard to be accepted by teachers on an equal footing with others, but that it helped if one 'hung around' with white students. A distinctive complaint of neglect came from an Asian Christian student, who claimed that while plenty of attention was given both to British versions of Christianity and to stereotypical 'Asian' religions at the school, Asian Christians were ignored.

Various kinds of opportunities were, it was claimed, denied to individual students as a result of them being from ethnic minorities. There were reports of a curriculum option denied, and of an examination entry being refused, when white students had not been so denied. Two other complaints were directly related to students' ethnic loyalties. One of these was that Muslim students lost opportunities because schools make no official allowance for Ramadhan; and the other was that an Urdu class had been organized for those who wished to take it at the same time when their fellow-students had their tutorial form period, with various very attractive activities and opportunities to discuss future special events being missed as a result.

Several young people expressed opinions about how students from groups other than their own behaved and were treated. In particular, several of those interviewed made comments about Asian girls and the ways in which they were treated in schools.

Two of these were Asian boys. One simply suggested that Asian girls at his school tended to be given more attention than Asian boys were given. The other said that Asian girls were treated by teachers 'in a gentler way' than white girls were. Teachers believe Asian girls more, for example requiring less evidence before allowing them time off for something like going to the dentist; and he said, Asian girls were allowed to be late, and to hand work in late, in ways that other students were not.

The two white students interviewed, both young women, had their own distinctive stereotypical understandings of how Asian girls tended to behave, why they did so, and how they were treated by teachers. Both perceived a large proportion of Asian girls to be lacking in academic motivation and to be quite disruptive. Both attributed this to the expectation among most Asian girls that they would be married very young and to the fact that they were in school only because 'they have to be'. One claimed to have experience of teachers being exceptionally tolerant of bad behaviour from Asian girls while the other claimed that when Asian girls were disciplined for bad behaviour 'quite a few' would react with the suggestion that 'You're only doing that to me because I'm coloured'.

Finally, one male student of Afro-Caribbean origin, when asked about discrimination, indicated that Asian students got into more trouble than white or black students. Teachers, he thought, expect the Asians to be trouble-makers. When an Asian student gives a right answer, he suggested, the teacher (and the other students) always act surprised. The teachers 'patronize' the Asian students. If one acts up, especially if he is a good student, the teacher threatens to report the behaviour to the student's father. Asian students are more likely to get thrown out of school, whereas others will just get detention (which he described as 'a joke').

The same student mentioned that there are 'some teachers who try too hard . . . try to come across as if they're not racist'. He described a teacher who always put on a West Indian accent to intimate a kind of familiarity. Such strategies were unnecessary and patronizing: 'All ethnic children want is just to be treated equally'.

Curriculum for a multicultural society

About half of the young people interviewed had things to say about the extent to which their school curricula were designed for a multicultural society.

In general, these young people tended to feel that their schools did little to recognize their ethnic cultures or to help students generally towards multi-cultural understanding. Some of them were quite resigned to this. One young woman, who said that her school did not celebrate the presence of non-

European cultures, was unwilling to suggest any ways in which the school could improve itself in this respect.

Others were less content, and talked of schools' token gestures but their general failure to teach about cultures other than the traditional Anglo-Saxon. One student remembers that 'once, a long time ago' the school had had a Bengali day, but never a Pakistani or Indian day, and concluded that 'the school isn't *seriously* interested in other cultures'. Another, asked about experiences in school that acknowledged her heritage, said that the school was 'one-sided, involved with only some people'. She could remember three weeks of religious education (RE) devoted to other cultures, but said that the students 'didn't get to understand the other religions or anything'. She also remembered a unit in Year 11 on 'US and African race relations', commenting that that was the only study on race relations she had had; she added, 'Because the teachers don't talk about racial issues or do anything, the kids see them as racist, but there's no behaviour that's racist'.

Another student remembered an occasion in a history or RE class when a student asked 'What about the Asian community?' and the teacher said 'Oh, skip that' and then 'went on about Jesus and things'. One student compared Oxford schools with those in the English city where she had previously lived, which had celebrated Divali and Dasehra: 'In Oxford, teachers are just not interested'. Some, however, believed that one could not generalize so easily about Oxford schools; one compared his own school unfavourably with another where the Open Evenings were 'based all over the world, not just on the school or England'. He had attended one of these Open Evenings and 'everybody mixed, were treated the same, and found out something new'.

Several of the interviewees talked about opportunities to use and to learn South Asian languages. One talked of the loss and deprivation of not being able to speak 'his own language' at school. The opportunities to learn Asian languages were, however, acknowledged. One young woman regretted not having taken the opportunity to learn Punjabi as her young brother was now doing. Students at another school spoke of their Urdu studies there. Here again, however, there were charges of tokenism and of school image-building while actual practice was constrained by teacher turnover, lack of materials and timetabling frustrations.

Two students talked of the tensions which had resulted when a live issue, that of the Gulf War, on which students had different cultural perspectives had intruded into classrooms. One of them said that his teachers did not like it when he had spoken about the west 'squashing' the Third World in the war.

Two accounts of what was seen as bad practice in attempts at multicultural education were described. One was the showing of a Third World film in geography, described by a student as

A baby's crying ... flies everywhere ... and all the white kids make fun, they just laugh. ... I feel so shamed ... When they talk they

show poverty not the good things, not the big houses, not good things ...
I get upset ... I feel downgraded ... go quiet ... leave their
classrooms.

The other was of an arrangement whereby a man came to the student's school
to talk about Afro-Caribbean issues; but 'No one went. It was on Wednesday,
our afternoon off. We'd go home.' This student and her friends felt angry
about being treated as a group for whom distinctive provision was to be made.
Whoever the man was, he was not seen as a positive resource.

Another black student went further, rejecting the whole idea of ethnic
issues being part of school experience. She commented 'The schools think
they're helping us, but it's only for *their* reputation. It's insulting to us. They
didn't ask us what we want.' Similarly, a Chinese student considered that
there was nothing the school should or could do to acknowledge his ethnic
identity.

The confusions and ambiguities of a notion of multicultural education as
being targeted at particular ethnic groups are reflected in the comments of
one of the white students. She reported that while they were not 'swamped'
by attention to different ethnic group issues, one example was of a Pakistani
ex-student of the school speaking at assembly about what she was doing now.
She thought that it was mostly so that Asian girls could see that there was
something outside schools besides marriage. She considered that 'It didn't
benefit us the same way it would benefit them'. At the same time she didn't
like separate activities 'for Asians only', like the Asian drama club, because
things should be mixed.

Several students had their suggestions as to what a multicultural education
for all students might include. One in particular had quite fully developed
ideas:

I'd like to learn more about black history. I've always been interested in
that and there's never been anything ... The school should educate people
about each other's ethnic background, because people don't really understand what kinds of homes or families people are coming from ... The
subjects I'd teach would be personal studies, history of how black people
got to the West Indies from Africa ... things about the culture, not in
any depth but just so people would know ... and things that make me
laugh, the superstitiousness of the West Indian people, silly things like
that.

Home and school

The young people interviewed almost without exception indicated the
importance to them of their families, and of the close-knit and mutually
supportive nature of their families. There were recurring mentions of
extended family networks, of the importance of local (usually religious)

communities, of gratitude to parents and responsibilities to them, of help from older siblings and responsibilities to help younger siblings, and of strict and religious homes. There were also quite frequent mentions of parental unemployment, retirement, feared redundancy, old age, sickness and widowhood, with the added responsibilities which these implied for the young people.

The most constant theme, however, was of the importance attached by parents to the young people's educational success. The recurring message is that the young people recognize the efforts and sacrifices made by their parents, and realize that their parents hope that the fruits of these efforts will be found in their own future success. Education is valued as the means by which future success can be achieved. Education is important and 'doing well' – a frequently recurring phrase – is even more important, because it will allow you to 'make something of yourself', to 'get a good job', to 'be what you want to be'.

What one student's parents were quoted as repeatedly saying seemed to sum up the attitude of most: 'Work hard, do well, and life will be easier'. To promote such hard work and subsequent success, parents gave moral 'support', showed 'interest', communicated their 'hopes' and 'expectations', made clear what they 'valued', occasionally 'inspired', frequently exerted 'pressure', and most frequently 'encouraged' their sons and daughters in their school work.

Many, however, were not well placed to help their children with their schoolwork; or more generally in their dealings with school.

Parents varied widely in the frequency with which they visited school. A visiting Chinese academic had frequently visited his son's school during his first term until he was sure that the boy was well settled and that the school was looking after him. Another student's mother, who was also employed in a profession, had regularly visited the school when her daughter had been in conflict with her teachers. Other parents, however, were reported as visiting the schools rarely, if ever.

Among those who did visit their children's schools, it seemed from the students' accounts that there needed to be a very special reason for doing so. The sudden discovery that the student was not in the top maths stream (and could therefore get only a C in GCSE), the student's involvement in a major fight, the student's first day at school, or the student being beaten up by fellow students were reasons quoted. One young woman explained that there had never been any need for her parents to visit the school since she had never been really naughty. A young man explained that even when a major incident had arisen in which he was threatened by the headteacher with police involvement, he 'didn't bother' his parents about it .

Other young people described how they hid invitations or simply did not tell their parents about school meetings. There seemed to be three common reasons. One was that the parents 'wouldn't understand', both literally because of their lack of English and also more generally because of their lack of any experience of English schooling. A second reason was that the students felt shy or embarrassed at the thought of their parents in the school context. A third reason was that they wished to protect their parents from the discomfort that they would feel from any expressions of racism from their peer group: 'in case the rude children upset them'.

There was a similar widespread reluctance among the students to talk about school at home, and for similar reasons. 'I couldn't possibly', one young man said. The students were concerned not to upset their parents: 'I wouldn't tell them about the racism, because my mother would cry'.

Some clearly regretted not feeling able to, as reflected in this comment: 'I can't share with my mother like English children can maybe; my mother doesn't know about my school'.

Clearly some things about school were told to parents but only if necessary – 'only if I'm asked'. Only if it wouldn't be too upsetting and, especially, only if there was some obvious point in sharing the information. 'No point' was the most recurring phrase used on this theme.

There seemed, too, to be an almost equally strong barrier against talking about home at school. To one young woman this would obviously be inappropriate: 'They would be talking about home-type things and never get any work done'.

Others too said that it would 'feel strange' to bring home into school conversations, either in the classroom or informally. There was a strong suspicion that people would not be interested in one's religion, festivals or lifestyle, also that 'teachers would not understand and it might prejudice the way they mark my work'; and, at the informal level, a sense of the impropriety of the kind of conversations which might occur: 'English girls winge about home a lot. It's best not to. I didn't want to make fun of my parents at school.'

Where the worlds of school and home are so separate, there tends to be a serious lack of help for students and of information for parents. Those students who were fortunate enough to be able to, depended heavily for guidance on academically successful older siblings. Other students were expected not only to do their own homework, but also to help their younger brothers and sisters with theirs, a task which some felt poorly equipped for. Over and over again, students talked of the lack of help for them and their siblings at home, and the lack of anyone else to turn to for help with their studies. One talked appreciatively of the help given by the University voluntary service JACARI to his younger sisters. Another said, perhaps with JACARI in mind, that her parents had agreed to her being interviewed for this research in the hope that it would lead to some such help for her siblings; and another made the request 'Please find someone to help us'. One student said that her parents would have been prepared to pay for extra tuition if they had been kept adequately informed by teachers.

Information for parents about their children's needs and progress was another recurrent concern. Doubts were expressed both about teachers' commitment to keeping parents adequately informed and also about reliance on letters taken home by students as a method of communication. The incidence of truancy was one example given of how inadequately informed parents are; and one student exemplified from her experience the potential effects of successful school–home communication, resulting in teachers and parents together successfully 'hassling' her to change her ways.

On a broader decision-making level also, connected for example with option and career choices, students felt in need of help, and parents felt responsible but in need of advice and guidance. 'Someone to talk to' was how their parents' need was expressed by several; and they pointed out that 'There aren't Asian teachers to talk to' and that 'There isn't any place in Oxford where Asian parents can talk to people' and, repeatedly, that 'My parents don't know any educated people in Oxford'.

Peer-group racism

About one third of those interviewed talked about peer-group racism, generally in the form of name-calling, racist jokes or other verbal abuse. On occasion this verbal racism could become more violent, as when there had been threats from whites in one school to burn the Pakistani flag during the cricket World Cup. One student had concluded from his experience in different schools that the fewer students there were in a school from minority ethnic groups, the more racism there was likely to be.

There was a good deal of fatalist resignation about such racism, with comments like 'There are funny people with no manners everywhere' and 'There's bound to be racism wherever people of different colour come together'. At a more sophisticated level, one student whose closest friends were white did not feel able to discuss ethnic issues with them because 'they'll think I'm trying to uplift black people . . . all I want is equality'.

Another student, at the other extreme, seemed to have been socialized into a virtual acceptance of racist remarks: 'All my English friends joke about it. It's a good laugh ... silly words, you know ... Paki and curry, and whether it [skin colour] comes off.' He said that this happened inside and outside the classroom and he would not tell teachers about it because it was 'just a joke' and 'it would feel like I was a baby'.

The universal view among the students was that they had to find ways of dealing with peer-group racism themselves. This was because reporting it to teachers or others in authority would not be effective, or because it would not be 'cool', or because one would get beaten up by the racists for doing so, or because ultimately one would in any case have to learn how to deal with such racism for oneself.

The strategies suggested by interviewees for dealing with racism from peers included

- walking away
- treating it as ridiculous
- calling names back
- avoiding it
- accepting it as a joke
- ignoring it as not worth bothering about 'because there are also good people who are white'.

Perceptions of gender and schooling

It was mostly in relation to Asian students that interviewees had things to say about gender differences in behaviour and experience. In the perception of an Afro-Caribbean male student, Asian girls are put under a lot of pressure by white male students at school, presumably with demands upon them to conform to white English notions of normal behaviour. In his view, 'Asian girls really do suffer'.

There was a considerable consensus between the sexes that some Asian girls as well as some boys rebelled against teachers' demands and behaved in ways the teachers did not approve of, but also about the different styles of rebellion. Whereas girls talked a lot, quietly, and 'let the teacher do what the teacher wants', boys were more confrontational, noisier, tougher, 'loudly speaking always', and 'give more attitude back'. One Asian young woman theorized that 'boys act stronger because they have to prove to the white boys that they are tougher. This is something the Asian girls don't have to prove to white girls in the same way.'

A young Asian man's perception was that (perhaps for related reasons) 'I think girls have a tendency to get on well with each other, whether they are white or Asian. Boys are less friendly towards each other.' Whatever the truth of that, another male Asian interviewee considered that 'Life is harder for girls because they have to be more completely different at home from the way they are at school'.

Certainly our data are consistent with the idea that female Asian students' lives are much more constrained outside school hours than are those of the male students. The effect on female students of having to live two such different lives certainly puzzled one young man:

> This [British] culture had affected them [girls] very badly. They are not friendly with boys at all. Even if I talk to them in sister-way they still don't talk. The bad ones make all Bengali girls rude. Even the normal girls become changed in just two weeks. They are turning strange.

CONCLUSION

The statistical study of Oxford school students' attainments in public examinations showed some clear trends, despite the relatively small numbers of most ethnic categories. Apparently clear tendencies emerged for the two smallest groups, with Chinese students performing well in GCSE and Bangladeshi students performing poorly. Although these results are consistent with previous findings, the small numbers do mean that they must be treated with caution.

For the larger minority ethnic groups, those of Pakistani, Indian and Afro-Caribbean origins, the overall results of students in GCSE examinations were not significantly different from those of students in the majority white category. This should not, however, be used as a reason for complacency, for at least three reasons:

1 The analysis that was possible with the available data was very crude. In particular, it was not possible to take account of the important factor of social class.
2 The numbers involved were small, so that very large differences would be necessary for any clear trend to be apparent. It will be necessary for this statistical exercise to be repeated over several years before any confident conclusions can be reached about current inter-category differences.
3 These local results do not reflect apparent trends elsewhere in the country for students from some minority ethnic groups to perform rather better than those of the white majority.

Major gender differences were found in the GCSE results, in favour of girls, among white, Pakistani and, less clearly, Indian students. Although other recent results have shown some tendency for superior examination performance by girls, the phenomenon is relatively recent and has not yet reached the popular political agenda. The scale and pervasiveness of the gender differences in our results are therefore of considerable importance.

In the context of a study of students belonging to minority ethnic groups, the important points are that such gender differences are very far from distinctively associated with these groups, but that they do extend to at least some of these groups in a quite striking way. Thus, among South Asian students the GCSE results of girls were, with 54 per cent below the median, only marginally different from that of the whole population; but as many as 80 per cent of South Asian boys had GCSE scores below the median. The greater concern for the educational attainments of boys from South Asian communities to which such results should properly lead should not, however, lead to a neglect of the educational disadvantages which are clearly experienced by some South Asian girls, notably those from the Bangladeshi community.

Although again the numbers are small, there are no indications in our data that students from minority ethnic groups are performing more or less well at A Level than the majority white British group. Nor are there apparent differences in central tendency between boys and girls within minority ethnic groups, although there is some suggestion that boys, in contrast to girls, tend to do either rather well or very badly.

Our interview data show a complex and varied picture of young people's experience of schooling but none the less present certain clear patterns. Although it is important to be cautious in interpreting data based on single interviews with quite a small sample, the textured, richly exemplified and often emotional accounts of the young people's lives which the interviewers enabled them to provide seem to us plausible and persuasive. While not wishing to make any quantitative generalizations about the lives of students from minority ethnic groups in Oxford upper schools, we have some confidence that our accounts reveal important features of these lives.

One of the most disturbing features of the interview data is the considerable scale of racism experienced by students from minority ethnic groups, emanating both from their peer groups and from a small minority of teachers. The seriousness and unacceptability of this racism is only emphasized by the fact that many of the young people interviewed had come to see it as normal and even in some cases as acceptable, as a kind of 'joking'. There was too a large proportion of the young people for whom schooling had been marred and devalued by the impact of such racism.

Overt racism from teachers was the exception rather than the rule, although when it did occur it seriously undermined the work of the schools with these young people. On the other hand, the pervasive view among the many who talked about it was that schools' efforts to provide a multicultural education were completely inadequate. Those interviewed were not unanimous, or even in many cases very articulate, about what a satisfactory multicultural education would involve; but all those who discussed the issue were negative, and many were contemptuous or angry, about schools' efforts to provide – or to present themselves as providing – multicultural curricula.

In direct relation to their academic careers at school, our evidence reveals strongly felt needs by the students for help of various kinds from teachers. The many stories of the value placed on help from individual teachers are in our view of considerable significance. In particular, help in overcoming distinctive linguistic or other disadvantages, and help in being befriended by teachers who clearly cared about them as individuals seemed especially important. Equally, in contrast, the demoralizing effects of the unhelpfulness of other individual teachers could also be important; and students appeared especially concerned 'not to be given up on', even when their academic progress and their work habits were not impressive.

Of all our findings, those which seem to us most striking are the repeated reports from students of the wider gaps between their lives at home and at school. We are left in no doubt that these gaps represent a considerable handicap for many students from minority ethnic groups. Not only does the need to live two separate and unrelated lives impose an extra burden on them, but in addition these gaps prevent the young people from receiving needed support, guidance and practical help from their homes. This is especially unfortunate in view of the great importance which most of these students' parents attach to education. It is in the area of developing more effective communication and collaboration between the homes and schools of minority ethnic group students that initiatives beyond the schools themselves would seem to be most needed.

Chapter 15

Family matters

H. S. Mirza

There is a genuine need for a cultural reappraisal of definitions of social class in the UK to be made immediately, not least because of the present misrepresentation of the African Caribbean family in contemporary British class analysis. African Caribbeans living in Britain are no more homogeneous in their class make-up than their white British counterparts, yet they are often discussed as one group.

In the same way that class affects occupational location, access to economic, political and social resources, values and lifestyles among the white British population, so too does it influence these factors for blacks. However, just as black families differ among themselves, so too do they differ from white families who have been 'objectively' classified in the same social-class grouping. If black people's class position is defined in terms of their relations to the means of production (that is, ownership), they appear to hold a similar position to that of their white compatriots (Miles 1982). If on the other hand their class experiences (lifestyles) are taken into account, substantial differences between black and white become evident.

As a consequence of various historical, cultural, economic and social factors, black working-class and middle-class families do have a fundamentally unique experience in the workplace, at school and within the family compared to their white counterparts who occupy 'objectively' the same class position. The racial dimension of the class experience is crucial to an understanding of the distinct aspirations and expectations of black working-class people in Britain. The process of migration has had a significant impact on the experiences, and hence attitudes and values, of working-class West Indians in the UK.

My research indicated that in many West Indian working-class households the woman can often be found in an occupation that may be defined objectively as middle class (such as social work). However, this fact is largely obscured by the tradition of taking the man to be the head of household. Other distinctions are often misinterpreted because of similar ethnocentric evaluations. For instance in the life-cycle of the black working-class woman (and sometimes the black working-class man) single parenthood is a not uncommon stage. Furthermore, the presence of relative autonomy between men and women in many black working-class households means that both partners are found to contribute equally to the family income. West Indian attitudes to education are also positive, the meritocratic ideal being a very important determinant of occupational and educational aspirations. Home ownership is also a black working-class aspiration as are a number of other values typically identified with a white middle-class orientation.[1]

A recognition that there is a cultural context to social class does not, as Miles (1984) suggests render a class analysis invalid. To acknowledge that there exists a black working class with cultural and historical origins distinct from the white working class does not imply that race is subsumed by class. On the contrary, it enhances its meaning, for not only does it incorporate a fundamental recognition of blacks with regard to their relations to the means of production but also it allows a more satisfactory reappraisal of working-class black consciousness.

EDUCATION AND HOME BACKGROUND

A curious state of affairs persists in the study of educational inequality and social class. On the one hand, those studies that investigate the influence of race and gender inequality in education often display a lack of understanding of the fundamental role of social class. On the other hand, studies that address the issue of social class distinctions in education nearly always fail to integrate a consideration of race and gender disadvantage into their analyses.

This compartmentalization of the various aspects of educational disadvantage seems especially surprising when we consider that they are fundamentally interconnected. For how could an analysis of social class, widely acknowledged to be a major factor in educational inequality not take into account the fact that blacks and females are the two groups known to suffer the most from the effects of educational disadvantage?

In studies of education and the black experience the consistent misinterpretation of social-class factors is clearly a response to the rigid and ethnocentric interpretation of social class that these studies assume. It is often the case that social class (often referred to as 'parental influence') is not found to be a significant factor in black educational performance. Many studies conclude that the effects of ethnicity override that of social class when accounting for black under-achievement (for example, Sillitoe and Meltzer 1985).

When parental background *is* discussed with regard to black educational performance, it is nearly always done so in a negative light. The logical assumption is made that black children from low socio-economic backgrounds must be influenced in the same way as their white counterparts, only worse (for example the Swann Report: Department of Education and Science 1985).

Some studies fail to give a satisfactory account of social class because of its apparent inconvenience to their analysis. For example, a positive appraisal of West Indian class characteristics was incompatible with the Eggleston Report's emphasis on under-achievement and institutional racism (Eggleston et al. 1986).

In a bid to account for scholastic success among black pupils, Bagley et al. (1979) makes the assumption that a positive orientation to education is solely a black middle-class phenomenon. But should low socio-economic status always be considered as reliable predictor of poor educational outcomes?

Clark (1983), in his study of why poor black families succeed, is one of the few researchers to offer insight into what he calls the 'quality of life' in poor black homes. Though his analysis is fundamentally flawed by its emphasis on individual motivation, he does draw our attention to the importance of family disposition, not composition, as a means of explaining the positive orientation of black children from materially deprived backgrounds.

It is a convention in studies that assert there is an important link between the parental background and educational outcome to use the paternal occupational yardstick (for example, Halsey et al. 1980). Likewise, the limited research that exists on social class and educational outcome among black pupils also always uses fathers' social status as a measure of parental background (for example, Sillitoe and Meltzer 1985; Mortimore et al. 1988; Inner London Education Authority 1986). This assumption begs to be questioned.

In order to investigate the effects of home back ground on outcome it was important to examine if there was measurable influence between the job aspirations of the young black women in the study and their fathers' social background. The findings showed that young black women, whatever the social status of the father, were very likely to aspire to a job of a high social status. This trend was very evident among young women with fathers who themselves were in higher social status jobs. The daughters of men in manual occupations deviated from the pattern only slightly, a small percentage choosing occupations that were classified as non-manual and manual. Those girls with fathers not working in the household, either due to unemployment or because they were not present, aspired by and large to professional and managerial occupations.

Can we assert from the evidence that fathers' occupation influences their daughters' job choice? The data appear to indicate that these young women were not reproducing their fathers' social status, making their choices independently from paternal influence. This was made clear by the fact that many young women whose fathers were in lower-status occupations were aspiring to the same occupational group as those young women who had fathers in the higher professions. Fathers' occupational status could be seen to have some effect when it is observed that girls with fathers in manual occupations were more likely than those from non-manual and professional backgrounds to choose non-manual and manual occupations. However, if the type of work that these jobs entail is investigated, it is evident that they were not choosing to do the same type of work as their fathers. These jobs were regarded as high-status female work and so in a sense represented mobility for these young women.[2]

If the relationship between fathers' job and daughters' aspirations is tenuous, we must then investigate if there is any direct link between mothers' job and daughters' aspirations. It has been argued that the mother plays a central role in influencing the educational attitudes and aspirations of their children (Jackson and Marsden 1963; Hoggart 1957). Other aspects of the maternal influence have been ascertained. Some studies, for example, investigate the psychological aspect of the maternal influence. Rutter (1981) emphasizes its impact on child cognitive development and Chodorow (1979) on 'sex socialization'. Research on white working-class women highlights the direct and indirect role of the mother in the occupational choice process of girls (Holland 1983).

In studies on the black female a similar case is made for the positive role model of the mother, to account for both the *occupational* and educational orientation of black girls (Fuller 1982; Phizacklea 1982; Dex 1983; Eggleston *et al.* 1986). It has even been asserted that the black mother plays a crucial part in the maintenance of educational disadvantage among her children in general (Brewer and Haslum 1986).

What the findings of my study showed was that young black women, whatever the occupational status of their mothers, were more likely to aspire to a high-status career than simply mirror their mothers' occupational experience.

It could be argued that there was some degree of influence of maternal social class, made evident by an increased likelihood among girls with mothers in skilled non-manual and manual work to choose jobs of that social class, compared with the decision of girls with mothers in social class 1 and 2, who were less likely to take up a career as a manual or non-manual employee. This was further shown by the fact that 25 per cent of the young women whose mothers were in semi-skilled and unskilled occupations opted to do this same type of work.

However, this social class influence can be seen to be marginal in the light of the more marked trend in the evidence that strongly suggests that the aspiration to a high occupational status was being made regardless of mothers' social status, even among girls from lower maternal social background. That the girls' occupational decisions appeared to be made independently of their mothers' occupational status was further supported by the fact that even girls whose mothers were in social class 1 and 2 (the most common occupational category all round for both mother and daughter) did not necessarily choose the same job as their mothers were doing: 20 per cent chose jobs classified as social class 3. Thus, in conclusion, the dynamic that determined high occupational aspirations among young black women appeared to be something other than the mothers' occupational status. It is to a further investigation of this question that I now turn: an investigation that examines the influence of *family* occupational background.

If we are adequately to gauge the social background of the young black women in the study who themselves are not yet in employment, and so cannot define their own social status, then we assess as best we can the most representative social status of the family. Given that we are not in a position to redefine social classification schema,[3] the most operative way to achieve this end would be to take the social class of the parent who could most adequately fulfil the head of household requirements laid down by conventional stratification theorists themselves. Goldthorpe (1983), articulating the conventional view, puts forward the following definition of the 'head of household'. He writes: 'The family "head" is the family member who has the greatest commitment to and continuity in the labour market' (p. 470). However, he then assumes: 'that this member is usually male is then an independent empirical observation' (p. 470).

It is my proposition here, contrary to conventional wisdom, that employed, married West Indian women in Britain can be defined as the 'head of household', and this is the important part, even when a husband is present. Furthermore I wish to argue that they can be defined as such by Goldthorpe's own criterion that states that the family head is the one who has the greatest commitment to and continuity in the labour market.

Goldthorpe regards any attempt to include married women into the class schema as 'problematic'. This he claims is because of the 'discontinuity so characteristic a feature of the employment histories of women' (Goldthorpe 1983: 475). He makes the ethnocentric assumption that the majority of employed married women are working part-time and that their economic participation may have a somewhat impermanent and intermittent character as they enter or leave the labour force in response to the needs of childcare or the demands of a husband's career. However correct this may be for the majority of women in Britain (and that is questionable – see Beechey and Perkins 1987), it most certainly is not true for all and is particularly misleading with regard to the West Indian woman in Britain.

The evidence of this study, and indeed that of the Policy Studies Institute (PSI) survey, *Black and White in Britain* (Brown 1984), suggests that there is no cultural precedent for making this ethnocentric assumption concerning West Indian women's commitment to the labour market. The characteristics of the black female workforce indicate that the social and economic contribution of the black woman to the British labour force is substantial. It is sufficient to merit recognition by any credible schema. Thus in the West Indian context to employ a convention that marginalizes the female contribution and presumes that the male should be head of household when both partners equally contribute to the family would, in effect, distort social reality (Gill 1984; Massiah 1982; 1984; 1986; 1988).

Nancy Foner (1979), in her study of the West Indian migrant to Britain, makes an interesting observation. She presents evidence to suggest that to ignore the West Indian woman's occupational status in her own right would be problematic when trying to calculate occupational mobility. She shows that in fact the husbands of nearly all the white-collar and skilled women in her London sample were in jobs of a lower status than their wives, and many of them had experienced downward mobility in England. Thus, to consider the husband's occupational status and mobility experiences, rather than the woman's, would result in mis-classifying them as downwardly mobile instead of upwardly mobile.

In the same way it was apparent that not to take the females' occupational status into consideration when establishing the family background of the girls in the study would result in a misrepresentation. The families in my study would appear downwardly rather than upwardly skewed in the occupational hierarchy.[4] This was clearly illustrated by the figures which showed not only that the social class of the black male was much lower than that of the female, but the social class of the West Indian family to be substantially altered if the female was correctly incorporated into the schema.

In every respect the West Indian woman's labour-market commitment earns her the right to be recognized as capable of defining her family's social position. However, it is often the case that in determining parental background the conventional wisdom is to take the occupation of the male head of household. Studies of black occupational mobility persist in conforming to this methodological convention by maintaining that males are in every cultural setting still the most committed and involved in the labour market. It is this ethnocentric convention in established stratification analysis that has yet to be refuted successfully.

Returning to a consideration of the effect that family background has on occupational aspirations, we shall now consider data which show the relationship between the family social status and daughters' occupational aspirations. The social status of the West Indian families in the study is defined here in terms of occupation of that parent, either male or female, who most adequately fulfils the requirement of family head according to Goldthorpe's own definition. If both members appear to contribute equally to the family position then the parent with the higher social status was taken to be the definer of the family's social background.[5]

There appears to be a pattern in the data that indicates much the same trend that has been observed in our previous consideration of maternal and paternal occupational influence. The evidence suggests again that young black women are choosing labour-market destinations independently of the occupational status of the head of household. This is shown by the fact that the majority of young women (over 70 per cent under any head of household grouping) chose careers in social class 1 and 2 (that is, professional and intermediate occupations). Girls from social class 3 families (namely, non-manual and manual) are as likely to choose occupations from their own social background as social class 1 and 2 girls, 20 per cent of whom wanted to do work classified as social class 3 occupations.

Other findings indicate that the majority of heads of households classified as professional and intermediate workers are in fact female (68 per cent). In the same way, male heads of household tend to be skilled manual workers (46 per cent). This finding, together with the observation that young black women aspire to high-status professions, whether the heads of households are themselves manual or professional workers, presents further evidence that maternal or paternal social status is of little consequence in the decision-making process.

Among West Indians in Britain the link appears weak between the first and the second generation with regard to their occupational aspirations. This suggests that young black women do not necessarily wish to reproduce their social-class status, however defined. The question then arises as to how the West Indian parents influence their child.

RE-EVALUATING PARENTAL INFLUENCE

In this study there appeared to be two ways in which parents influenced aspirations: one, the positive orientation to education, and the other, the black female orientation to work, both of which can be regarded as British West Indian working-class characteristics. I shall now turn to an assessment of these two important class characteristics in order that we may move towards some explanation for the high aspirations of young black women.

First- and second-generation attitudes to education

It is often the case that people migrate for 'a better life'. This is as true of the West Indians who came to the UK as any other group of people. West Indians came to Britain in the 1950s, in what can be argued as both a male- and female-headed migration, in search of better opportunities for themselves and their children. While objectively occupational opportunities for migrants are restricted by specific constraints with regard to their disadvantaged labour-market position, there is another dimension to migrant life: that of their own subjective occupational orientation.

This internal cultural dynamic of migrants, what I call the 'migrant effect', refers to the degree to which migrants themselves pursue the goal of upward occupational mobility, particularly for the next generation, by striving for educational achievement and qualifications. The influence of this 'migrant effect' on educational outcomes may vary according to the culture of the migrant group, the country of settlement, and economic and social conditions (especially significant is the extent of racial exclusion and discrimination), but it nevertheless remains a characteristic feature among many migrant groups (Alba 1985).

Glazer and Moynihan (1963) discuss in *Beyond the Melting Pot*, their study of American migrant society, the drive for educational credentials among the many migrant groups in the USA. They describe the Jews' 'passion' for education; the Italian concept of (family) social status through the professional occupations of their children; the Puerto Rican capacity for hard work and the value they place on schooling. Of the West Indian migrants who went to the USA in 1920–5 Glazer and Moynihan write: 'The ethos of the West Indians ... emphasized saving, hard work, investment and education ... buying homes and in general advancing themselves' (1963: p. 35).

They remark that West Indians, such as Marcus Garvey, 'furious' at the prejudice they encountered in the USA (which they felt was far greater than that among the whites in their home islands), turned to radical politics.

Leggett (in Bettelheim and Janowitz 1977) supports this thesis of political involvement, claiming that blacks, having the lowest ethnic status, have therefore the highest level of class consciousness. Indeed, a degree of political consciousness among early black migrants to the UK has been demonstrated by the 'Black Education movement' set up by this generation of migrants (Chevannes 1979; Tomlinson 1985). The struggle for basic educational rights has been a political focal point for the 'black community' since the 1960s. However, as Tomlinson observes, it is not so much a radical movement as one that seeks to ensure equality of opportunity for migrant children within the education system. Confirming that migrant parents have strong educational aspirations for their children, Tomlinson writes:

> The parents very much aware of the discrimination their children could face in seeking employment after school placed great faith in the acquisition of educational qualifications to help overcome this.
>
> (Tomlinson 1982: 34)

Parental recognition that the British education system discriminates against the black child has resulted in the establishment of black supplementary schools, spearheaded by the action, in particular, of black women. These separate black schools embody the belief that education will ultimately help black children to succeed in an 'English' system by providing them with the credentials necessary for employment, or further education and training in the majority society.

It was found in the study that black parents wanted improved educational standards for their children, and despite the general feeling of disillusionment and mistrust towards the schools their daughters attended, still retained their faith in the meritocratic ideal. Among the parents interviewed it was clear that securing educational opportunities for their children was of central importance, as one father explained:

We work to give our children opportunity. We earn to pay rent, buy a little food. Man, there was no time for bettering ourself. Our children, they now have the benefits to better theyself, education and so on. We didn't have these opportunities, our childrens now have these opportunities and we's work hard for them. [*sic*]

(Mr Burgess, London Regional Transport maintenance)

Parents were 'realistic' about employment opportunities, and their knowledge of British racism, gained from their own experience, made them anxious for their children. They had a clear understanding of the 'make-or-break' situation that faced their children in Britain, as Mrs Pierre, a mother of one of the girls, explained:

When we came here, there was so many jobs, we could've move from one to another. The first night I arrive I get a job with my cousin. But the more of us come the less work, but we had relatives then an' that make it easier. But now these children, they don't understand. They have it harder to get a job now, there is much against them that we not have then. But now they have opportunity. We are here to help them get on and we can help them educate themselves. They don't have to find the money for rent. You see, we had our children here and so they grow up expecting different things.

(Mrs Pierre, auxiliary night nurse)

Clark (1983) puts forward a theory as to why poor black families succeed in education. He argues that too often studies emphasize family composition (that is, single-parent families or others) and not family disposition (beliefs and values). This is an important point; black girls in the study did seem to derive much of their determination for 'getting on' from their parental orientation and both the passive and active support this engendered. It was apparent that West Indian parents did encourage their daughters and were proud of their successes in many different ways. A parent, a canteen worker for twenty-four years since her arrival from Jamaica in 1954, outlined her ideas and values on education and her daughters' success:

It is important that she does what she wants, then she will do well. . . . Anita should stay on and finish her studies. I does see many that leave, hang around the streets, what is the point of leaving school to do this? Our other daughter, Sheila, she went to John Henry school, did well and then went on to college, then a Government job. They send her on a social work training course, CQSW I think it called. She probably out working today, she's a residential social worker now. The next one she does something, with computers. Me, I don't understand a thing about that. My's only fear is Anita, now she start saying she want to be a nun. It's that school, you know. What will she do when we want to play we music, drink and relax? [*sic*]

Parental attitudes to their children's education varied from those who took strong disciplinarian measures to those who adopted a passive approach. The passive approach was an attitude that relied heavily on trust between parent and child, and much responsibility lay with the child. Ms Dean, a cleaner in a West End hotel in London, describes what was the passive support role of many parents in the study:

> She's a good girl, goes up and works on her own. Some children at school disturb her. Some children want to work, others don't. You know there are just some children like that. We never force them to work, there is no point, it must come from themselves.

This type of parental support was often misunderstood by the school. Teachers argued that this form of parental concern was not sufficient for the girls' needs, and often complained that it led to over-ambitiousness among the pupils. For example, Ms Parker, a fifth-form (Year 11) mistress, had this to say of one parent who was an educational welfare officer: 'The problem is that she believes you must work hard to get anywhere, to move out of your circumstances, this philosophy has got through to Sherry who is just too over-ambitious for her ability.'

It was clear that teachers, rather than considering it an asset, considered passive parental encouragement to be negative, as the following comment made by a teacher concerning a black parent shows:

> The mother wants too much of her daughter, she is far too over-ambitious for her. Just to show you she really hasn't a clue about her daughter, she's only capable of a low-grade CSE and she wants her to do O Levels.

Another teacher had this to say of the passive, but supportive, role of one family: 'The parents are not unduly worried as she works hard but she is just not able enough to carry it off, she is not geared up to the exam level'.

The evidence showed that in many cases black parents attempted to provide whatever support they were able to give, mostly of a moral and where possible a material nature. It was clear that many working-class black parents, not least because of their own educational background or the restrictions induced by difficult working conditions, rely heavily on the school to provide the less accessible material and academic help they were often unable to give.

Nevertheless, it must be noted that however 'conservative' the parental attitudes towards education appeared to be, this acceptance of the status quo was not reflected in the cultural ideology of the West Indian working class. They often referred to the racism they knew existed in society and in the classroom. The setting up of supplementary schools, with its emphasis on high educational standards, bears witness to this fact. The apparent contradiction between the desire for a traditional education and the need for radical politics did not appear to be problematic to the West Indian working-class community who found it a logical stance in the light of their migrant experience and the racism they had encountered. Ms Arnold rationalizes these seemingly opposite views in the following passage:

I does get real angry when they say the Queen's prejudice, she invited us here. I remember the day my friend brought a *Gazette* and showed me the headline, 'Immigrants Welcome, Queen Welcomes Immigrants'. We was sitting under a tree in the shade, that's when I make up me mind to come. She invited us here, how can they be prejudiced if they ask us to come? She is Head of State in the West Indies. The problem is they don't know their history here, these English people. [*sic*]

However, Mrs Arnold went on to explain the reality of life and bringing up children in Britain and in so doing presented different ideological position:

It's bad, real bad. . . . The school has a lot of it [racism]. I know because it real difficult to get Verne in the school . . . there are so few blacks there and you know the reason why. I know the teachers are racist, but you must be careful because they are the teachers and until you leave that is a problem. Them can be vengeful and harm your child's prospects, this is a real racist place. [*sic*]

Parents were also aware of the problems faced by black youth but did not associate the difficulties they encountered with the police with anything other than racism and state coercion. Despite their disciplinarian values, which often prompted them to complain of the laziness of young people, parents were aware of the political issues involved. Mrs Davis talked about the bad media publicity blacks get and the level of police harassment which they encounter:

I tell you there's no wonder there so much trouble. They [the police] really ask for it the way they treat us black people. But the way the papers report it you'll never know what really go on, you see. In Brixton I was in the middle of it. The things I saw . . . pushing two black boys into a van, then they just start kicking and beating upon them on the floor. A next boy he run up to help but they just turn on him too. Man, I just turn and ran. [Daughter, listening, says, 'I hate them'.]

In the late 1970s, Nancy Foner made the following observation about the likely orientation of West Indian migrants' children towards education in the years to come:

The struggle to get a good education may, however, become a central focus in their lives; the second generation set their goals higher than their parents have and measure their achievements and prospects by English rather than Jamaican standards.

(Foner 1979: 217)

Indeed, as Foner predicted, the second-generation West Indian girls in the study did show a strong commitment to education and in particular identified with the meritocratic ideal as a means of 'getting on'. This was clearly illustrated in the girls optimistic statements:

Black people work hard and want to really make something of themselves. I want to get on in my life.
(Marsha: aspiration, social work; mother: office worker; father: carpenter)

I believe you can really change things for yourself, it is up to you but you really can.
        (Laurie: aspiration, journalist; mother: secretary; father: telephonist)

The strategy of 'staying on' in pursuit of educational qualifications was the way many working-class black women expressed their aspirations for 'getting on' in life, as the following extracts show:

My plans are to stay in education until I get my A levels. Then I plan to go to college to become a social worker.
        (Sherry; mother: social worker; father: BR engineer; ability high)

I want to stay on and then go to college so that I might study journalism.
        (Veronica; mother: cook; father: mechanic; ability average)

While West Indian working-class parental attitudes were an important factor in motivating the girls, there was substantial evidence that the specific choice of career was greatly influenced by a realistic self-appraisal of their academic capabilities. Girls did not aspire to careers that they felt they would not be able to achieve whatever the parental occupational status, as a comparison between the following statements shows:

I would like to do medicine especially something to do with women and the curing of disease.
        (Isabel; mother: midwife; father: labourer; ability high)

I would like to be a legal secretary and work in an office.
        (Joy; mother: insurance officer; father: accountant; ability low)

If I leave school I would go to college and do a BTec general course, after that I would do a BTec national and then HND so then I have got a wide range of jobs which I will be able to do.
        (Selma; mother: nurse; father: telephone engineer; ability average)

I would like to study and learn about computers. I'd like to do data processing as it is something interesting and that I will be able to do.
        (Sharon; mother: cleaner; father: absent; ability average)

It was notable, however, that the higher the social status of the parent the more likely it was that the daughter would choose to go on into higher education, rather than further education, as a means of qualifying for a profession. Two statements set against the context of their parental status, illustrated this process of exclusion:

I would like to go on and do a degree in psychology, preferably at a polytechnic.

(Jackie; mother: cook; father: welder; ability high)

I would like to do a BA degree in business studies, in accounts and then study for a chartered accountant degree at university.

(Floya; mother: playgroup leader; father: chartered accountant; ability high)

In this way social class can be seen to have some effect on the accessibility of higher education. However, as Tomlinson (1983) in her study on black women in higher education shows, many of the young women at university were from working-class social backgrounds. Indeed, the aspiration towards a university education was not exclusive to girls of professional parents, and several young black women from working-class backgrounds did indicate that they would like to go on to university:

I would like to stay on at school and do three A levels. After I would like to get into a university and get a degree in law. I intend to be a barrister and practise law.

(Ruby; mother: nursery teacher; father: clerk; ability high)

I want to do a degree course somewhere that I know.

(Frances; mother: social worker; father: postman; ability high)

Their coming from single-parent backgrounds did not necessarily limit the girls' aspirations, especially if their ability was high:

I have already got six O levels. Now I am doing three more and some A levels so that I can study interior design. I want to go to the London School of Furniture.

(Debra; mother: local government officer; father: absent (postman); ability high)

I would like, finally, to do art therapy, after doing a course at Goldsmiths' [University of London].

(Avril; mother deceased; father: painter-decorator; ability high)

None the less, the goal of higher education among black working-class girls of high ability was the exception rather than the rule. It was notable that the majority of young black women did aspire to Further Education college whatever their ability, most of them seeking work in a social/caring profession.

An explanation for high black female aspirations has been attempted by Fuller (1982). While she was right to observe the girls' commitment and resoluteness in their efforts to achieve their goals, she was less correct in describing this positive orientation as a 'subculture of resistance', the outcome of a reaction to negative parental and societal pressures towards black females.

The explanation for their positive orientation seemed to lie within an under-standing of the transmission of the West Indian migrant, working-class ethos, the values of which had filtered down to the girls from their parents, and had subsequently been modified.[6] Many of the young women in the study described how their parents had an important role to play not only in influencing their cultural identity, but also in shaping their specific educational outlooks, both of which combined to make them what they were today:

> Both my parents brought me up in the West Indian way. They brought me and are still bringing me up in the way their parents brought them up. I would like to pass this West Indian tradition down to my children so that this tradition lives on and never dies.
>
> (Karen; mother: nurse; father: London Regional Transport maintenance)

> As we grew up my parents used to talk about 'back home' and how it differed from England. Although I was born in England I always felt attached to my parents' country. . . . If our parents did not pass down some of their culture black people would lose out on a lot of things, e.g. who their ansister [sic] was, and how they lived and how they differed from white people and their culture.
>
> (Merle; mother: cleaner; father: bus conductor)

The Church was also an important part of West Indian working-class life, and it was not uncommon to find the girls expressing a religious influence in their career decision.[7] One girl stated: 'I would like to be a successful business woman with God's help, it gives me strength to know He guides me' (Janet; mother: teacher; father: carpenter). Several other girls who stated that God was a major source of encouragement also taught at Sunday school at the weekend.

Being second-generation West Indian meant that, unlike their parents, these young women also saw themselves as British. Having a black British identity was not considered problematic.[8] The girls had few illusions about being accepted as being British, and maintained a second-generation modified form of 'West Indianness' among them, as the following statements reveal:

> I may have been born here but I do not feel that I am English, simply because I have not been given the chance to feel English. I do feel that I am black though, but that I live in England.
>
> (Karen; mother: nurse; father: London Regional Transport maintenance)

> I am me because my parents have taught me a lot of their ways, and being brought up in a British society has combined to make me what I am today.
>
> (Julie; mother: cook; father: absent)

> I have only ever lived in England, but my parents are Dominican. I think England is a nice country but the people are false. Because one minute they are talking to you and the next they are talking behind your back, which

is not very nice. In England there are a lot of prejudices which you do not find in other countries. So even though I have a British passport I don't only class myself as British but as Dominican too.

(Denise; mother: cook; father: unemployed)

The girls were aware of managing the separate spheres of school and home life. In the following extract of a classroom conversation, the teacher asks the black girls in the class about the problems of a 'generation gap':

Ms James: But do you not find there to be different aspirations between you and your parents?
Dianne: You get used to it.
Merle: You don't do it at home, you'll get told off, but you do it at school, you don't bother.

The strong emphasis on discipline and doing 'what was expected of you' in the West Indian household was acknowledged by the girls to be part of their culture and ultimately practised by their parents in their best interests.

My mother came here to get a better education for her children, sometimes if you feel you don't want to go to school . . . well, you just have to feel you want to.

(Dianne; mother: dinner lady; father: ticket collector)

Back home it's stricter there, beating and all that. Sometimes it's not good. They expect too much of you for your age. Beat you if you don't pass a test and all that, but I tell you it makes you work!

(Ann; mother: nurse; father: plumber)

My parents brought me up very well, a little bit restricted but it doesn't bother me.

(Dawn; mother: cook; father: unemployed)

It was found that the girls held similar expectations about discipline and control to those of their parents. This accounted for their often stated preference for strong discipline in the classroom, which they identified as 'control', and organized, structured lessons which they regarded as 'good teaching'. In the girls' statements it was clear what they considered a good education to be:

Since I have been here things have got so bad. Miss Grey [the headmistress] has got no control, things are out of hand, I would say.

(Kara: upper-sixth-form [Year 13] student)

There is no discipline downstairs [i.e. lower school] . . . it's disgusting.

(Frances: upper-sixth-form [Year 13] student)

As a consequence of their educational expectations, it was not uncommon to find that girls were often disillusioned with the type of teaching they were receiving. It was clear that the young women had developed a strategy by which they gauged those lessons and teachers that were worth listening to. The girls were obviously bored and uninterested in the 'liberal teaching' approach of some teachers. In these often relaxed and less structured classes the girls would sit in the back of the room and carry on with 'prep', neither being disruptive nor participating.

This was also the case with teachers whom the girls judged to be indifferent or uncaring and with lessons they considered a waste of time.[9] Fuller (1982) suggests that the negative classroom stance which she also observed among the girls in her study was a manifestation of the 'subcultural' resistance to authority prevalent among alienated black females. However, there was little evidence to support this view of their often obvious classroom dissent. The girls appeared to be getting on with their own work as a means of rationalizing what they considered to be unproductive and wasteful lesson time. Their response to certain (though not all) teachers was the outcome of the girls' particular and unique orientation to education, which was clearly the product of their West Indian social-class background.[10]

The black female working-class orientation to work

> Women are socialised to be resourceful. Each succeeding generation learns from the preceding one what it takes to survive in an environment often unfavorable to women.
>
> (Justus 1985: 447)

While there appeared to be no direct association between the maternal social-class occupational status and aspirations, data from other sources indicated that the second-generation girls were greatly influenced by their mothers' work experience. The way in which the previous female migrant generation affected their daughters' orientation to work was clearly illustrated in the statements and decisions made by young black women. Within the context of a cultural consideration of social class, a unique female work tradition is revealed which clearly has an important influence on the aspirations of succeeding generations.

If we begin with an investigation into the characteristics of this unique black female work tradition, the distinctive nature of their experience *vis-à-vis* their white working-clsss counterparts becomes evident. In the study, 84 per cent of the black mothers worked, 69 per cent in full-time employment. This contrasted sharply with the other mothers in the study, of whom only 46 per cent worked, 28 per cent full-time White women were also almost twice as likely to be unpaid workers (29 per cent) – a type of work often referred to as housework – than black women (13 per cent).

Despite the limited scale of this investigation this was by no means an unrepresentative sample. The PSI (Brown 1984) statistics and the Labour

Force Survey (OPCS 1987) revealed similar trends in the national population. For example, PSI stated that 74 per cent of black women in the UK worked, and of these women only 29 per cent were in part-time employment. In the indigenous population, 46 per cent of the women worked and most of these were in part-time employment (46 per cent).

The black female cohort differed from the white women in the sample in other ways too, in that black women were more likely to head their households: both in terms of the traditional definition of a female-headed household (that is, one where a husband is not present) and according to the more equitable definition (the most economically committed and better situated in the occupational hierarchy). This study showed that 45 per cent of West Indian women headed their household compared to 11 per cent of white women.

Sutton and Makiesky-Barrow (1977), in their study of Barbadian society, make this comment about the West Indian female orientation to work:

> Women are expected not only to contribute to their own and their children's support but also to acquire and build separate economic resources, control their own earnings and use them as they see fit. Men readily accept the idea of their wives working; in fact a man might boast of his wife's position and earnings.
>
> (Sutton and Makiesky-Barrow 1977: 307)

Clearly the evidence does suggest that West Indian women do have different relationships within their families and, in particular, with the males in these families, that contribute to a unique working tradition. Barrow (1986) suggests that men and relationships with men were an important part of enhancing female economic autonomy and were not a restriction in the traditional Euro-centred sense; nor, as some authors suggest (Wilson 1969), only a means of gaining social respectability. Explanations as to why this may be so point to the central concept of an ideology of meritocracy in West Indian working-class life, in which both men and women appear to participate equally (Jules 1991). As Sutton and Makiesky-Barrow observe:

> The position a woman acquires often results from her own achievements rather than her spouse and women tend to be individually ranked even if they are married. Although both sexes speak critically of status ranking and its negative role in the social life of the community, status mobility is in fact a major concern. Women as well as men are preoccupied with finding a way of 'rising' a notch above within the social hierarchy, and both look to the occupational system for doing so.
>
> (Sutton and Makiesky-Barrow 1977: 302)

Lee (1982) makes the following interesting observation with regard to the ideology of meritocracy and its effects on the equality of opportunity between the sexes. He writes with regard to the Irish situation:

The less a culture emphasises merit, the more resistant to equality are the males likely to be ... if only because the supremacy of the dominant males does not depend on superior merit. They are therefore likely to feel vulnerable to what they perceive as a threat posed not so much by women, as by ability in women.

(Lee 1982: 10)

In a culture that places a value on merit, such as the West Indian working-class culture in Britain, this syndrome that Lee describes in the Irish situation does not appear to arise. It would seem from the evidence given by the males in the study that female labour-market participation is not perceived as a threat to their own economic and social status.

Barrow (1986) also moves some way towards accounting for the character-istically positive labour-market orientation and tradition of economic inde-pendence evident among working-class West Indian women in the Caribbean. She argues that the struggle for economic autonomy was a necessary strategy for survival, a form of self-reliance should other forms of economic support fail, or be insufficient to meet their often most basic requirements. Barrow makes the important observation that the black women's rationale for working was not about gaining social mobility nor even escaping from poverty, but rather a means to 'achieve mere survival and mark time with occasional improvements in standards of living' (Barrow 1986: 170). It could be argued that this strategy, evident among the migrant generation, has been passed down and modified by the second generation, who themselves, seeking a modicum of upward mobility, still appear to employ a similar rationale.

In the interview data provided by the young black women, strong feelings about the need to work were evident. In their expression of this desire, these women located the essential role of their mothers (or female guardian or relative) as an important inspiration, as the following statements show:

I want to be like my mother, well liked, sociable, outgoing and most of all successful.

(Joanna; aspiration: teacher; mother: secretary)

Both my mother and sister do book-keeping and accounts. I would like to follow in their footsteps and do as well in my job as they have done in theirs.

(Trudi; aspiration: office work; mother: book-keeper)

My mother has had to work hard to bring us up, and she brings us up in the West Indian ways. She's had to take shit at work, but I think she's brave.

(Anita; aspiration: social work; mother: cook)

In response to the question 'Who do you admire most?', a total of 20 per cent of young black women positively indicated their mother, other female relative (such as grandmother, aunt or sister) or female friend. This was in contrast to their white female peers of whom only 8 per cent said that they were influenced by any female associate, whether mother or sister.

When asked if they would like to do the same type of work as their mothers, however, the girls nearly always replied 'No'. It was clear, therefore, that it was not the mothers' actual job that influenced the girls as much as their mothers' (and other black females') attitudes and rational strategies. This aspect of occupational influence can be seen if a comparison is made between actual maternal occupation and daughters' aspirations.

For example, while 20 per cent of black girls' mothers were employed as nurses, only half as many of their daughters wished to pursue such a career (10 per cent). In fact, when asked what job did they most dislike, 32 per cent of the young black women indicated that nursing was the job they would like the least, suggesting that a reason for the decision was the type of work and that they knew of women, often their mothers, who did it.

Although a large number of mothers were engaged in unskilled and semi-skilled 'caring' and 'service' work (for example, 27 per cent of the mothers were employed as home-helps, dinner ladies and cleaners), virtually none of their daughters showed any inclination to undertake such work. The only work that they desired to do that was classified as unskilled or semi-skilled was associated with childcare. Another popular choice being made by the girls that did not reflect their mothers' labour-market experience was their desire to do office work. Whereas 20 per cent stated their desire to do such work, only 10 per cent of their mothers had been successful in securing such jobs.

On the whole the careers being selected by the girls reflected a much broader range of jobs than those in which their mothers were currently employed. Jobs in journalism, artistic careers of various sorts, jobs in business and the medical and academic professions, were some of the careers chosen by the girls of which their mothers had little experience.

CONCLUSION: THE CULTURAL CONTEXT OF SOCIAL CLASS

A conventional examination of the influence of social class, examining paternal, maternal and heads of households' occupational status on young black women's career choices demonstrated that by this method no association could be found. Young black women, whatever the occupational status of their parents, maintained, in general, high aspirations of social class.

However, a detailed consideration of West Indian working-class, migrant cultural characteristics revealed that, in fact, young black women were strongly influenced by their parents' orientation to work and education. It could be argued positive attitudes to education and the lack of restrictions on female labour-market participation within West Indian families account for the high aspirations of social class among these girls. The case for a cultural reappraisal of social class therefore appeared valid in view of this evidence.

NOTES

1   In my study 59 per cent of the working-class West Indian households lived in owner-occupied homes compared to only 26 per cent of the white working-class families. The white families were far more likely to live in council homes: 64 per cent compared to only 34 per cent of black families.

2   For example, these jobs are classified as lower-status occupations (i.e. office/administrative work is grouped as SC3NM, or trained nursery nurses as SC3M).

3   There have been attempts to incorporate women into a classification schema. For example, Helen Roberts (1987) presents the 'City Classification Scheme' which takes on board the feminist critique of stratification analysis by her recognition of the domestic responsibility among women hitherto invisible in the economy (see also Acker 1973; Delphy 1981; Delphy and Leonard 1986).

4   In this study the social status of the women who were 'heads of household' was higher than that of the males. Of West Indian women classified as 'head of household' 68 per cent were in social class 1 and 2, whereas only 15 per cent of black males were. The majority of black males who were 'heads of household' were in social class 3, manual occupations (i.e. 46 per cent).

5   The parents' commitment to the labour market was judged by work characteristics such as if they engaged in full-time work or part-time work. Other aspects such as distance travelled to work helped to assess their level of involvement in the labour market. With a more adequate questionnaire administered to the parents (and not to the children, as this was) such aspects of length of employment and time off work for child rearing could be included.

6   For example, parents often had 'conservative' social values particularly when it came to such matters as intermarriage and family respect. Many second-generation girls with their experiences of being black British wished to challenge many of what were often regarded as redundant values, as the following statement suggests:

> If I was to bring a dreadlock home my mother go mad! She'd say 'He, not decent; what will the family think!' ... My mum is more against a Rasta than a white boy, but it's not about the colour or the hair but what a person is like.
>
> (Merle)

7   See Justus (1985) on the central role of the Church in West Indian society. Tomlinson (1983: 73) also notes the influence of the Church and God on black female aspirations in higher education.

8   In answer to the question 'Who do you most admire?', 49 per cent of the girls in the sample said that the person they admired most was themselves. This was in contrast to their white peers, only 25 per cent of whom gave this answer.

9   With regard to standards of teaching and classroom reactions in particular the girls in the lower streams felt classes were often a form of containment. One girl explained:

> I am sure if you put the black kids in the high groups they would work but as they put blacks in a low group they will be bound to do no work. I have been streamed low when I know I could do better.
>
> (Gina)

10   Some teachers were respected and admired by the girls. The response to these lessons was markedly different from those whom the girls did not regard as 'good teachers'.

REFERENCES

Acker, J. (1973) 'Women and social stratification: a case of intellectual sexism', *American Journal of Sociology* 78.

Alba, R. D. (ed.) (1985) *Ethnicity and Race in the USA: Towards the Twenty-First Century*, London: Routledge & Kegan Paul.

Bagley, C., Bart, M. and Wong. J. (1979) 'Antecedents of scholastic success in West Indian ten year olds in London', in G. K. Verma and C. Bagley (eds) *Race, Education and Identity*, London: Macmillan.

Barrow, C. (1986) 'Finding support: strategies for survival', *Social and Economic Studies*, special issue, J. Massiah (ed.) *Women in the Caribbean* (Part 1), Institute of Social and Economic Research, Cave Hill: University of the West Indies 35(2).

Beechey, V. and Perkins, T. (1987) *A Matter of Hours: Women, Part-time Work and the Labour Market*, London: Polity.

Bettelheim, B. and Janowitz, M. (1977) 'The consequences of social mobility', in J. Stone (ed.) *Race, Ethnicity, and Social Change*, North Scituate, MA: Duxbury.

Brewer, R. I. and Haslum, M. N. (1986) 'Ethnicity: the experience of socio-economic disadvantage and educational attainment', *British Journal of Sociology of Education* 7(1).

Brown, C. (1984) *Black and White in Britain: The Third PSI Survey*, London: Heinemann.

Chevannes, M. (1979) 'The Black Arrow supplementary school project', *Social Science Teacher* 8(4).

Chodorow, N. (1979) 'Mothering, male dominance, and capitalism', in Z. R. Eisenstein (ed.) *Capitalist Patriarchy and the Case for Socialist Feminism*, New York: Monthly Review Press.

Clark, R. M. (1983) *Family Life and School Achievement: Why Poor Black Children Succeed or Fail*, Chicago: University of Chicago Press.

Delphy, C. (1981) 'Women in stratification studies', in H. Roberts (ed.) *Doing Feminist Research*, London: Routledge & Kegan Paul.

Delphy, C. and Leonard, D. (1986) 'Class analysis, gender analysis and the family', in R. Crompton and M. Mann (eds) *Gender and Stratification*, London: Polity Press.

Department of Education and Science (1985) *Education for All: The Report of the Committee of Inquiry into the Education of Children from Ethnic Minority Groups*, Swann Report, Cmnd 9453, London: HMSO.

Dex, S. (1983) 'The second generation: West Indian female school leavers', in A. Phizacklea (ed.) *One Way Ticket*, London: Routledge & Kegan Paul.

Eggleston, J., Dunn, D., Anjali, M. and Wright, C. (1986) *Education for Some: The Educational and Vocational Experiences of 15–18 Year Old Members of Minority Ethnic Groups*, Stoke-on-Trent: Trentham.

Foner, N. (1979) *Jamaica Farewell: Jamaican Migrants in London*, London: Routledge & Kegan Paul.

Fuller, M. (1982) 'Young, female and Black', in E. Cashmore and B. Troyna (eds) *Black Youth in Crisis*, London: Allen & Unwin.

—— (1983) 'Qualified criticism, critical qualifications', in L. Barton and S. Walker (eds) *Race, Class and Education*, Beckenham, Kent: Croom Helm.

Gill, M. (1984) 'Women, work and development in Barbados, 1946–1970', in J. Massiah (ed.) *Women in the Caribbean Research Papers*, vol. 6, *Women, Work and Development*, Cave Hill, Barbados: Institute of Social and Economic Research, University of the West Indies .

Glazer, N. and Moynihan, D. P. (1963) *Beyond the Melting Pot: The Negroes, Puerto Ricans, Jews, Italians and Irish of New York City*, Cambridge, MA: MIT Press.

Goldthorpe, J. H. (1983) 'Women and class analysis: in defence of the conventional view', *Sociology* 17.

Halsey, A. H., Heath, A. F. and Ridge, J. M. (1980) *Origins and Destinations: Family, Class and Education in Modern Britain*, Oxford: Clarendon.

Hoggart, R. (1957) *The Uses of Literacy*, London: Chatto & Windus.

Holland, J. (1983) *Work and Women*, 2nd edn, Bedford Way Papers no. 6, Institute of Education, University of London.

Inner London Education Authority (1986a) *The Junior School Project*, London: Research and Statistics Branch, ILEA.

—— (1986b) *Investigating Gender in Schools: A series of in-service workshops for ILEA teachers* 385/1135m/MH 4.

Jackson, B. and Marsden, D. (1963) *Education and the Working Class*, London: Routledge & Kegan Paul.

Jules, V (1991) 'Race and gender as factors of students' survival to the fifth form in Trinidad and Tobago', in S. Ryan (ed.) *Social and Occupational Stratification in Contemporary Trindad and Tobago*, St Augustine, Trinidad: University of the West Indies.

Justus, J. B. (1985) 'Women's role in West Indian society', in F. C. Steady (ed.) *The Black Woman Cross-culturally*, Cambridge, MA: Schenkman.

Lee, J. (1982) 'Society and culture', in F. Litton (ed.) *Unequal Achievement: The Irish Experience 1957–1982*, Dublin: Institute of Public Administration.

Massiah, J. (1982) 'Women who head households', in J. Massiah (ed.) *Women in the Caribbean*, Research Papers vol. 2, *Women and the Family*, Cave Hill, Barbados: Institute of Social and Economic Research, University of the West Indies.

—— (1984) 'Indicators of women and development: a preliminary framework for the Caribbean', in J. Massiah (ed.) *Women in the Caribbean*, Research Papers vol. 6, *Women, Work and Development*, Cave Hill, Barbados: Institute of Social and Economic Research, University of the West Indies.

—— (1986) 'Work in the lives of Caribbean women', *Social and Economic Studies*, special issue, J. Massiah (ed.) *Women in the Caribbean* (Part 1), Institute of Social and Economic Research, University of the West Indies 35(2).

—— (1988) 'Researching women's work: 1985 and beyond', in P. Mohammed and C. Shepher (eds) *Gender in Caribbean Development*, Women and Development Studies Project, St Augustine, Trinidad: University of the West Indies.

Miles, R. (1982) *Racism and Migrant Labour*, London: Routledge.

—— (1984) 'Marxism versus the sociology of "Race Relations"', *Ethnic and Racial Studies* 7(2): 217–37.

Mortimore, P., Sammons, P., Lewis, L. and Ecob, R. (1988) *School Matters*, London: Open Books.

OPCS (1987) *The Labour Force Survey 1985*, Series LFS No. 5, London: OPCS, HMSO.

Phizacklea, A. (1982) 'Migrant women and wage labour: the case of West Indian women in Britain', in J. West (ed.) *Work, Women and the Labour Market*, London: Routledge & Kegan Paul.

Roberts, H. (1987) 'The social classification of women: a life-cycle approach', in P. Allatt, T. Keil, A. Bryman and B. Bytheway (eds) *Women and the Life-Cycle Approach*, London: Macmillan.

Rutter, M. (1981) *Maternal Deprivation Reassessed*, Harmondsworth: Penguin.

Sillitoe, K. and Meltzer, H. (1985) *The West Indian School Leaver*, vol. 1, *Starting Work*, OPCS Social Survey Division, London: HMSO.

Sutton, C. and Makiesky-Barrow, S. (1977) 'Social inequality and sexual status in Barbados', in A. Schlegel (ed.) *Sexual Stratification: A Cross-cultural View*, New York: Columbia University Press.

Tomlinson, S. (1982) 'Response of the English education system to the children of immigrant parentage', in M. Leggon (ed.) *Research in Racial and Ethnic Relations*, vol. 3.

—— (1983) 'Black women in higher education: case studies of university women in Britain', in L. Barton and S. Walker (eds) *Race, Class and Education*, Beckenham, Kent: Croom Helm.

—— (1985) 'The "Black Education" movement', in M. Arnot (ed.) *Race and Gender*, Oxford: Pergamon in association with the Open University.

Wilson, P. (1969) 'Reputation and respectability: a suggestion for Caribbean ethnology', *Man* 4(1).

Index

A levels: ethnic groupings 199–200; grades 197–8

Abberley, P. 93, 94

ability: in capitalist society 108–9; and disability 90, 95–6; job success 121, 127–8, 129; labels 96; meritocracy 119–21, 129–30; nature–nurture 34, 35; and social class 108, 119–21, 129; social mobility 116–19, 120, 125–6

ability tests, bias 126, 129

abuse 42, 78, 176, 181

achievement: boys 142–4, 145–6, 147; girls 140–2, 147; home background 77–8, 83–4, 105–6; social class 222–3

adolescence, gender identity 161

adult education specialists 69

Advisory Centre for Education 69

African/Caribbean pupils: boys 164–5; diversity 165, 221; girls 184; masculinities 172–6; racism 110; visibility 167–8, 169, 185; *see also* Bad Boys

Alba, R. D. 228

Althusser, L. 108, 155

Anderson, M. 9, 15

Anne Devlin County Primary School 166–7

Archer, H. 53–4

Ariès, P. 20

Arnot, M. 89, 108, 109, 110

Articled Teacher Scheme 55

Asian boys 169, 176

Asian girls 176, 181–4, 211, 217

Audit Commission 79

Back, L. 169, 175

Bad Boys, Anne Devlin County Primary School 186; Black culture 174–5; masculinities 172, 186; racism 172–6; sexuality 176–81; taboo themes 173–4, 177; visibility 167–8, 169, 185

Bagley, C. 223

Baldwin, S. 95

Ball, S. 150

Banks, O. 89

Barker Lunn, J. 106

Barnes, C. 94

Barrow, C. 237, 238

Bart, D. 90

Barton, L. 91

Bastiari, J. 82

Becker, H. 96

Beechey, V. 225

Bell, C. 22

Bernbaum, G. 107

Bernstein, Basil 25, 66

Bettelheim, B. 228

Billig, M. 180

Bines, H. 97

Black Education movement 228

black feminism 151

black girls: African/Caribbean 184; nationality 234–5; role models 224, 238–9; West Indian 231–2, 234, 235–6, 237–8, 240 (n7); work tradition 236–9; *see also* ethnic minority pupils

black power movement 110

Black and White in Britain (PSI Survey) 225, 236–7

blaming, and labelling 164, 171, 172

Blank, M. 66

Bloom, B. S. 77

Bottomley, V. 55

Boulton, M. G. 22

Bourdieu, P. 122, 164
Bowlby, John 22
Bowles, S. 108, 155
boys: achievement 142–4, 145–6, 147;
    African/Caribbean 164–5, 167–8,
    169; Asian 169, 176; disciplined 144;
    equality issues 141–2; race 169; see
    also Bad Boys; gender
Brewer, R. I. 224
British nationality 234–5
British Society 49
Brod, H. 164
Brown, A. 75
Brown, C. 225, 236–7
Brown, J. 9, 12
Bruner, J. 47
Bryant, B. 47

Calder, P. 62, 150
capitalism: ability 108–9; production
    93–4, 153, 154
Carrington, B. 90, 169, 185
Central Advisory Council for
    Education 37
Certificate of Pre-Vocational Education
    135, 137
Chester, R. 9
Chevannes, M. 228
child development 36, 44–5, 54, 66–7
Child Protection Register 78
childcare: fathers 22, 160; NVQs 59–62;
    paid/unpaid 141–2, 239; standards
    for carers/teachers 58–9; training for
    55–62; wage scales 55–6; women
    workers 55–7
childhood 20–1
children: academic/technical/practical
    105; nursery education benefits 39,
    41, 45–7; and parents 23, 30, 81–2;
    playspaces 42; social worlds 73–4; see
    also under ethnicities; see also boys;
    ethnic minority pupils; girls
Children Act (1989) 56, 86
Chisholm, L. 165
Chodorow, N. 160, 224
Church, influence 234, 240 (n7)
city technology colleges 132, 144
Clark, D. 25
Clark, R. M. 83–4, 223, 229
class: see social class
classroom management, racism 167–8
Coard, B. 98
Coffield, F. 26

Cohen, P. 164, 166
Cohen, S. 166
Cole, T. 97
Coleman, J. 103
Collins, R. 12, 26
Commission for Racial Equality 109
Committee of the Secondary School
    Examinations Council 105
community education centres 85–6
community relations, conflict 191–6
compensatory education 38, 46, 67, 106
comprehensive schooling 107
confrontations: primary school 169–70;
    racial 171; reports of 172–3;
    territorial 166
Connell, R. W. 159
Connolly, P. 167, 169, 176, 186
consumerism, bounded 69
Council for the Accreditation of
    Teacher Education 50
Craft, M. 106
crime, costs 80
cultural capital 25, 122, 124, 129, 190
cultural deprivation 105–6
culture: Black 174–5; dominant 68,
    107–8, 110; gender as school
    construct 138–44; plurality 190–6;
    popular 174–5; and socialization 24;
    school awareness 190–1; see also
    multicultural opportunities
curriculum: assessment 135–8; hidden
    144, 161; hierarchy of standards 66;
    multicultural opportunities 211–13,
    219; nursery education 45–7; social
    structure 107; see also National
    Curriculum
Curtis, C. 59

Dalla Costa, M. 154
David, M. 90
Davidoff, L. 17
Davies, B. 150
Davies, L. 89, 159
daycare 42–3, 64; see also nursery
    education
Deem, R. 110
Demaine, J. 90
demography, historical 15
Department of Education and Science:
    (1972) 39; (1978) 94–6; (1985) 222;
    (1986) 57; (1990) 52, 60; (1991) 58
Department of Employment 57, 58–9
deschooling 107

Dessert, T. 90
deviancy 90, 91
Dex, S. 224
difference, politics of 98
disabilities, pupils with 90, 93–4, 95–6, 98; *see also* special needs
discipline: gender differences 144; parental 23; public 168–9; race 168–9, 209–11 discrimination in schools 110, 209–11, 228–9, 230–1
divorce 9–11, 18, 25, 78
Dollimore, J. 164
Donald, J. 165
Douglas, J. W. B. 89, 106
Dowling, Marion 43

Ebbeck, M. 52
educability, social determinants 89, 105
education: ability/disability 90, 95–6; budget cuts 133–5; compensatory 38, 46, 67, 106; cooling out 155–6; family function loss
14, 15–16; feminism 151–2, 155–6, 158–9, 161, 162–3; gender equality 132–3, 217; home background 222–7; inequalities 25, 89, 102, 103–7, 155; learner centred 79; Marxism 152–3; new sociology of 107–9; post new sociology 109–11; reforms 133–8; selection 106, 107–8; sociology of 89–91; tripartite system 105; universal 103; vocational 57–62; waste 79–81; West Indian girls 235–6; *see also* parental involvement
Education: Framework for Expansion (DES) 39
Education Act (1944) 105
Education Act (1981) 94
Education Reform Act (1988) 89
Education and Training for the Twenty-First Century (DES and DE) 58
Educational Priority Areas 37–8
effort 121–2, 129–30
Eggleston, J. 223, 224
employment: families 12–13, 78; lifecycle 13; parental expectations 229–30; social class 117; *see also* jobs; labour
Engels, Friedrich 153
English, as second language 39, 68, 203
Enlightenment 103
Ennis, R. 111
environment, learning ability 34, 35

equal opportunities: budget cuts 134–5; gender 132–3, 141–2, 237–8; governor training 146; multiculturalism 192–3; sociology of education 90; special needs 97; taxation 138
Equal Opportunities Commission 60, 109, 132
ethnic minority pupils: differentiation 208–9; examination results 197–200, 201, 218–19; facilities/resources 206–9; family 213–16, 219–20; gender/schooling 217; interview study 200–9; loyalties 210; stereotyping 110, 209–11, 219; teachers' influence 204–8; tokenism complaints 212–13; *see also* African/Caribbean pupils; Asian boys/girls; Black girls; West Indian girls
European Childcare Network 55
European Commission 55
European Union, teachers 51
examinations: competitive 104; ethnic groupings 197–200, 201, 218–19; gender 200; league tables 137–8; *see also* A levels; GCSEs; NVQs
exclusion 144
experts, family relationships 18–19, 23, 78–9, 86–7

family, in Britain today 4–13; composition/disposition 229; deprived 83; employment 12–13, 78; ethnic minority pupils 213–16, 219–20; expert help 18–19, 23, 78–9, 86–7; function specialization 14, 15–16; historical changes 13–19; husband–wife relations 17–18; inequalities 103; learning 40, 67, 77–8, 79, 81–4; life cycles 8–9, 16–17; nuclear/extended 6, 10–11, 15–16, 42; nursery education benefits 41–4; pedagogy 83; power balance 18; privacy 16–19, 23; radical feminism 157; social mobility 122–4, 225
fathers 22, 160
feminism 149; black 151; education 109–10, 151–2, 155–6, 158–9, 161, 162–3; liberal 150–2, 154; patriarchy 109–10; psychoanalytic 160–1; radical 151, 154, 156–9; socialist 152–6
Ferri, E. 40

Finch, Janet 11–12
Firestone, S. 158
Floud, J. 89, 105
Flude, M. 110
Foner, N. 226, 231–2
football 147, 176
Ford, J. 91
Freeman, A. 95
Fulcher, G. 91, 95
Fuller, M. 165, 224, 233, 236

Garland, C. 47
gender: children's rhymes 174;
    discipline 144; education 132–3, 217;
    equal opportunity 132–3, 141–2,
    237–8; examination results 200; from
    popular culture 174–5; inequalities
    26, 89, 90, 237–8; labour market
    141–2; male domination 157, 159;
    Marx 153; meritocracy 237–8; power
    relationships 18, 149–50, 162, 178–81;
    race 176; in school culture 138–44;
    segregation 159, 190–1; social
    practices 24; subordination 155–6,
    157
gender identity 161, 165, 169, 171
General Certificate of Secondary
    Education 135, 136, 137, 138, 197–9,
    218
General National Vocational
    Qualification 135, 136, 137; see also
    NVQs
Gill, M. 225
Gillborn, D. 90, 110, 165, 167, 185
Gintis, H. 108, 155
girlfriends, racism/sexuality
    181–4
girls: achievement 140–2, 147;
    African/Caribbean 184; Asian 176,
    181–4, 211, 217; disciplined 144;
    football 147; job choices 223–5, 226;
    as property 170–1, 177–8;
    school/home learning 67, 81; science
    subjects 145; sexism towards 176–7,
    181–4; studies 109–10; West Indian
    231–2, 234, 235–6, 237–8, 240 (n7);
    see also gender
Glass, D. V. 89
Glazer, N. 228
Goldthorpe, J. H. 12, 117–19, 131 (n3),
    225, 226
Gorbutt, D. 107
governor training, equal

opportunities 146
Grace, G. 97–8
Gray, H. 95
Greer, G. 157
group loyalty 170; see also peer groups
    Groves, D. 12

Hall, C. 17
Hall, S. 166
Halsey, A. H. 38, 105, 106, 223
Hammer, M. 110
Hancock, R. 81
Hannon, F. L. 81
Hannon, P. 65, 75
Hargreaves, A. 108
Hargreaves, D. 96
Hargreaves, D. H. 107, 108
Harris, D. 108
Haslum, M. N. 224
Hatcher, K. 159, 185
Headstart programmes 39
Hearn, G. 161–2
Hearn, J. 164
Hevey, D. 55, 56, 58, 59, 61
Hewitt, R. 169, 170, 175
hidden curriculum 144, 161
Hobsbawm, E. 103
Hoggart, R. 224
Holland, J. 224
Holstein, J. A. 102
home: and achievement 77–8, 83–4,
    105–6; education 222–7; ethnic
    minority pupils 213–16, 219–20; as
    learning environment 79, 82, 88; and
    school, gap 235; and social-emotional
    development 36; traumas 78; see also
    family; parents
home–community link 39–40
home–school links 39–40, 64, 67, 82, 106
household: black 221–2; defined 5–6,
    7–8; employment 12–13; experiences
    11–12; female-headed 221–2, 225–6;
    heads 221–2, 225; size/composition
    7, 15
housework 12, 154
Hudson, L. 108
Hughes, M. 67, 70, 81–2
husband–wife relations 17–18

identity: constructed 166–7, 169, 185;
    gendered 161, 165, 169, 171;
    racialized 165; resistance 185–6
ILEA 98

IMPACT maths 79
inequalities: education 25, 89, 102,
    103–7, 155; family 103; gender 26, 89,
    90, 237–8; social class 105–6, 107, 233
infancy 20
Inner London Education Authority 223
intelligence: genetically determined
    104–5; social class 104; social
    environment 105–7
interaction: child/parent 23, 30, 81–2;
    and socialization 19–20; symbolic 73,
    74, 75
Ireland, gender inequalities
    237–8

JACARI 215
Jackson, B. 89, 106, 224
James, A. 165
James, S. 75, 154
James Report (1972) 49
Janowitz, M. 228
Jarecki, H. 40
Jessup, G. 60
jobs: choices 223–5, 226; expectations
    231–2; father's 223–4; mother's 37,
    42, 224; stereotyping 141–2; success
    121, 127–8, 129; see also employment;
    labour
Jones, S. 175
Jules, V. 237
Justus, J. B. 236, 240 (n7)

Kelly, A. 161
Key to Real Choice (EOC, 1990) 60
Kirp, D. 95
kiss-chase 176–7, 179

labels: ability 96; behaviour 171; blame
    171, 172; professionals 98; racism 98;
    stigmatizing 90, 91
labour, paid/unpaid 12, 141–2, 154
labour division 12, 13, 18, 26, 154, 155
Labour Force Survey (OPCS 1987)
    237
Lacey, C. 107, 108
Land, H. 12
language spoken at home 39, 68, 203,
    204
Laslett, P. 15, 103
Leach, B. 97
learning: beyond school 86–8;
    environment 75–6; in family 40,
    77–8, 79, 81; in home 40, 79, 82, 88

learning difficulties 94, 95; see also
    special needs
learning society 84–6
LEAs: administrative reforms 138;
    examination tables 137; gender
    equality 134, 136; new equal
    opportunity practices 145–7 Lee, J.
    237–8
Lewis, C. 22
Lewis, I. 95
liberal feminism 150–2, 154
liberalism 150, 190–6
Licensed Teacher Scheme 55
life cycles 8–9, 13, 16–17, 25–8
lifestyle 221
literacy 104
LMS (local management of schools)
    132, 134, 138
Loenen, A. 72

Mac an Ghaill, M. 110, 165, 167, 185
McFadden, M. 162–3
Mahony, P. 159, 180
Makiesky-Barrow, S. 237
male domination 157, 159; see also
    ownership of girls
management committees 64
Manor Park estate 166
Manpower Services Commission 57
marriage, power balance 18
Marsden, D. 89, 224
Martin, F. M. 106
Marxism 108, 152–4
masculinities: adult themes 173–4;
    caring and creative 141–2; identity
    169, 171; power balance 161–2;
    racism 172–6; of resistance 185–6;
    working-class 164–5
Mason, M. 97
Massiah, J. 225
mathematics 67, 79
Mead, G. H. 73
Measor, L. 110, 161
Meltzer, H. 222, 223
men: childcare 160; domination 157,
    159; employment 12–13; as fathers
    22, 160; see also masculinities;
    patriarchy
meritocracy 116; ability 119–21,
    129–30; effort 121–2, 129–30; gender
    237–8; multiple regression models
    126–30; success 125
Merttens, R. 67

Messenger, K. 59
middle classes 103, 106; *see also* social
    class migrant effect 227–8
Miles, R. 221, 222
Mill, John Stuart 150, 151–2
Miller, G. 102
Mills, C. W. 90
Minns, H. 81
Mirza, H. S. 110, 165
Mitchell, J. 160
Mittler, P. 95
Morgan, D. 164
Mortimore, P. 223
mothers: Bowlby 22; as household
    heads 221–2, 225–6, 240 (n4);
    influence 224–5; paid work 12, 37,
    42, 141–2, 154, 224; single parenting
    42
motivation 124, 129, 141–2
Moynihan, D. P. 228
multicultural opportunities 192–3, 210,
    211–13, 219
Muslim community: representation
    193–5; swimming lessons 190–1, 192

nannies 55–6
National (and Scottish) Vocational
    Qualifications in Child Care and
    Education 59–60, 61
National Child Development Study
    116–19, 122
National Childcare Staffing Study
    (USA) 56–7
National Children's Bureau 83
National Council for Vocational
    Qualifications 57, 60
National Curriculum 67–8, 69, 89,
    110, 132, 135, 136, 137
National Union of Teachers 40
National Vocational Qualifications
    57–62; *see also* GNVQs
nature–nurture debate 34, 35
NCH Action for Children 78
neglect 78
new sociology of education 107–9
Nigeria: nursery school environment
    31–5; parental control 30; preschool
    education 31–4; primary education 32
Norwood Report 105
numeracy 104
nursery education 38–41; aims 39, 46,
    47; benefits 39, 41–4, 45–7;
    curriculum 45–7; environment 34–5;

freeing mother to work 35; home–
    school transition 43–4; Nigeria 31–5;
    provision 37–8, 55
nursery nurses 44, 69
nursery teachers 44–5, 50–1, 69

O'Brien, M. 22
Oakley, A. 12
occupation: *see* employment; jobs;
    labour
Office of Population Censuses and
    Surveys 37, 117
Office for Standards
    in Education (OFSTED) 135, 137,
    140, 143
Oliver, M. 93, 94
open learning environment 75–6
oppression, and disability 93
ownership of girls 170–1, 177–8

PACT reading 79
Pahl, R. 13
parent education 83, 85
Parent Link 83
parental involvement: equal
    opportunities 66–8; home-learning
    79; methods 70–5; open learning
    75–6; preschool 64–5; professional
    distancing 67
parents 21–3, 68–70; Asian/White
    190–6; and children 23, 30, 81–2,
    84–5; class 82, 83; as consumers 64,
    68, 69–70, 191; contribution to
    nursery education 41–2; as customers
    69; deficit model 66, 67, 68–9, 77–8;
    discipline 23; as educators 70, 77;
    encouragement 230; ethnic minority
    pupils 213–16, 219–20; expectations
    68, 229–30; influence 227–39; 'liberal'
    190–6; management committees 64;
    racism awareness 215, 230–1; single
    42, 78, 221–2; social class 22, 66, 119,
    122, 130 (n1); West Indian 227–36;
    see also parental involvement
Parry, M. 53–4
paternity leave 22
patriarchy 17–18, 21–2, 109–10, 149–50,
    157, 158
pedagogy of family 83
peer groups 169–72, 216–17
Perkins, T. 225
personal and social education 141, 144–5
Phizacklea, A. 224

playground rhymes, racial/gendered 174
playgroups 40
Plowden Report 37–8
Policy Studies Institute 225, 236–7
politics: of difference 98; radical
    feminist 156–9; of resistance 228;
    socialist feminist 152–6
Pollock, L. 20
popular culture 174–5
post-new sociology of education 109–11
poverty 223
power balance, between sexes 18,
    149–50, 162, 178–81; see also male
    domination
Pre-School Playgroup Association 40,
    56
pregnancy, schoolgirls 144
preschool institutions 31–4, 52, 64–5,
    66–8; see also nursery education
primary caretakers 32
primary school: Asian/White parents
    190–1, 193–5; group loyalty 170; in
    Nigeria 32; peer groups 169–72;
    racism 164–5, 167–9, 172–6
Pring, R. 107
Pritchard, O. 97
privacy 16–19
production 221
professionals 52, 65, 67, 91, 98
    prophecy, self-fulfilling 171, 177,
    185–6
Prout, A. 165
psychoanalytic feminism 160–1
psychology 104
public/private sphere 17, 23
Pugh, G. 64–5, 68, 83
Pumfrey, P. 95
Pupil Ethnic Monitoring 197

qualifications 127–8, 135–7; see also
    examinations
Quicke, J. 90

race 164–5
Race Relations Act (1975) 109
racism: children's rhymes 174;
    classroom management 167–8;
    discipline 168–9, 209–11;
    discrimination 110, 209–11, 228–9,
    230–1; gendered 176; inequalities 89,
    90; labelling 98; masculinity 172–6;
    parental awareness 215, 230–1;
    parental conflict 190–6; peer group

216–17; primary school 164–5,
    167–9, 172–6; pupil–pupil 172;
    resistance 172–6; sexuality 181–4;
    stereotyping 110, 209–11, 219; teacher–
    pupil 172; violence 166
radical feminism 156–9
Rattansi, A. 165
reading, home–school 67, 79
relatives 11; see also family
religion 190–5, 234, 240 (n7)
remarriage 10
Renaissance 103
reproduction: sexual 158, 159; social
    23–7, 90
resistance: Black culture 175; identities
    185–6; masculinity 185–6; politics
    228; racism 172–6; subculture 233–4
Rieser, R. 97
Road, C. 97
Roberts, Helen 240 (n3)
Ross, D. 61
RSA 82
Rubinstein, D. 106
Rumbold Report (DES) 52, 60
Rutter, M. 224
Ryan, J. 90

school–community link 39–40
school–home link 39–40, 81
schools: administration/organization
    132, 138; as community focus 87;
    gender breakdown of staffing
    139–40; gender cultures 138–44; LMS
    132, 134, 138; management/culture
    139–40; racism 167–9; see also
    comprehensive school; primary
    school
Scull, A. T. 90, 91
Segal, L. 164
segregation: gender 159; special needs
    90, 98
selection, educational/social 106,
    107–8
self-fulfilling prophecy 171, 177,
    185–6
service sector 239
Sex Discrimination Act (1976) 109
sexism 110, 176–7, 181–4
sexual abuse 176
sexual harassment 159
sexuality: Bad Boys 176–81; power 162,
    178–81; psychoanalytic feminism
    160; racism 181–4; radical feminism

157–8
Shaw, J. 159, 161
Short, G. 185
Sillitoe, K. 222, 223
Simon, B. 105, 106
single parents 42, 78, 221–2
Smith, M. 91
Smith, T. 39
social advantages/disadvantages
    hypothesis 116, 120, 122–4, 125,
    126–30
social class: ability 108, 119–21, 129;
    achievement 222–3; child
    development 66–7; and cultural
    deprivation 105–6; divorce 25; by
    employment 117; and household
    heads 221–2; inequalities in
    education 105–6, 107, 233;
    intelligence 104; masculinity 164–5;
    parents 22, 66, 119, 122, 130 (n1)
social constructionism 102, 111–12
social mobility: downward 125–6;
    family 122–4, 225; fluidity 27;
    historical 103; job choice 224; NCDS
    116–19, 120
social problems 102
social reproduction 23–7, 90
Social Trends 8
socialist feminism 152–6
socialization 19–23, 24, 26, 73–4
sociology of education 89–94
special needs: depoliticized 90–1;
    Education Reform Act (1988) 89;
    entitlement 89; equal opportunities
    97; pathological 90; provision 98–9;
    sociology of 91–4; as term 95
sports, gender/race 147, 176
Squibb, P. 108
standard assessment tasks 135, 136, 137
standards, educational 58–9, 66, 110
Stanworth, M. 110
stereotypes: occupations 141–2; racism
    110, 209–11, 219 stigmatization 90
streaming 106–7
structural functionalism 89
subcultures, anti-school 110
subject specialism 50, 54–5
support agencies 78–9; see also experts,
    family
Sutton, C. 237
Swann Report 222
swimming lessons, conflict 190–6
Sykes, P. J. 110

Sylva, K. 47
symbolic interaction 73, 74, 75

taboo subjects 173–4, 177
teacher training 49–55
teachers: assessment of competence
    60–1, 97; for early years 52–4; ethnic
    minority pupils 204–8;
    multiculturalism 195–6; nursery
    education 44–5; parental involvement
    67, 70–3; and pupils 81, 172, 205;
    subject specialism 50, 54–5; turnover
    206
Technical and Vocational Educational
    Initiative (TVEI) 135, 136, 137
territorial disputes 166
Thomas, F. 90
Thorne, B. 185
Tizard, B. 39, 66, 67, 69, 81–2
tokenism 212–13
Tomlinson, S. 91–2, 228, 233
Tong, R. 163
Topping, K. 67
Tough, J. 66
trade unions, equal opportunities 138
training, vocational/professional 49–55,
    61–2; see also qualifications
Troyna, B. 159, 185

unemployment 13, 25–6, 162
universal primary education, Nigeria
    30–1
urbanization 17, 31, 42
US: cultural deprivation 105–6; Family
    Policy Council 87; high achievers
    from low-income backgrounds 83–4;
    National Childcare Staffing Study
    56–7
Utting, D. 77, 78

value systems, curriculum 66
Van der Eyken, W. 42
Vass, J. 67
Veritas 83
Vernon, P. 105
victim-blaming 164
Vincent, C. 69–70
violence 78, 166
vocational education 57–62
Vulliamy, G. 95

wages, childcare 55–6
Wagg, S. 165

Walkerdine, V. 150, 165, 173–4,
    178, 186
Ward, E. 52
Warnock, Mary 95
Warnock Report 94–6
Watts, B. N. 52
Wedge, D. 61
Weiner, G. 90, 110
Wells, Gordon 81
West Indians: achievements 223; girls
    231–2, 234, 235–6, 237–8, 240 (n7);
    households 221–2, 225–6, 240 (n4);
    parents 227–36, 239; women, job
    status 226
Westwood, S. 185
White, J. 107
White, S. 47
Whitebook, M. 57
Whitty, G. 107, 108
Wicks, M. 9
Williams, B. 111
Williams, J. 90
Williamson, B. 107
Willis, E. 151

Willis, P. 155, 178–9
Wilson, P. 237
Windle, K. 55, 61
Wolfendale, S. 67
Wolfensberger, W. 90
Wollstonecraft, Mary 150, 151–2
Wolpe, A. 159, 178
women: childcare, paid 55–7;
    classification scheme 240 (n3);
    employment 12–13, 26; see also
    mothers
Women's National Commission 55
Wood, D. 47
work: see employment; jobs; labour
Working with Under Sevens Project 55,
    58
working-class: ability wasted 89; high
    ability children 104–5; masculinity
    164–5; streaming 106–7; see also
    social class
Wright, C. 167, 185
Wright, D. 110

Young, M. F. D. 107